A Narco History

A Narco History

How the United States and Mexico
Jointly Created the "Mexican Drug War"

CARMEN BOULLOSA
& MIKE WALLACE

OR Books
New York · London

© 2015 Carmen Boullosa and Mike Wallace

Published by OR Books, New York and London
Visit our website at www.orbooks.com

For all rights information: rights@orbooks.com

Cataloging-in-Publication data is available from the Library of Congress.
A catalog record for this book is available from the British Library.

ISBN 978-1-944869-12-0 paperback
ISBN 978-1-944869-25-0 e-book

Cover and text design by Bathcat Ltd.
Typeset by AarkMany Media, Chennai, India.

FOR THE DEAD, THE DISAPPEARED,
THE CHILDREN LEFT BEHIND.

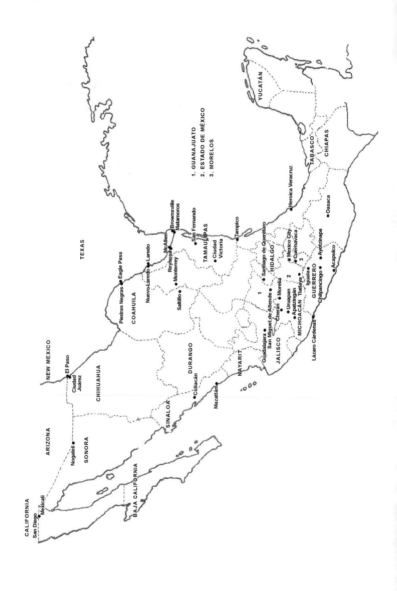

CONTENTS

INTRODUCTION
The Forty-Three

Ayotzinapa is a small village, located near the town of Tixtla, in a remote and mountainous region of Guerrero, a state in the south of Mexico. Though best known in the U.S. for its Pacific coast port city of Acapulco, a famed tourist resort since the 1950s and 1960s when stars like John Wayne, Elizabeth Taylor, Frank Sinatra, and Lana Turner flocked there, Guerrero is a poor state, and Ayotzinapa lies in one of its poorest regions.

The village is built around a teacher training school. Its construction dates to 1933, when a colonial-era hacienda was transformed into an institution that aimed to educate the isolated, low-income population of rural Mexico. It was one of a network of "normal schools" imbued with a vision of social justice rooted in the Mexican Revolution (1910–1920). These schools were tasked with educating their students in both literacy and politics: ultimately in creating students who could transform their society. Ayotzinapa's alumni include two 1950s graduates—Lucio Cabañas and Genaro Vázquez—who became famous leaders of agrarian guerilla insurgencies during the 1960s and 1970s. The school today celebrates this tradition. Its buildings feature murals of Marx and Che and its entryway bears the inscription: "To our fallen comrades, who were not buried, but seeded, to make freedom flourish."

Much of the radical energy of the 522 students (all male, between eighteen and twenty-four years old, many of Indian descent) goes into preserving the school itself. It has been widely believed that the authorities want to shut it down, along with the other sixteen rural teachers' schools, despite the fact that roughly a fifth of Guerrero's 3.4 million citizens do not know how to read or write. Students are given one peso a day (about seven U.S. cents) for their personal expenses, and the funds allotted for meals and housing are skimpy. To survive, the students grow much of their own food, raise chickens, look after dilapidated buildings, and share bare rooms containing more occupants than beds.

Periodically they head into nearby cities and towns to *botear*—or "pass the can"—to raise money for the school. They also hold demonstrations to push for more funding, and for the creation of more jobs for those who obtain their degree. In 2014, allotments were trending down, and the students were up in arms. "If we don't demand things, nothing comes," said one nineteen-year-old student. "We just get leftovers."

Occasionally they have "borrowed"—forcibly commandeered—commercial buses from national companies. The state doesn't provide enough vehicles, and it's a long walk to the schools in remote hill towns where they do their practice teaching, or to the cities where they go to fundraise or demonstrate. More aggressively, they have used the buses to blockade tollbooths along the superhighway that runs from Acapulco north to Mexico City, the nation's capital; at these temporary barriers they chant protest slogans and demand contributions from infuriated drivers. As these buses (and their drivers) have always been returned, the authorities, to the annoyance of the companies, have basically tolerated the practice.

On Friday afternoon, September 26, 2014, at the end of the second week of classes, roughly a hundred students—almost all freshmen—went on an expedition. Details of the trip's purpose, its progress, and even its horrific outcome are still unclear, which is amazing considering the national, indeed global attention that has been riveted on it. Nearly every aspect of what happened that day is contested—partly due to the usual Rashomon effect of contradictory witness accounts, partly due to incompetence, corruption, and lies.

There is no universally accepted account of what happened to those students during that day—particularly to forty-three of them. The following Introduction draws on the findings of many independent journalists (among them surveys by John Gibler and Esteban Illades), the recollections of student participants, the confessions of alleged perpetrators, and the evidence and analysis presented by official investigative bodies. It is "a" history" —not "the" history—of that 48 hour period, and, as we will see, has been subject to challenge.

◆ ◆ ◆

On September 20, 2014, at a conclave attended by students from the network of normal schools, it had been agreed that on Thursday, October 2, students from various institutions would assemble at Ayotzinapa and from there travel together up to Mexico City, 240 driving miles to the north. There they would attend a demonstration held each year to commemorate the students massacred during a demonstration in 1968. The convoy would need approximately twenty-five buses, and the Ayotzinapans promised to "borrow" them all. On September 22, a group of students drove down from the hills and headed west on a valley road for about ten miles, to Chilpancingo, the capital city of Guerrero, which sits on the Acapulco–Mexico City highway. There they took possession of two more buses. But on a return visit the following day they were repulsed by federal police. On September 25 they headed to a less well-defended locale, and returned with two more. But this left them far short of their goal, and they decided to dispatch a much bigger contingent the following day.

The task was turned over to roughly a hundred freshmen, who had only been at the school for two weeks, barely enough time to get their hair cropped (an initiation ritual). The short-haired task force would be commanded by eight seasoned second- and third-year veterans of former bus-fishing campaigns. The students headed north in two buses toward the city of Iguala (population 118,000). Before arriving, the leadership, headed by Bernardo "El Cochiloco" Flores, decided to split up. One bus swung right onto a road heading east toward the town of Huitzuco (population twenty thousand) and parked at a roadside restaurant, a likely pit-stop for buses heading toward Iguala. The other continued north, halting short of the city at a highway toll booth, where the Ayotzinapans succeeded in snaring an Iguala-bound passenger bus. Coming to terms with the operator, ten students boarded this third vehicle, and headed on to a bus terminal in the city center, arriving around 8:00 p.m.

There the youths encountered two unpleasant surprises. First, after the passengers had disembarked, the bus driver went off to apprise the bus company, saying he'd be right back, but he didn't return, and the students discovered he'd locked them in. The inexperienced youths, panicky, called El Cochiloco in his bus outside the city, who immediately headed to their assistance. In the meantime the students had broken the windows and exited. The second surprise was that municipal policemen had arrived and were heading toward them with guns drawn and cocked. At just this moment, the first fifty reinforcements arrived; minutes later another thirty brought them to their full and formidable complement of ninety or so, armed with rocks grabbed on the way. The police decided to retire. But something unusual was clearly afoot. There was a long history of bad blood between the Iguala police and the radical students, but gunplay, though not unheard of, was not customary. What the students didn't know (though there are conflicting opinions as to who knew what, when) was that the police were on hyper-alert because there was a massive public event underway a few blocks from the station, being run by Iguala Mayor José Luis Abarca and his wife María de los Ángeles Pineda Villa.

◆ ◆ ◆

The mayor and his wife were not people to trifle with. Abarca was closely linked to a violent drug trafficking gang, the Guerreros Unidos ("United Warriors"), which had been a military arm of the once powerful Beltrán Leyva Organization. When the latter collapsed in 2009, leaving the Guerreros to their own devices, they took over the production and processing of opium paste (the base for making heroin) and shipped it directly to Chicago, secreted in commercial passenger buses. The Guerreros Unidos supplemented this income stream with collateral criminality, notably kidnapping and extortion, both in Iguala itself—where they were notorious for donning masks at night and grabbing people on the street and giving them an hour to come up with $1000—and throughout Guerrero. They also did battle with other fragments of the progenitor Beltrán Leyva cartel, notably a gang called Los Rojos (The Reds), for control of the drug trafficking business in Guerrero. Their incessant shootouts, which filled mass graves in the countryside, helped drive the state's murder rate to sixty-three for every one hundred thousand inhabitants, approaching that of Honduras, the homicide capital of the world.

Abarca's principal connection to the Guerreros came courtesy of his wife. Pineda came from a family of drug dealers—her father and three brothers had worked with the Beltrán Leyva Organization in its heyday, then became Guerrero warriors (two brothers died in battle in 2009). Federal police opened a case against María de los Ángeles herself in 2010 for *"delitos contra la salud"* (drug trade–related crimes), but dropped it for reasons unknown.

Abarca had started his business career as a sandal salesman in the local market, but had a meteoric rise. Using mysteriously assembled funds, he became a major property owner, acquiring real estate, jewelry stores, and a shopping mall (the land for which was donated by the Ministry of Defense after intense lobbying on Abarca's behalf by officials of Guerrero state). He snared the mayoralty in 2012, despite warnings that putting him in office meant turning the city over to organized crime. (One of those protestors was found dead a few weeks after Abarca assumed office). The new mayor proceeded to stuff eleven relatives onto the city payroll. He made his cousin Felipe Flores chief of police, and it was generally believed that the department was now a de facto branch of the Guerreros Unidos, who, in addition to extorting the citizenry, used Iguala as a base for their drug trafficking, and provided the mayor with muscle when needed.

In May 2013, Abarca had turned them loose on local activist Arturo Hernández Cardona, who had led a demonstration in Iguala by aggrieved farmers and miners. According to witnesses, Abarca arranged the kidnapping and torture of Hernández Cardona, and then showed up personally to inform the victim, "You fucked with me, so I will have the pleasure of killing you," just before shotgunning him to death. The Ayotzinapans, who had had close ties with Hernández Cardona, demonstrated in front of town hall. The local Catholic bishop, Raul Vera, called for an investigation into the killings. He even took the case to human rights organizations in the U.S.—but the authorities decided the mayor was constitutionally immune from prosecution, and nothing was done. Impunity had been formalized. "Butchers have come into power," Bishop Vera said, and indeed it is very hard to discern where the state ends and the criminals begin.

It is even harder in the case of the mayor's wife. When she and her husband came to municipal power in 2012, it was María de los Ángeles herself who, according to one of the gang's leaders, became Iguala's "key operator," the organizer of the city's dark side. In her daylight role as first lady, however, Pineda loved to play Lady Bountiful. She had endless photos taken of herself posing with the beneficiaries of her benevolence. And on September 26, 2014, she was due to give her annual report as president of the local chapter of the National System for Integral Family Development, a state-funded organization. According to many observers, she also intended to use the occasion to launch a campaign to succeed her husband as mayor. The ceremony, held in the downtown Civic Plaza, was to be followed by an open-air party. To ensure an imposing audience, they brought in four thousand *acarreados*, poor people rewarded for attending and applauding. This gathering was in full swing when word arrived that Ayotzinapa students were once again in town, possibly intent on ruining her big day. The imperious first lady—stylistically a cross between Marie Antoinette and Maleficent (the Disney villain)—spewed abuse about the students, with whom she had crossed swords before: "filthy," "criminals," "hustlers," and "profiteers" were among the sputtered adjectives. Then either she or the mayor gave the order to "Stop them, contain them, and teach them a lesson."

◆ ◆ ◆

Meanwhile, back at the terminal, the massed one hundred students discarded the bus with broken window and commandeered two new ones. Sure that the police would be back, they decided to get out of town as fast as possible. The caravan of now four buses proceeded north on a main north-south street, through thickening traffic, heading straight for the Civic Plaza.[1] It seems like they intended to make a right turn just before it, and head east to an entrance to the *periférico*, the circumferential highway that would take them back to Ayotzinapa. Only one bus was able to do so before police cars began pouring into the area. The remaining three vehicles had no choice but to plow straight ahead, past the Plaza, where the event was just breaking up, and make for another entrance to the highway. The police gave chase, running behind and alongside them, shooting in the air, until other patrol cars cut in ahead of the procession, just before the on-ramp, forming a barricade and boxing in the three buses.

Then they began shooting to kill. They were joined in this by reinforcements dispatched by the police department of the neighboring town of Cocula, which was even more a creature of the Guerreros Unidos than was the Iguala department. In addition, two unmarked cars showed up, out of which stepped some masked men in black commando outfits, almost certainly Guerrero members, who began firing bursts from semi-automatic weapons. Several students were killed or wounded, and twenty-five to thirty were rounded up (principally from the last bus in line) and driven off in police vans.

---

1   It seems odd that the buses didn't make a left on Eutimio Pinzón, and left again on Avenida General Álvaro Obregón, and then head south nine blocks to the highway, rather than driving north, into the congested and likely dangerous center. But perhaps there was some obstruction at the critical juncture. Such things are always clearer in hindsight, and at a calm distance from the tempestuous reality.

Others scattered into the night, seeking shelter. Some were suc-cored by householders—one elderly woman took in a group of stu-dents, a "gentleman" rescued another group—others were spurned. One contingent of students carried a wounded comrade to a nearby clinic. A doctor agreed to call an ambulance. Instead he phoned the army. The 27th Infantry Battalion had a garrison at Iguala, in part to deal with thugs like the Guerreros Unidos, but they proved anything but helpful. Around midnight they showed up in full battle gear, lined the students up against a wall, took their data and photos, confiscated their cell phones, and threatened to turn them over to the municipal police, saying, "You had the balls to stir things up, so have the balls to pay the price." In the end, however, they let them go.

All these in flight from the blocked column of buses were pro-foundly fortunate compared to another of their colleagues, Julio César Mondragón, known as "El Chilango," meaning he came from Mexico City, an unusual home town for an Ayotzinapan. Sometime during that dark night he was captured by persons unknown. They tortured him, gouged out his eyes, ripped the skin from his face, then shot and killed him and dumped his body in the street.[2]

◆ ◆ ◆

In the meantime, the lone bus that had gone off on its own suffered the same fate as the ambushed trio. Intercepted just before reach-ing the highway and making their escape, they were surrounded by police, who began shooting at them. Some of the students shouted out they were not criminals, but students, thinking perhaps they'd

---

2   One of the many remaining mysteries is why, if the murders committed that night were done by gangsters intent on hiding their deeds, they would signal their involvement by dumping a mutilated corpse in a public place, a signature method of cartel assassins. As we will show, the narco modus operandi for dealing with dead victims was either to make a great public show of the murder—hanging bodies from highway overpasses, dumping them at town hall doorsteps, videotaping the killing itself—*or* to hide the bodies, usually in mass graves, or dissolving them in acid, or burning them down to ash and bone. It is odd that in this case they did both at the same time.

been misidentified, to which the police responded, "We don't give a fuck!" Others gathered rocks to throw, but with the arrival of more patrol cars, they broke and ran. Some escaped, two were killed, several were wounded, and around ten of them were captured and bundled into police cars.

At roughly the same time, in a quite different part of the city, another bus, also full of youngsters, was shot up by the police, thinking they were Ayotzinapans. They were in fact soccer players from Chilpancingo, in town to play against Iguala, and having won their match, were on their way home to celebrate. Two aboard the bus were killed (the chauffeur and one of the passengers) and several were wounded. The police, realizing their mistake, called an ambulance.

At that point the police had killed six and injured twenty-three.

◆ ◆ ◆

Throughout all this mayhem, Guerrero's Governor Ángel Aguirre was receiving phone calls from state officials reporting on the shootings in Iguala. It's not known whether the governor talked with the mayor, but he had talked that day with the mayor's wife (with whom, people say, he was having an affair; Pineda also appears to have channeled funds into Aguirre's gubernatorial campaign). In the end, the governor decided against intervening in the police assaults; it was not in his jurisdiction, he would say.

The mayor would claim to have been entirely out of the loop that evening. He allowed as how he had heard that students were disturbing the peace downtown, but insisted he had only ordered the police not to respond to their "provocations." While the bus shootings were happening, Abarca argued, he could not have been involved, as his wife's post-event party was in full swing: "I was dancing," he said, and even reeled off the ditties he and his wife had danced to. After which he had gone home and slept soundly. In fact he and Pineda were on the case throughout the night, with ten calls registered from his cell phone and twenty-five from hers, the last of which was placed at 3:00 a.m.

Also burning up the wires that evening was Gildardo "El Cabo Gil" López, the number two man in the Guerreros Unidos, whose particular remit was as liaison with the Iguala and Cocula police departments. El Cabo Gil arranged for the captured students to be sent to his home in Loma del Coyote, a village west of Iguala on the road to Cocula. He in turn contacted his superior, Sidronio Casarrubias Salgado, the reigning boss of the Guerreros Unidos. The message he texted said that "Los Rojos are attacking us!"—adding yet another layer of complexity to the swirling events of the evening. El Cabo Gil was perhaps especially sensitive to possible incursions by Los Rojos, his father having been killed by the rival gang, but it's hard to see how he could have come by that notion in this instance, given that the police with whom he was in touch were under no such delusion. In any event, Casarrubias returned a BlackBerry message: "Stop them, at any cost."

At this point, control of the operation was transferred to the gangsters. The police departments delivered two groups of students, some thirty that had been captured at the caravan, another ten who had been rounded up at the second confrontation site, and then departed. The students were tied up with rope or wire, and packed into two pick-up trucks, a Nissan Estaquita and a 3.5-ton Ford. Most were piled on top of one another in the Ford; the five who didn't fit were laid out in the Nissan. Then the trucks, flanked by a sixteen-man motorcycle escort, headed toward Cocula, then branched off on a bumpy dirt road that led to a garbage dump, arriving between 12:30 and 1:00 a.m. It was drizzling—no more than seven millimeters accumulated during the night—and it was dark, the only lights being those of the trucks and motorcycles.

The sixteen gangsters dragged the students from the trucks onto the ground near the edge of a ravine. Roughly fifteen of them had died en route, apparently from asphyxiation. Roughly thirty were still alive, crying and screaming. These were then, according to one of the confessed perpetrators, "interrogated." The Guerreros claimed they demanded to know if the students had a Los Rojos connection, which they of course denied, until under beatings and torture one cracked and "confessed," after which, around 2:00 a.m., they were shot, one after another. (We do not know if all were killed before the final stage; one can only hope so.)

Then the bodies were heaved down to the bottom of the ravine, where they were stacked, like cordwood, in alternating layers. The resulting tower of bodies was doused in diesel fuel and gasoline, and set on fire. The blaze was kept burning through the night and into the following afternoon of Saturday, September 27, perhaps fifteen hours or so, by feeding the flames with whatever inflammable materials happened to be in the dump—paper, plastic, planks, branches, tires—and with a continuous supply of diesel fuel ferried in by motorcycle. Finally the bodies were reduced to ashes and bits of bone, which were then pulverized. "They'll never find them," El Cabo Gil texted to Casarrubias.

◆ ◆ ◆

Before concluding this narrative, we must note it is being challenged by those who propose a counter narrative which is even more horrible than this one. It argues that the students were in fact captured by the army, taken to the battalion's barracks, and there killed and burned in the military's professional grade crematorium. Proponents do not advance a scenario that lays out how this came to happen—presumably it would have involved a transfer not to gangsters but to soldiers—and their hypothesis, as they acknowledge, requires accepting that an elaborate cover-up ensued at the highest levels of government.

This is not inherently implausible. The army has long been at loggerheads with leftists; indeed decades ago they were responsible for the killing of Ayotzinapa guerilla graduate Lucio Cabañas, but only after he had humiliatingly held out against several years of massive military campaigns. More recently, they've been accused of using excessive and indiscriminate force against civilians, including torture, and specifically of committing a particular massacre and then altering the crime scene to cover up their culpability. There's also the question of how a narco municipality managed to exist with an army garrison in town.

It's possible to imagine that they arrested those they considered as dangerous radicals, perhaps just to "teach them a lesson," and then, when they realized admitting this might be politically problematic, decided to eliminate the students and pin the blame on gangsters. Federal authorities also have a dismal track record when it comes to admitting official wrongdoing, and conceivably could have participated in a cover-up, which included torturing the captured gangsters into taking the fall.

This scenario has been adopted by substantial numbers of Mexicans, and crowds have been demanding the military open the barracks to inspection. We do not find this narrative persuasive, given the large number of people who would have had to participate in such a mammoth conspiracy, and the as yet complete absence of evidence for such an approach. But if it should prove to be true, and the military and the federal state were responsible for this particular mass murder, the ramifications would be immense. And even if it's not, the conviction that it might be suggests how profoundly alienated much of the population has become from the established order.

◆ ◆ ◆

All of these horrific details of the gangster-run massacre only emerged six weeks later, after key participants were caught and had confessed. In the interim, from September 27 on, with the students' fate as yet unknown, a hunt got underway to find the vanished forty-three, spurred by the students' distraught parents who desperately hoped their children had been "only" kidnapped and hidden away. "They Took Them Alive, We Want Them Back Alive" became the endlessly chanted demand.

On September 28, all 280 members of the Iguala Police Department were brought in for questioning, after which twenty-two were held. Of these, sixteen, found to have used firearms, were arrested and sent to a maximum-security prison, charged with aggravated murder.

On September 29, Mayor Abarca denied having any involvement in the police attack. Nor did he admit to the "Will no one rid me of this troublesome priest?"–style injunction to "teach them a lesson." The next day, however, the mayor requested and received a thirty-day leave of absence, and immediately skipped town with his wife and his cousin, the police chief.

On October 4, searchers combing the countryside near Iguala discovered three mass graves containing the bodies of twenty-eight people (later revised to thirty-four). But on October 14 it was declared that DNA analysis proved none were the missing students. Who they *were* was a new mystery, soon compounded when more mass graves turned up, containing an undetermined number of bodies. Other families now came forward to demand investigation to see if *their* disappeared relatives were among those whose bones had been uncovered. ("*Six* mass graves," wrote one appalled columnist, "and they still haven't found the *right* mass grave.")

The next day, October 5, a 250-person federal police contingent—the elite National Gendarmerie—removed all the Iguala police from office and took over their duties. October 6 saw shockwaves and protests rippling out from the vigil at Ayotzinapa that the parents had begun to keep. President Enrique Peña Nieto, whose initial response to the incident had been muted (on September 30 he'd said the state of Guerrero should assume responsibility), addressed the nation, promising to expand the search and bring the perpetrators to justice. Students who had escaped the initial police shooting held a press conference and described the attack on the buses. A guerrilla group from Guerrero—the Popular Revolutionary Army (EPR), which dates to the mid-1990s and has been largely inactive in recent years—YouTubed its solidarity, promised to take action, and called on the public to enact "popular justice."

On October 8, students from the school led their first large-scale demonstration, and solidarity protests were held the same day in Berlin, Buenos Aires, London, San Francisco, Los Angeles, New York, Chicago, Montreal, Barcelona, Madrid, Brussels, and Manchester, England. On October 13, masked protesters stormed and burned a state office building in Chilpancingo. On October 16, there were student strikes around the country, and Peña Nieto declared finding the students to be a priority of his government. Within days, the federal state dispatched special police forces to take control of thirteen other gangster-ridden municipalities in Guerrero. Thousands of security forces scoured the countryside, using horses, vans, tanks, helicopters, motorboats, and diving gear. At the state level, in Acapulco, thousands of students, teachers, and machete-wielding farmers called for the resignation of Governor Aguirre over his handling—or non-handling—of the case. That same day on a highway near Mexico City, federal forces captured Casarrubias, the top-ranking member of Guerreros Unidos.

On October 22, Mexico's Attorney General Jesús Murillo Karam announced that, according to the gangster's confession, the mayor and his wife had indeed ordered the interception of the buses. Later that day in Iguala, as thousands marched peacefully demanding the missing students be returned alive, dozens of masked protestors broke away and firebombed City Hall. In Mexico City over fifty thousand demonstrated, peacefully.

The next day, October 23, Governor Aguirre stepped down, pressured by his party and public opinion. He was not, however, accused of any culpability. On October 27, authorities arrested four other members of the Guerreros Unidos. They directed attention to the garbage dump, which was cordoned off by the army and navy. Forensic teams arrived to investigate the scene.

On October 29, parents of the students had a five-hour meeting with Peña Nieto at Los Pinos, the presidential residence, and then held a press conference at a human rights center in the city. One father, declaring, "We are not sheep to be killed whenever they feel like it," asserted he had come to demand the children be found "because I am a citizen of Mexico, and I have rights."

On November 4, the mayoral couple was tracked down by federal police, hiding in a working-class neighborhood of Mexico City. Abarca admitted he had been collapsing under the strain. Pineda, haughty as ever, disdainfully ordered the police arresting her to "Take your hands off me" before adding, "How dare you!" Both were imprisoned. None of the couple's responses to questioning were released.

Finally, on November 7, Attorney General Murillo, having met with the parents first, held a somber press conference at which he presented the findings to date. Drawing on the confessions of several who had participated in the mass murder, he laid out the story whose essential lines we have presented above. He also added a disturbing postscript to the atrocity.

After the fire had burned out, the executioners were told to cool and pack the remains—ashes and bone fragments (the latter first smashed to powder)—into large black plastic garbage bags and to dump the contents in the nearby San Juan River. The first, and seemingly least experienced, flung two bags, *intact*, off a bridge into the current below. His colleagues explained they were supposed to *empty* the bags into the river, and this was done with all the remaining ones. But the error allowed Navy divers to salvage some remains. The parents, not trusting Mexican officials, demanded that attempts to glean some DNA information from these tiny bits of bone include, as independent agents, a team of forensic experts from Argentina, who were grimly experienced in tracking the remains of those disappeared by the dictatorship. Material was also sent to the world-class laboratories at the University of Innsbruck in Austria. For the moment, Murillo said, the students were still officially categorized as "missing," and the case remained open.

In December the Austrians announced that DNA found on one of the bone fragments was that of Alexander Mora Venancio, one of the Forty-Three. The Argentinian forensic team accepted the analysis, but noted that as they had not been present when the remains had been discovered, they could not ratify the government's assertion that the burning had taken place at the dump.

In January 2015, Attorney General Murillo Karam declared the case closed, arguing that no new information had been unearthed that would require revising the official narrative. Many of the parents insisted that, given the absence of any forensic evidence as to the fate of forty-two of the forty-three missing students, their sons might still be alive. They called for turning the case over to an international criminal tribunal.

◆ ◆ ◆

The story of the Ayotzinapa students has shaken Mexico profoundly. Immense demonstrations have taken place all across the country. Students at universities and technical schools have been particularly vociferous, appalled at the fate of their fellow students, but artists, actors, writers, lawyers—one trade and profession after another—have also marched in solidarity. Catholic bishops have spoken out (as has Pope Francis). Over the six agonizing weeks from massacre to unmasking, hope faded but anger grew, and with it the size and fury of protests against municipal, state, and federal authorities. Not only have individual politicians been discredited to a remarkable degree, but the leading political parties have also been bitterly denounced. The PRD, the major left opposition party, has been badly tarnished, as both Abarca and Aguirre ran for office on their ticket. Peña Nieto's ruling PRI party has been attacked for its belated concern with the students' fate, and more broadly for its inability or unwillingness to crack down on criminality; huge citizen assemblies have called on the president to resign. Most of these protests have been peaceful, but some have flared into violence, as when the doors of the Presidential Palace in Mexico City were set ablaze, or when Acapulco International Airport was seized. This led critics to denounce the disorder, and to dismiss the Ayotzinapans themselves as radical troublemakers not worth all the uproar. But the overwhelmingly predominant responses have been shock, shame, sadness, and outrage.

This reaction is something of a mystery. Not because the massacre does not warrant such responses, but because it is only the latest in a lengthy sequence of horrors. Apart from the identity of the victims—poor rural youth determined to improve themselves and their communities by becoming teachers—there is not a single aspect of the killing spree, and the nexus of corruption and criminality that spawned it, that has not been commonplace in Mexico's recent history.

Mass murder (in one instance producing three hundred corpses); grisly torture (one victim's face was skinned and sewn onto a soccer ball); collusion between mayors, governors, and militarized drug traffickers; rampant kidnapping and extortion; police on the payroll of cartels possessed of vast drug profits available for bribery; the wholesale arrest of police departments; a criminal justice system that all but guarantees criminals impunity from prosecution; the inefficiency or disinterest of higher political officials; and even the eruption of protests from civil society—all these have been routine in the last dozen years.

Forty-three bodies? Since 2000, more than one hundred thousand have been killed. Mass graves? Tens of thousands have been disappeared, many likely moldering in such pits. Horrific executions? Roughly two thousand of the hundred thousand suffered death by decapitation.

So, why now the nationwide explosion? In part, it was the militant determination of the parents not to let this latest atrocity get lost in the endless slipstream of murder and mayhem. In part it was precisely *because* of the long train of abuses that had preceded it—the patently metastasizing cancers of corruption and criminality—of which people had finally had enough. "We are angry because this is not an isolated event," said one woman demonstrating on behalf of the Forty-Three. "Many of us are parents and we see very ugly things in this country that we want to fight."

This is a book about that long train of abuses. It seeks to provide readers, especially those in the U.S., with a general context, without which this particular outrage is largely incomprehensible. Much of our story will focus on what is generally known as the Mexican Drug War, a phenomenon conventionally dated from 2006, when the Mexican military was sent into action against powerful drug cartels exercising effective control over vast stretches of Mexican territory. Most

Americans know that something horrible has been going on below the Rio Grande during the past decade (2006-2015). They have seen the occasional stories detailing blood-drenched massacres, the capture of drug kingpins, the murder of journalists. They may have read U.S. State Department Travel Warnings alerting them that murder and kidnapping await the unwary (and the wary as well). But it has been difficult to get a grasp on the drug war's extent or nature.

It is our contention that just as the story of the Forty-Three needs contextualization, so does the drug war itself. We suggest that it, too, is inexplicable if one scrutinizes only the narrow time frame in which it is customarily confined. That decade has a lengthy and complicated backstory that needs to be situated in the preceding century (1914-2015) of which it was the sanguinary dénouement.

In addition, we argue that the very term "Mexican Drug War" is profoundly misleading, as it diverts attention from the American role in its creation. Americans understandably view the blood-drenched bulletins from below the Rio Grande as dispatches from a different world. They are reports from a distant battlefield, limning a *Mexican* Drug War—presumably a conflict of Mexico's making, hence Mexico's responsibility alone. But we believe the term to be a misnomer, as the complex phenomena to which it refers were jointly constructed by Mexico and the United States over the last hundred years.

Americans are probably aware that the vast bulk of illegal drugs consumed in the United States—cocaine, heroin, marijuana, and methamphetamine—arrive from Mexico. Some are also aware that the vast bulk of weaponry used by drug cartels in their battles with each other and with the Mexican state flows south from the U.S.A. But what is perhaps less appreciated is how much the present situation dates to America's long-ago coupling of a voracious demand for drugs with a prohibition on their use or purchase. Just as the prohibition of alcohol in 1919 summoned American organized crime into being, along with hyper-corruption of politicians and law enforcement, so its even earlier proscription of narcotics in 1914 (which, unlike the ban on alcohol, was never repealed) spawned a drug-trafficking industry in

Mexico, the enormous profits from which were used to corrupt Mexican politicians and law enforcement.

Mexico was not a helpless, hapless victim. Powerful forces within the country profited hugely and happily from supplying gringos with what their government forbade them. But when the U.S. began bullying its neighbor into trying (and failing) to interdict the torrent of drugs moving across their joint border (something it had been unable to accomplish itself), it led, eventually, to the "Mexican Drug War," which would cost tens of thousands of Mexican lives and spur an explosion of corruption and criminality.

These assessments underlie the organization of this book. We will first undertake an overflight of a century of U.S./Mexico relations, setting the commerce in drugs, and the attempts at its repression, in the context of the larger political, economic, and ideological transformations experienced by both countries. Then we will track in greater detail the last decade's drug war proper, when a tsunami of violence swamped Mexico. Finally we will return to the story of the Forty-Three, which by then, we hope, will have become more comprehensible, and conclude with some thoughts on how both the U.S. and Mexico might turn some new pages in their respective and joint histories. In particular, we will suggest that the fury aroused by the Forty-Three affair, and the subsequent determination of Mexicans to pursue fundamental changes, might best be directed not only into indispensible remakes of its political, economic, and criminal justice systems, but also into ending the century-old criminalization regime itself, which we believe has in large part been responsible for the current situation.

—Carmen Boullosa and Mike Wallace
Brooklyn/Coyoacán
January, 2015

CHAPTER ONE
1910s–1930s

We begin north of the Rio Grande, the source of the insatiable demand for, and interdiction of, narcotics from Mexico. In the United States, the use and sale of various psychoactive drugs—notably opium, marijuana, and cocaine—had been perfectly legal in the nineteenth century and into the early years of the twentieth. Indeed, drug peddling had become big business. Pharmaceutical and patent medicine companies added opium derivatives (morphine, laudanum, heroin) to home remedies for assorted ailments, opiates being one of the few effective forms of pain control available. The typical opium user was a middle-aged, middle-class, white woman. Cocaine, too, was added to medicinal and recreational commodities ranging from cigarettes to soft drinks. Coca-Cola was tinctured with coca leaves until 1903.

Slowly during the 1890s, then with mounting determination during the 1900s and 1910s, a variety of players promoted the criminalization of narcotics, a movement that paralleled the simultaneous push to outlaw alcoholic beverages. These drug prohibitionists included: doctors newly aware of the additives' addictive capabilities (and who now had, in aspirin, an effective substitute); muckrakers who denounced corporations for using drugs to hook customers on their products; and anxious racists of various stripes, such as southern whites who claimed cocaine drove Negroes to rape white women, and anti-Chinese activists who charged them with using opium to seduce white women. As David Musto notes, it was not fear of drugs per se that drove the prohibitionists, so much as fear of the social groups who used them.

First, some state governments were won over to prohibition. Then, in 1906, the Pure Food and Drug Act required manufacturers to list the ingredients in their narcotics-laden products, alarming many of the housewives who unwittingly had been spooning opiates to their children. In 1909 the Smoking Opium Exclusion Act successfully barred importation of the form in which most Chinese ingested the drug— putting opium dens out of business—while exempting medicinal versions used by white Americans. The 1909 initiative was prompted, also, by American businessmen's desire to break Europe's (and especially England's) grip on the lucrative China market, as it was thought (correctly) that banning opium would play well with the Chinese authorities who were then trying to stamp out the widespread use of a drug that, since the 1840s, had been pushed on them at gunpoint by the British.

These proscriptions had several unanticipated consequences. Scarcity drove up the price, which attracted criminal traffickers. It also induced former opium smokers to switch to more potent and more dangerous derivatives, like morphine and heroin. The prohibitionists responded by tightening restrictions. They also pushed for international criminalization—winning in the Hague Convention of 1912 commitments from several nations to restrict opium and cocaine. In the U.S. they won passage of the Harrison Act in 1914, which prohibited all non-medicinal use of opiates and cocaine, though not cannabis, which was (correctly) adjudged to be relatively harmless.

The United States had declared war on drugs.

The subsequent shortages, and skyrocketing prices, drew a new generation of gangsters to the trade (Lucky Luciano's first arrest, in 1916, was for peddling opium). With passage of the Eighteenth Amendment and the Volstead Act in 1919, the production, distribution, and sale of alcoholic beverages were banned, triggering the shift from licit to illicit purveyors that spawned modern organized crime in the U.S. Gangster entrepreneurialism was further accelerated by criminalization of the manufacture, importation, and possession of heroin in 1924—which promptly galvanized yet another underground market. Arnold Rothstein, New York's master criminal, alerted by his protégé Luciano about the profit potentials—a kilo of heroin could be bought for $2,000, then cut and resold for $300,000—shifted out of rum-running in the mid-1920s, and turned instead to importing opium and heroin from Europe. Purchasing a well-reputed mercantile firm as cover for his wholesaling operations, Rothstein began distributing to a national market, dispatching the goods by rail.

◆ ◆ ◆

The booming U.S. demand for narcotics also attracted attention in Mexico. While the climate in the United States was not suitable for poppy horticulture, Mexico was situated in a latitude zone that provided the perfect temperature for cactuses (at lower altitude) and poppies (at higher elevations). Conditions for opium cultivation were particularly ideal in the Golden Triangle, a region in the western Sierra Madre mountains (of *Treasure* fame) where the states of Sinaloa, Durango, and Chihuahua come together. (See map, page vi.) It was there that poppy production blossomed—introduced in the 1880s by Chinese migrants who had been forced out of the U.S. or had arrived by sea to Sinaloa, a state that runs for four hundred miles along Mexico's Pacific coast. Most worked on the railroads and in the mines, but some rural Chinese families entered into production of opium and marijuana. Their numbers increased after the United States banned further immigration, with passage of the baldly titled Chinese Exclusion Act of 1882 and its subsequent iterations in 1892 and 1902. In the first decade of the twentieth century the number of Chinese living in Mexico quintupled (from 2,660 to 13,203), and more opted to engage in cultivation. During and after the Revolution, in the 1910s and 1920s, they were joined by some of the many Mexican farmers who had been impoverished by the war's devastation.

Over these decades Chinese immigrants and their descendants fashioned a rough-hewn drug trafficking network. After harvesting the poppies and extracting the *goma* (gum, latex paste) from the poppy seedpods, they conveyed raw or cooked opium to Chinese dealers in the U.S. (chiefly Los Angeles) via a series of outposts in towns between Sinaloa and the cities on Mexico's northwest border, notably Tijuana. More and more Mexican peasants, middle-class townsfolk, and some wealthy merchants jumped into the business. It was easy to enter—there were no significant start-up costs. Nor was there significant danger: there was room for everybody, hence no need to employ violence to stake out market share.

The U.S. border—360 miles to the north—was not only close to Sinaloan traders and producers (called *gomeros* after the *goma*) but also notoriously porous. It had been so for a long time, ever since the Mexican War (*La Invasión Norteamericana* [1846–1848]) had violently redrawn the line of demarcation, shifting vast holdings of gold, coal, iron, and copper, along with great tracts of fertile agricultural land, to the U.S. side of the ledger, including all or parts of California, New Mexico, Arizona, Nevada, Utah, and Colorado. The newly inscribed frontier (enhanced by an additional strip purchased in 1853) became one of the longest borders on the planet, stretching two thousand miles. It ran from Tijuana, on the Pacific coast, through deserts and arid hills to Ciudad Juárez at roughly the halfway mark, and from there it jagged southeast, running along the Río Bravo (as Mexicans call the Rio Grande) down to the Gulf of Mexico.

Almost immediately the border was transgressed more or less at will. In the 1850s slaves smuggled themselves across to freedom: Mexico, having abolished slavery, awarded citizenship to runaways who headed not toward the North Star (Canada) but the Southern Cross. In the 1860s Confederates smuggled cotton to Mexico for transshipment to Europe, and gun runners sent munitions to help Benito Juárez fight the French. Cattle rustlers ambled over from both north and south, stealing herds and driving them across the border for rebranding and sale. A brisk commerce in tequila, pulque, mescal, and rum also sprang up, flowing north to the U.S. from Mexican distilleries, avoiding tax collectors and, later, prohibition agents.

There was also an easy flow of people back and forth. Border crossing was a breeze because there were no official restrictions or quotas on Mexican movement north; even after the U.S. imposed stringent quota laws in the 1920s, Latin Americans remained exempt. The U.S. Border Patrol, created in 1924, focused on Europeans or Asians seeking to circumvent the barriers erected on the Atlantic and Pacific frontiers. In the early 1900s, about sixty thousand Mexicans entered the U.S. each year at the behest of U.S. agricultural employers; the majority returned home in the winters. The number doubled in the 1910s, as the Revolution set off tidal flows of migrants.

Mexico's people and produce obtained easier passage after the Sonora Railroad—operating from 1882 between Mazatlán (Sinaloa) and Nogales (Sonora)—was integrated northward in 1898 into the Southern Pacific's U.S. rail grid, and extended southward to Guadalajara. The renamed Southern Pacific of Mexico transported millions of passengers and millions of tons of freight, both within Mexico and across the northern frontier.

Opium eased its way into these well-traveled routes. The three crossing points closest to the mountain seedbed of Sinaloa were Tijuana and Mexicali (both astride the border between Baja California and California) and Nogales, where Sonora interfaces with Arizona. Channels were also being created in the center of the country, at the major metropolis of Ciudad Juárez, situated in the state of Chihuahua just below New Mexico and Texas (at El Paso). And farther east, transit points grew up at three medium-size towns dotted along the river—Nuevo Laredo, Reynosa, and, finally, Matamoros on the Gulf of Mexico.

◆ ◆ ◆

Not all drugs crossed the border. Some were destined for local consumption. During the nineteenth and early twentieth centuries, psychoactive agents were commonly used in Mexico, for medical and recreational reasons. Opium smoking was chiefly a pastime of the Chinese minority; morphine, heroin, and cocaine appealed to bourgeois artists and intellectuals; and marijuana was primarily the province of the poor. But drug use was not a mass phenomenon. Ingestion levels were nowhere near those attained in Gringolandia.

In part this was because Mexico, unlike the U.S., had a long tradition, inherited from the Spanish, of keeping a regulatory eye on drug use. Constraints of varying degrees had long been imposed on the consumption of alcohol, of peyote and other psychoactive substances used in rituals (which were seen by the Inquisition as theologically suspect), and of herbs, notably potentially dangerous ones like belladonna, henbane, hemlock, digitalis, and jimsonweed.

Surprisingly—from a contemporary perspective—one of the drugs most frowned upon by officialdom was marijuana. Not an indigenous plant, the weed had been introduced by Spanish imperial authorities in the sixteenth century because hemp was highly prized as a nautical fiber, used for making ropes and sails. Gradually it became available from herboleros—indigenous pharmacists—and by Porfirian times (dictator Porfirio Díaz reigned from 1876 to 1911) it had become the drug of choice for the lower classes, particularly soldiers and prisoners. Marijuana had also gained the reputation of being able to trigger temporary insanity and murderous violence. There were indeed hundreds of well-documented cases, especially in jails and army barracks, of sky-high *machos* running amok, even when vastly outnumbered. But as Isaac Campos argues persuasively, this is better chalked up to context than to cannabis. The effect of marijuana, as with most psychoactive chemicals, depends on the setting in which it is consumed, which includes prevailing mindsets. It should not be surprising that its use in highly stressful situations, where defending one's honor (and person) often demands an aggressive response to a perceived slight, could engender paranoia rather than mellowness, and promote a lashing out.

A patchwork of state, local, and federal laws grew up during the Porfiriato. In 1883, marijuana and opium were among the two dozen drugs that could be sold only by prescription, and only through pharmacies, not *herbolarias*. The regulation was not aimed primarily at recreational users, but was intended to diminish the number of accidental (or purposeful) poisonings. The edict was reaffirmed in the first Federal Sanitary Code (1891). And in 1896, even Culiacán, capital of drug-friendly Sinaloa, banned the sale or use of marijuana without a prescription. So did Mexico City, a decision that municipal authorities reaffirmed in 1908, though they outlawed only cultivation and commerce, not possession of pot, nor giving it as a gift. By the 1910s there was substantial but not overwhelming support in Mexico for restrictionist policies, though most drugs, if prescribed by doctors, remained available in pharmacies.

The Revolution strengthened prohibitionist forces. In 1917, the country was still reeling from a dizzying succession of events—the electoral defeat of the long ensconced Porfirio Díaz by Francisco Madero in 1911; Madero's overthrow and murder by Victoriano Huerta in 1913; the outbreak of war against Huerta by the combined forces of Venustiano Carranza, Álvaro Obregón, Emiliano Zapata, and Francisco "Pancho" Villa, their anti-Huerta campaign aided and abetted by the United States, which briefly occupied Veracruz; Huerta's overthrow in 1914; the seizure of power by liberal reformer Carranza in 1914, the recognition of his government by the United States in 1915, and his election as President in 1917. It was in the subsequent window of (very relative) tranquility and stability that Carranza and his immediate successors set in motion a change in Mexico's approach to the business of narcotics, one that dovetailed with simultaneous developments transpiring north of the Río Bravo.

In 1912, Francisco Madero's government had signed the Hague Convention (though Mexico would not ratify the treaty until 1925). In part this was done because the still-shaky regime felt the need to align itself with the international movement being promoted principally by the United States. But in truth Mexico had preceded the U.S. on the road to regulatory regimes and was way ahead of it in its opposition to marijuana.

The issue was put aside in the ensuing whirlwind of revolutionary combat, but once Carranza came to power, restrictionists took a further step. Determined to restore political order, Carranza convoked a Constitutional Convention, which opened in the city of Querétaro in December 1916. Battles between relatively moderate Carranza forces, and radical younger turks seeking social and economic as well as political change, were for the most part won by the radicals, with key provisions drastically curtailing the power of the Catholic Church, laying the basis for major land reform, establishing national rights to subsoil minerals, expanding lay education, and creating a powerful executive branch.

There was, however, little disagreement about drug policy. In January 1917, Brigadier General José María Rodríguez, personal physician of Carranza, argued passionately that Mexico's position in the "competition of nations" was imperiled because the Mexican "race" had become "infirm" and "degenerated" under Porfirian rule. Some delegates even charged the dictatorship had sought to stupefy and distract the populace through drink and drugs, gambling and prostitution. Stern revolutionary elites associated alcoholism, opium addiction, and marijuana consumption with lower-class illiterates and (mistakenly) with indigenous Indians—"backward" social sectors. Drugs were perceived as obstacles to forging a new model citizenry, one that could build a modern, progressive, and civilized Mexican nation.

Rodríguez proposed an amendment to the Constitution that would give Congress the power to prohibit the "selling of substances which poison the individual and degenerate the [Mexican] race." He named alcohol, opium, morphine, ether, cocaine, and marijuana (the latter being "one of the most pernicious manias of our people"). He also urged writing into the revolutionary charter a provision for a federal department of public health, whose recommendations on issues of civic hygiene would have the force of law. This was done; the new Constitution was approved in 1917, and in 1918 the agency was established, with Rodríguez as its head. He now pushed for draconian measures and, during the last days of the Carranza regime, had the department promulgate "Decrees on the Cultivation and Commerce of Products that Degenerate the Race." These banned the growing of opium and the extraction of its narcotic latex without special permission; banned completely the production and sale of marijuana, nationwide; required drug wholesalers to obtain special permission to import opiates or cocaine; and mandated that such importers sell those drugs only to licensed medical distributors, or to doctors who had received specific permission to receive and prescribe them.

Mexico had declared war on drugs.

Implementation was forestalled by renewed revolutionary chaos, as Generals Álvaro Obregón and Plutarco Elías Calles, among others, took up arms against the Carranza regime. In May 1920, with rebel forces closing in, Carranza left the capital for Veracruz but never made it, having been murdered (or committed suicide) on the way. Obregón was now elected to succeed him, and Mexico entered a period of (again relative) tranquility. In 1923 Obregón peacefully passed the presidential torch to his comrade-in-arms Calles, who during his term in office (1924–1928) resuscitated the delayed assault on illicit substances.

Calles was determined to realize the transformative visions embodied in the Constitution but not yet wholly enacted. In preparation, he had undertaken a 1923 tour of Europe to study contemporary socialist practice. He consulted particularly with German Social Democrats, and also corresponded with Turkey's Mustafa Kemal Atatürk, who was just then embarking on an analogous program of political, economic, and cultural reforms to transform the former Ottoman Empire into a modern and secular nation-state. In particular, Calles set about ruthlessly enforcing constitutional curtailments of Catholic prerogatives—breaking the Church's grip on the educational system, and prohibiting religious rituals outside of churches, which themselves became the property of the nation. This sparked a furious resistance by Catholic peasants that spiraled into the ferocious Cristero War (1926–1929) in which seventy thousand to ninety thousand died.

For all his anti-clericalism, Calles sought the moral betterment of the Mexican people. As had his Revolutionary predecessors, he saw combating drug use as one way to accomplish this. Alcoholism was his original bête noire. As governor of Sonora he had prohibited by decree the importation, manufacture, or sale of intoxicating beverages. Violators were to be punished with five years in prison, though he underscored his determination by summarily executing one poor drunkard. As president, he lit into narcotics.

In February 1925 the *New York Times* reported, in a story head-lined "Calles Orders Drug War," that the new president had announced he would "punish all drug handlers and users of drugs in Mexico." He had, moreover, fired policemen who "were recently implicated in the drug traffic through protecting importers." Follow-up stories hailed Calles' announcement that he would "clean out" traffickers from border towns, shut down retail outlets in Mexico City, and go after transshipments from Asia and Europe. (Opium and heroin arrived to Acapulco and other west coast ports on Japanese vessels, sometimes hidden inside fish, or were transported to east coast ports like Tampico and Veracruz from Germany, Belgium, and France.) The government also assaulted opium growers—destroying several hundred acres of Chinese-cultivated poppies in the states of Nayarit and Durango—and went after pot producers too.

"Mexico Bans Marihuana," declared a December 1925 *New York Times* story recounting industrious efforts by public health department inspectors to arrest farmers and incinerate their crops. Marijuana leaves, the paper explained, retailing an emerging north-of-the-Río-Bravo version of Mexico's conventional wisdom, "produce murderous delirium" that often drives addicts insane, adding: "Scientists say its effects are perhaps more terrible than those of any intoxicant or drug." In 1931, Luis Astorga notes, drug consumption and trafficking were defined as federal crimes.

◆ ◆ ◆

Calles also set in motion momentous changes in the nation's political structure that would greatly impact once and future drug wars, albeit in contradictory ways. In 1928 he proposed ending *caudillismo*—the seemingly endless battle for preeminence between rival generals—by bringing all factions together inside one capacious political entity, the PNR (*Partido Nacional Revolucionario* or National Revolutionary Party). Established the following year, the PNR solved the vexing problem of presidential succession by allowing the outgoing president, in consultation with other party chieftains, to choose the incoming one. The procedure became known as *el dedazo*—"the tap of the finger"—with the announcement serving as a sort of secular Annunciation. The term of office was changed from four to six years (a period that became known as the *sexenio*). Reelection was strictly prohibited, thus barring any replay of Porfirian-style "elective" dictatorship.

This was no small achievement, given the fate of most other Latin American nations: there would be no dictators-for-life, no Somozas or Trujillos in Mexico's future. Calles, to be sure, did not completely follow his own script. After his term expired, he managed to select and de facto dominate his three de jure successors, with each serving only two years; hence he became known as the behind-the-scenes *Jefe Máximo* ("Maximum Leader"). In 1934 he fingered Lázaro Cárdenas, and even chose his cabinet for him. But in 1936, Cárdenas finally put Calles' principles into practice by having him pulled from his home at midnight and bundled off to exile in San Diego.

Cárdenas, a Depression Era president whose 1934–1940 term overlapped two of FDR's, extended and deepened the Revolutionary legacy: nationalizing oil and railroads; redistributing forty-five million acres of hacienda land to peasants; reviving the system of *ejidos* (communal land, parcels of which were possessed and worked by individuals, but not owned or sellable by them, forestalling re-accumulation of giant *encomienda* tracts); expanding social services and secular schools; and supporting strikes that lifted workers' wages. He also sought to organize core sectors of society into consolidated entities—like the CTM (Confederation of Mexican Workers), a vast collection of unions—with equivalent corporatist bodies for peasants, businessmen, professionals, the military, and others. These were then incorporated into the PNR, which in 1938 he renamed the PRM (*Partido de la Revolución Mexicana* or Party of the Mexican Revolution). The political order had been transformed from an elite to a mass-based system. Within a year, the PRM claimed some 4.3 million members.

What the PRM was *not* was democratic. The new political system concentrated power overwhelmingly in the hands of the party-selected president, reducing the legislative and judicial branches to rubber stamps. Rivalries and disputes were to be settled inside the party, after which a united front was to be presented to the outside world. Internal factionalism was moderated by patronage. Federal and state officials dispensed contracts, jobs, political promotions, educational opportunities, and social services only to loyal and accommodating party adherents. Leaders of trade unions and *campesino* (peasant farmer) organizations delivered votes and suppressed rank-and-file protests, in exchange for personal favors to leaders and concessions to their constituencies.

Challenges to this one-party rule were derailed by muscle and electoral fraud. In 1940 the radical Cárdenas, seeking stability after so much upheaval, chose a moderate successor, Manuel Ávila Camacho. A more radical faction decided to run an opposition candidate, who gathered considerable support. But the labor confederation and the army collaborated in manipulating ballot boxes; PRM gangs provoked street fighting in which dozens were killed and hundreds wounded; and the party declared its official candidate the winner by a preposterous 99 percent margin. (In all this they were following a trail long since blazed by politicians in the United States, the quintessential example being New York City's Tammany Hall, which since the 1830s had been hiring gangsters to drive away opposition voters, using "repeaters" to "vote early and vote often," and stealing ballot boxes to purge them of unwelcome votes.)

The PRM elite did much the same in 1943 when first confronted with a truly independent rival party. In 1939, a group of conservatives led by Manuel Gómez Morín—economist, former director of the Bank of Mexico, and former rector of the National University of Mexico— had founded an oppositional political party, the PAN (*Partido Acción Nacional* or National Action Party). As businessmen and Catholics close to the hierarchy, they were opposed to Cardenismo's anticlericalism, land reform, and oil company expropriation, and to the ruling party's monopolization of politics (though the PAN's democratic credentials were tarnished by their sympathy for Franco's regime).

When the new party first ran candidates, in 1943, the PNR dispatched hooligans to break up their meetings and deployed tested methods of electoral fraud. When the PAN disputed the outcome, the PNR leaders had the official certifying body (which they controlled) award themselves all the contested seats. In 1946 the party bosses adopted a slightly more sophisticated strategy, allowing a handful of victorious opposition representatives to take their seats in the Chamber of Deputies, and one mayor to occupy a single city hall. But they maintained absolute control of the presidency, the senate, and every one of the thirty-two state governorships, and would for decades. Their conviction that they had established a lasting primacy was reflected in their final name change. In 1946 Ávila Camacho rechristened the PNR as the PRI—the *Partido Revolucionario Institucional* (Institutional Revolutionary Party). The Revolution had been institutionalized. The party had declared itself the agency of permanent revolution.

Yet the PRI was not quite the monolith it claimed to be; the pyramid of power was not perfect. If their command of the country's center was all but total, their grip on the periphery, while potent, was more compromised. Many of the circumferential governors were, as they had been under Porfirio Díaz, powerful local *caciques* (chiefs) who were allowed great leeway in ruling their fiefdoms, so long as they obeyed PRI dictates and channeled votes and resources up the chain of command. Many were former generals who had in effect been bought off by being dispatched to the provinces, allowing party politicians to steadily shrink the power of the officer class at the center, furthering demilitarization.

◆ ◆ ◆

One of the perquisites of local power was the freedom, subject to presidential will, to engage in profit-making ventures, notably illicit ones. Drug trafficking was one such business that could be permitted to powerful members of the "Revolutionary family," and this opportunity was most thoroughly seized upon in the northern states nearest the U.S. frontier. Cultivation and commerce of narcotics thus became incorporated into the political system—despite official strictures against it. More precisely, *because* of those strictures: criminalization gave politicians the upper hand and opened up profitable opportunities. Local police and military authorities could exact tribute from traffickers in exchange for guaranteeing no interference from police or military forces. At the same time they regulated the business by forestalling would-be competitors from entering the trade—thus keeping a lid on intramural violence—while also banning operators from themselves engaging in political activities.

Colonel Esteban Cantú, arguably the first major Mexican racketeer, had been sent to the border town of Mexicali in 1911, at the outset of the Revolution, to protect the northern region of Baja California from possible U.S. incursions. In 1914 he declared himself governor and proceeded to preside over a vice economy (prostitution, gambling) aimed at tourists. He also allowed opium dealers to sell their goods to the United States. Cantú lasted until 1920—partly because of Mexicali's geographical isolation and the center's preoccupation with revolutionary upheaval—when General Abelardo L. Rodríguez was dispatched to reaffirm federal authority. According to Paul Kenny, et al., Rodríguez more or less picked up where Cantú had left off. By 1930, after a ten-year reign in Baja California harvesting profits by providing parched Prohibition-era *Norteños* with drink and drugs, he had become a millionaire.

In the 1920s, alcohol smuggling proved an even bigger bonanza than drug dealing. Mexico did not impose a national counterpart to U.S. Prohibition, and such state laws as existed were completely ignored in the rush to profit from northern puritanism. Distilleries and breweries that were criminalized in the U.S. flocked south and reopened all along the border. Saloons shuttered on one side of the frontier stepped across the line and did a roaring business. When U.S. alcohol manufacturers and retailers were required to ship their remaining supply out of the country, Kentucky distilleries alone dispatched thirty-nine million gallons of whiskey south by rail, principally to Ciudad Juárez, from where they were promptly smuggled back north. Mexican capitalists, too, seized the moment and began constructing breweries along the border to quench the insatiable U.S. thirst. Much of the liquid contraband was conveyed in automobiles modified to carry one hundred gallons of booze in side-panel or under-the-rear-seat tanks. (Customs officials would rock suspicious cars and listen for the slosh.) Other smugglers ferried their cargoes across the river, with bribed Mexican authorities providing armed cover against U.S. Border Patrol agents on the farther shore, at times leading to international gunplay.

The glory days ended abruptly with the repeal of Prohibition in 1933, but what the U.S.A. took away by wiping out liquor super-profits, it gave back by criminalizing marijuana. The Marijuana Tax Act of 1937 imposed punitively high taxes on the cash crop, driving it from the free market to the black market and increasing both its scarcity and profitability. Some of the decision to belatedly add cannabis to the list of previously banned psychoactive commodities could be put down to efforts at bureaucratic and personal self-preservation by Harry Anslinger, Commissioner of the Federal Bureau of Narcotics (FBN). Seeking to stave off plans to fold the agency into a larger body (and fire Anslinger), the FBN chief gathered up news stories about marijuana's ability to drive men to violence and madness, and deployed them as evidence that it was an extremely dangerous drug, requiring oversight by an independent federal authority.[3] His criminalization campaign was also backed by southwestern states which, in the prosperous twenties, had welcomed Mexican agricultural laborers and mine workers, but in the depressed thirties, embarked on a massive forced and illegal deportation, as described by Balderrama and Rodríguez. Estimates of those driven back across the border

---

3   The commissioner's scrapbook of horror stories included many that had first been published in the *Mexican Herald*, an English-language newspaper in Mexico City, and were then picked up (as the *Herald* had an Associated Press franchise) and circulated by sensationalist papers in the United States. Anslinger did, however, tailor his alarmism to North American anxieties, arguing that marijuana released sexual inhibitions, and led to rape as well as murder.

range from several hundred thousand to as many as a million, many of them U.S. citizens. Among the justifications for the expulsion was the Mexicans' use of the "killer weed." Lawmakers again declared a drug guilty by association with a "dangerous" population—adding marijuana/Mexican to cocaine/black and opium/Chinese.[4]

Anslinger had succeeded in creating a major new market demand for a product that easily could be cultivated in Mexico. But Anslinger's impact south of the Río Bravo was far greater: he proceeded to intervene directly and heavy-handedly in Mexican affairs, contributing mightily to a fateful turn of events.

In 1937, drug policy and its enforcement in Mexico was still, as since Carranza's day, in the hands of the public health department—Cárdenas having refused to shift it to the attorney general's purview—and the health authorities now headed off in a direction diametrically opposite to that of Anslinger. Dr. Leopoldo Salazar Viniegra, head of the Federal Narcotics Service (part of the health department), was a physician highly regarded for his years of work in Mexico City's Hospital for Drug Addicts, and his extensive research into the effects of drugs. In October 1938 he published a paper entitled "The Myth of Marijuana." He argued that it was a relatively innocuous substance; that it did not (contrary to popular and scientific belief) induce psychosis or provoke violent, criminal behavior; and that Mexico should repeal its prohibition. Instead, the state should establish a government-regulated monopoly on drug distribution, cutting out the criminals by authorizing official dispensaries (or state-licensed physicians) to give addicts maintenance doses at cost. He also called for a public health campaign to educate people about truly dangerous drugs (notably alcohol), and for an expansion of the drug-treatment system. He openly criticized U.S. anti-drug policy as inappropriately

---

4   South of the border, the Chinese were also subjected to forced removal during the Depression, evicted from the opium business by Mexicans long envious of their prosperity. The process had begun in the 1920s, when Calles and prominent politicians had backed a xenophobic campaign whipped up by the Mexican press. It picked up steam after the crash and Repeal with a wave of expropriatory racial violence, packing Asians into boxcars, shipping them out of state, and taking over their homes, property, and businesses.

punitive and inherently unworkable: "It is impossible to break up the traffic in drugs," he declared, "because of the corruption of the police and special agents and because of the wealth and political influence of some of the traffickers." Public health authorities backed his proposal, and the first clinics were opened.

Anslinger hit the roof and struck back fast, imposing (as his office was empowered to do) an embargo on the export of all medicinal drugs to Mexico.[5] He also launched a campaign to discredit Salazar Viniegra, saying his plan was "fantastic" and "amoral," and insisting that drug addiction was not an illness to be treated but an "evil" that "should be rooted out and destroyed." Given inherited anti-marijuana attitudes prevalent in elite Mexican circles, Anslinger's assault gained traction, especially after he wheeled in the U.S. State Department to apply additional pressure. In short order the clinics and the legalization regime were snuffed out.

Anslinger also contained a brush fire closer to home. In 1938, soon after marijuana was proscribed, New York City Mayor Fiorello La Guardia, who had been a vigorous opponent of Prohibition, commissioned a study of the drug by the prestigious New York Academy of Medicine. After extensive study, its very distinguished Marihuana Committee concluded (as had Salazar Viniegra) that the drug was not connected to crime, violence, or sexual predation. Nor was there any evidence (pace Anslinger) that it was being peddled to schoolchildren. Nor was it addictive; indeed they thought it might prove useful in withdrawing from other truly harmful addictions. Completed by 1941, the report was published in 1944. La Guardia might have used its findings to call for reconsidering the 1937 law, but the wartime mayor had far more pressing issues to deal with, and did not follow up. Anslinger was left in possession of the federal field.[6]

---

5   Anslinger later played the embargo card against Cuba, with more justification, when it seemed Batista might allow Lucky Luciano to stay in Havana. Luciano had come there from Sicilian exile in hopes of working with Meyer Lansky and others to make Cuba a major way station in a revived post-war heroin trade. Batista caved and sent the capo packing.

6   And soon, as Carruth and Rowe note, with the arrival of the Cold War, Anslinger tied narcotic addiction to the Red Menace , and doubled the FBN's budget in five years.

CHAPTER TWO
1940s–1950s

During World War II, Sinaloan opium output rose dramatically. Some say the U.S. prevailed on the Mexican government to give free rein to gomeros in order to procure morphine for wounded soldiers, the traditional supply line from Turkey having been severed. Others insist there is no evidence of such a deal, but agree that the trade certainly bloomed, as did the production of hemp, great quantities of which were needed for rope and cordage and other uses. Marijuana output declined after the war, but the opium trade continued to flourish into the fifties, and indeed its operators began to descend from their former mountain fastness. To market their crop, campesino entrepreneurs set up shop in Culiacán, capital of Sinaloa. Violent confrontations began to emerge between traffickers, or against the police, the town becoming (local papers worried) "a new Chicago with gangsters in sandals."

Partly in response to provincial disorder, partly heeding U.S. complaints about the post-war growth in drug trafficking, the PRI—under President Miguel Alemán (1946–1952)—broke with Cárdenas' public health approach and moved decisively toward a punitive prohibitionist regime, and one, moreover, that gathered law enforcement into federal hands. In 1947, Miguel Alemán moved anti-drug enforcement into the PGR, the *Procuraduría General de la República* (attorney general's office) and its subsidiary enforcement arm the *Policía Judicial Federal* (Federal Judicial Police [PJF]).

It quickly became apparent, however, that PRI honchos and their PGR agents had no intention of striving to eliminate the drug business. Rather they adopted a centralized version of what local *caciques* had been doing, establishing something of a public-private partnership. The federal police would take over the business of riding herd on narcotic operators—coordinating, steering, and containing their increasing propensity to compete by violent means. At the same time (a far from merely incidental benefit) they would generate a regular income for the state while also providing for their own pockets and for those of their PGR superiors, and so on up the ladder to the political authorities near or at the apex of the party structure. The PRI would seek not to extirpate but regulate—to establish a (profitable) "Pax Priista."

In the same year, 1947, and largely at the instigation of U.S. authorities, the Miguel Alemán government created the DFS (*Dirección Federal de Seguridad* or National Security Directorate) which was part political police, part national security agency. Something of a cross between the FBI and the then newly minted CIA, it would work particularly closely with the latter, a token of Mexico's alignment with the U.S. in the emerging Cold War. The CIA would come to count on DFS spies to provide it with information on the doings of Soviet, Eastern Bloc, and, later, Cuban officials in Mexico. The PRI would employ it as a domestic secret police, tasked with surveillance and repression of dissidents, populists, unionists, Marxists, communists, and other "subversives."

The DFS quickly strayed into PGR territory, using anti-drug operations as a device for quelling social movements and PRI political adversaries. The DFS also became actively complicit in regulating and profiting from the flow of narcotics to the United States. Colonel Carlos Serrano, a PRI senator and close friend and adviser of President Alemán, had been instrumental (notes Stephen Niblo) in creating the DFS and retained considerable power over its operations. He was believed by the CIA to be "an unscrupulous man, [who] is actively engaged in various illegal enterprises such as the narcotics traffic," though this was no bar to the CIA's working with him. The actual head of the DFS, Colonel Marcelino Inurreta (who had been trained by the FBI), and his top deputies were suspected by the U.S. State Department of being deeply involved in moving marijuana and opium.

In 1948, the Mexican government announced a "Great Campaign" to destroy illegal poppy plants. Police agents—supported for the first time by a contingent of soldiers—launched the effort in Sinaloa. During the 1950s the campaign was extended into Baja California, Sonora, Jalisco, Durango, Morelos, Guanajuato, and the Yucatán. Measured against its putative eradicationist goal, the campaign was largely ineffectual. The illegal plantations were scattered over a vast territory and growers who were discovered often bribed officials to leave their crops alone. But the effects of the campaign were nevertheless sweeping. The federal state had succeeded in prying drug policy enforcement from the hands of local *caciques*, drawn it to the national level, and shown drug dealers exactly who was their new boss. This had the additional if unintended consequence of centralizing the drug trade as well. Local traffickers soon realized that survival and prosperity now depended not only on winning protection from municipal and state authorities but required coming to terms with federal forces—the federal police, the military, the DFS, and PRI officials. That in turn required agglomerating into larger organizations, and expanding their horizons beyond the Sinaloan heartland to embrace the entire country.

CHAPTER THREE
1960s–1970s

In the 1960s and 1970s, this expansion of the drug industry was boosted further by developments in the United States, Europe, and the Middle East.

Marijuana—which had been the particular province of relatively small slivers of the U.S. population (mostly hipsters, urban blacks, and Mexicans)—now became an item of mass consumption. The boom in usage had an immediate impact on Mexican growers, providing them with a stable price and a steady demand, market advantages traditional crops like beans and corn could not match. Sinaloa alone could not meet the burgeoning demand, and farmers started raising it in neighboring Durango, then over in Jalisco, then in southern states like Oaxaca and Guerrero, transforming marijuana production from a basically low-key Sinaloan operation into a high-volume national industry spread over a dozen states. By 1975, the country was supplying about 95 percent of all marijuana consumed north of the Río Bravo.

Transformations were afoot in the opiate world as well. The heretofore reigning "French Connection" had been based on the transport by Corsican gangsters of raw opium purchased legally in Turkey to laboratories in Marseille, where it was processed into heroin, and then conveyed to New York, from whence *mafiosi* injected the drug into the continental commercial bloodstream. This complicated system had been set in place back in 1947, as Alfred McCoy has demonstrated, courtesy of the youthful CIA, which had backed Corsican gangsters against the French Communist Party in their battle to control the Marseille docks. By the late 1960s, when the U.S. was getting 80 to 90 percent of its heroin through this network, anxieties about the communists had subsided, while those about heroin dealers had grown, and anti-drug forces gained the upper hand. In 1972, encouraged by the U.S., Turkey banned opium growing. Though they reversed themselves in 1974, by then a series of spectacular busts had seriously crimped the connection, triggering a heroin drought in East Coast cities.

The period was also marked by spectacular corruption cases. Not long after a 1971 film (*The French Connection*) hailed an earlier record police seizure of drugs in New York City, it was revealed that most of that confiscated heroin had been spirited out of the New York Police Department Property Clerk's fortress and replaced with flour and cornstarch. Later, another three hundred pounds of stored heroin and cocaine, $73 million worth, flew the police coop, making it the then biggest robbery in United States history. The great bulk of the elite NYPD Special Investigations Unit (popularly known as "the Princes of the City") was cashiered for corruption.

The feds, too, were wracked by corruption. As Douglas Valentine shows, Anslinger's Federal Bureau of Narcotics was honeycombed with it. This was a state of affairs from which he averted his eyes until his retirement in 1962, only to have it blow up in a 1968 investigation, which demonstrated that the bureau was itself a major source of supply and protection of heroin. The report was suppressed, as Edward Epstein notes, but virtually every agent in the New York branch was indicted and convicted, fired, or forced to resign. The remains of Anslinger's operation were subsumed in 1968 by the new Bureau of Narcotics and Dangerous Drugs (BNDD) placed within the Justice Department. This successor agency was itself soon riddled with corruption. So much so that its chief appealed to the CIA to help clean up its house which, the CIA agreed, had been "heavily infiltrated by dishonest and corrupt elements, who were believed to have ties with the narcotics smuggling industry." In a parallel to events in Mexico, the regional office of the BNDD achieved a symbiosis with local mafiosi, accepting regular bribes to arrest only those dealers nominated by syndicate, which allowed federal agents to accumulate impressive arrest records and rapid promotion, while eliminating unwanted competitors for the mob.

With the French Connection disconnected, retailers looked elsewhere for wholesale suppliers. Mexico was the obvious choice, given its proximity to the United States, DFS willingness to ride shotgun for traffickers, an ideal geography and climate for a quality product, and an underclass of needy agricultural workers. The switchover happened rapidly. "Mexican mud," a brown tar-like heroin, began flowing north. Estimates suggest that in 1972, Mexico had supplied between 10 and 20 percent of the U.S. market for heroin; by 1975, this had increased to between 70 and 90 percent of a market that had itself (William Walker notes in his *Drug Control*) nearly doubled in size.

At first smuggling from Mexico was more decentralized than that from Europe, hence harder to police. A myriad of small-time smugglers organized a large number of small-scale runs across the border, thereby minimizing the costs of any one seizure. The influx of American dollars into the Sinaloan heartland enriched and transformed the gomeros, who were increasingly called *narcotraficantes* (or *narcos* for short) to signal their elevation in status from mere poppy growers to wealthy international smugglers. They began to adopt a style befitting their new station; in Culiacán they fashioned an entire neighborhood, called Tierra Blanca, and filled it with ostentatious houses.

The operation that broke out of the pack, however, was headquartered in Durango. The Herrera Brothers had been in the business since the 1950s and had established an outpost in Chicago, composed of other members of the extended and extensive clan. Now, with surging U.S. demand, it swelled to major league proportions and by the mid-1970s was moving more than ten tons a year, with a gross retail value of $2 billion. Most Herrera heroin was driven up from Durango to Chicago (a forty-nine-hour nonstop trip) hidden in compartmentalized gas tanks. As the "Heroin Highway" terminated in the Windy City, Chicago usurped New York City's traditional domination of the wholesale market: roughly a third of the product remained in Chicago; the rest was shipped around the nation on commercial flights. In Durango, the efficient organization of what was now being called the "Mexican Connection" was overseen by members of fifteen inter-related Mexican families, headed by patriarch Jaime Herrera-Nevarez. Managers oversaw the hiring of campesinos, the distribution of poppy seed, the development of new production areas, the oversight of gum collectors, the management of labs, cutting, and shipping. Profits were repatriated—cash was smuggled back in the same gas tanks or increasingly sent via wire transfer (using money orders and Western Union) to financial institutions in Durango City, as much a wholly owned subsidiary as any company town in the United States. Net income after wages, bribes, etc. (which Lupsha and Schlegel estimate at $100 million a year) was invested in ranches, land, dairies, apartments, and resort developments—a tremendous, if illicit, boon to the Mexican economy.

◆ ◆ ◆

Up north, during Richard Nixon's presidency (1969–1974), a tremendous amount of energy was being expended contesting the growing influx. Nixon revived Harry Anslinger's War on Drugs. Psychoactives were again associated with a feared social group—this time the large chunk of American youth that had begun smoking weed, getting high while chortling at late-night screenings of the Anslinger era's *Reefer Madness* (1936). Not even Nixon still believed that marijuana drove people to rape and murder, but he did believe, as did many cultural conservatives, that cannabis was doing something worse—undermining American civilization itself.

On July 14, 1969, Nixon sent a Special Message to the Congress on Control of Narcotics and Dangerous Drugs, in which he declared "the abuse of drugs" to be a "serious national threat to the personal health and safety of millions of Americans." Americans were not sufficiently aware of the "gravity of the situation," the President believed, which was why "a new urgency and concerted national policy are needed at the federal level to begin to cope with this growing menace to the general welfare of the United States."

At the same time, Nixon sent administration officials to Mexico to persuade their counterparts to spray herbicides on marijuana and opium crops. Mexican authorities refused, even those sympathetic to Nixon's project, fearing the ecocidal consequences: they pointed to the frightening side effects Agent Orange was producing in Vietnam. Balked, Nixon launched Operation Intercept in September 1969, overseen by Attorney General John Mitchell and largely devised by G. Gordon Liddy (both of later Watergate fame), with the (unannounced) goal of bullying Mexico into acquiescence. Two thousand inspectors began meticulously scrutinizing each car that tried to cross the frontier, searching (sometimes strip searching) each person, each vehicle, each piece of luggage (including purses and lunch boxes), backing up traffic for miles, in effect shutting down the border. After twenty painful days and a blistering barrage of complaints from all quarters, Nixon called it off. But it had worked, just as Anslinger's tactics had. Mexico was strong-armed into launching another Great Campaign (like that begun in 1948), this one submissively entitled Operation Cooperation. Nevertheless, Mexico (which called the joint program Operación CANADOR, an acronym of cannabis and *adormidera* [poppies]) was able to forestall U.S. demands for aerial defoliation by increasing its own efforts at manual eradication. Mexican soldiers were allowed to hack away at opium poppies and marijuana plants with sticks or machetes, at the price of allowing American law enforcement to enter Mexico and conduct surveillance of their operations.[7]

---

7   Among this round's unanticipated consequences was the discovery by drug traffickers that if the border could not be driven through, it could be flown over, which would soon lead to their adoption of an airborne delivery system. Operation Cooperation also had the effect of eliminating less-capable smugglers, thus consolidating power in the hands of bigger, better-financed criminal organizations like the Herrera brothers' operation. And in the States, a considerable number of youths responded unexpectedly to the short-term marijuana famine by shifting to LSD.

Nixon now turned to legislative action, winning passage of the Comprehensive Drug Abuse Prevention and Control Act of 1970, which consolidated previous federal statutes and increased the authority of federal narcotics agents. Title II—the Controlled Substances Act—provided the legal basis for a war on drugs. As his reelection campaign approached, Nixon plowed ahead, stirring up a full-scale moral panic. Bulling his way past the embarrassing findings of the National Commission on Marijuana and Drug Abuse he had established in 1971—it reported there was no evidence marijuana was harmful or addictive and recommended decriminalizing possession— he insisted (in June of that year), using wildly inflated statistics, that the "drug traffic is public enemy number one," against which "we must wage a total offensive, worldwide, nationwide, government-wide."

In 1973, once safely (he thought) returned to the White House, Nixon created the Drug Enforcement Administration (DEA) by executive order. Subsuming the rotted-out Bureau of Narcotics and Dangerous Drugs, along with other agencies, its assigned mission was to "establish a single unified command to combat an all-out global war on the drug menace." Nixon resigned in 1974, but the DEA—whose raison d'être was permanent war on drugs—would long outlive its creator. At its outset, the DEA had 1,470 special agents and an annual budget of less than $75 million. Today, it has 5,235 special agents, 227 domestic field offices, foreign offices in 62 countries, and a budget of roughly $2.5 billion.

◆ ◆ ◆

Despite his humiliation of Mexico, Nixon was not without his supporters there, most particularly President Gustavo Díaz Ordaz (1964– 1970), who was very much on Nixon's cultural wavelength. Personally revulsed by marijuana-smoking Mexican students, he proclaimed the universities to be "full of garbage and filth!" But like Nixon, Díaz Ordaz had deeper worries, rooted not only in personal rigidity but in perceived challenges to PRI power. Many of the rising generation saw the one-party state as repressive, its socialist rhetoric masking an actually existing authoritarianism. Like Nixon, his partner in paranoia, Díaz Ordaz equated political dissent with communist conspiracy, and he lit into those urging democratic reform—writers, journalists, editors, disaffected workers, and particularly students.

In 1966, Díaz Ordaz sent paratroopers to occupy universities where students had mounted demonstrations. In 1968, incensed by insubordinate street protests that threatened to blacken Mexico's image on the world stage just weeks before the country was to host the Summer Olympics, he dispatched armored trucks to disperse the thousands camped in the Zócalo, generating images that evoked those of Prague youth confronting Soviet tanks. Next, Díaz Ordaz orchestrated a massacre of students who were demonstrating in the Plaza de las Tres Culturas in Tlatelolco, a neighborhood in Mexico City, unleashing the army, police, and paramilitary gunmen who fired rifles, bazookas, and machine guns into the crowd from all sides. Two thousand were rounded up, stripped, and beaten; some of them were disappeared; estimates of the dead (indeterminate as bodies were trucked away and burned) ran as high as three hundred. The massacre sparked national and international outrage.

The 1970 shooting of Kent State students protesting Nixon's escalation of the Vietnam War into Cambodia was a pale echo of the Tlatelolco slaughter (in Ohio four were killed, nine wounded), though it did provoke a nationwide strike by over four million students. Similarly the emergence of the Weather Underground, and their bombing campaign in the early 1970s, was a shadow of the turn to armed resistance in Mexico by urban guerilla groups opposed to what they considered a brutal and unresponsive regime. What had no northern counterpart was the emergence of rural rebellions, feeding on a growing crisis in the agricultural sector.

In the mountains of Guerrero, Lucio Cabañas, a Ayotzinapa-trained teacher-turned-revolutionary, forged a small force dubbed the Party of the Poor that engaged in kidnappings and bank robberies to fuel an armed rebellion. By 1971, the new president Luis Echeverría

(1970–1976) had dispatched twelve thousand troops to the region. Though he developed closer ties with socialist governments in Chile and Cuba and offered refuge to victims of the infamous Operación Cóndor, Echeverría remained adamantly opposed to allowing guerrilla groups to develop within Mexico, and he dispatched DFS agents to infiltrate various leftist organizations. In 1974, after Cabañas kidnapped a multimillionaire PRI senator and candidate for governor, the president upped the military presence to twenty-four thousand. The army carried out sweeping roundups, interrogations under torture, and disappearances. In the municipality of Atoyac de Álvarez alone, the military disappeared some four hundred people. Cabanas was killed that year in a shootout with soldiers.

Echeverría's relationship with the U.S. had not been particularly warm, and he had been reluctant to expand the ongoing Operation Cooperation (CANADOR, in Mexico) inherited from his predecessor. But in September 1976, just as Echeverría was passing the presidential torch to his chosen successor, José López Portillo (1976–1982), his government did so. The turnabout was due partly to the insistence of the United States; partly to concern at the surging size of the drug industry (which then covered some six hundred thousand square kilometers, and included roughly thirty thousand opium plots, some of them exceeding forty acres); and partly out of alarm at the rising levels of trafficker-related violence. In Culiacán, gun battles on downtown streets had become daily fare, and Sinaloan papers were packed with complaints about the rising narco threat. The PRI was also dismayed by agrarian unrest—widespread land seizures and armed defiance of authority by desperate campesinos, hard-pressed by a deepening agricultural crisis. The two problems were in fact conjoined, as tens of thousands of these farmers had entered the drug economy and were prepared to defend their new economic lifeline at gunpoint.

The state decided on a full-scale ground assault, and green-lighted the up-till-then rejected U.S. urging of an aerial spraying campaign, as well as authorizing U.S. reconnaissance flyovers of the target area. The new López Portillo government's stated aim was "the total elimination of opium poppy cultivation and maximum cooperation with the United States and other countries in the endeavor." The Mexican attorney general predicted the end of drug trafficking in six months. Left unannounced was the determination to crack down on rural insurgents under cover of the anti-drug campaign. The program was soon renamed Operation Condor, the nom de guerre of the U.S.-supported campaign of political repression and assassination implemented after 1975 by right-wing dictatorships in South America against guerillas, dissidents, students, social activists, unions, and academics—a decade long "Dirty War" in which tens of thousands were killed or disappeared. This aspect of the Mexican operation was the purview of José Hernández Toledo, who had commanded military operations at the Tlatelolco massacre.

In early 1977, ten thousand soldiers stormed the Golden Triangle sierra of Sinaloa, Durango, and Chihuahua. Marauding through villages, they kicked down doors, dragging hundreds of young men away, some to be beaten and tortured (via electric shock, burns, and chili-laced water shot up noses), hundreds never to be seen again. Army units also ransacked houses, raped women, and confiscated belongings, which intensified the armed resistance. From the air, U.S.-supplied aircraft began spraying drug crops—using 2,4-D acid on opium and the toxic herbicide paraquat on marijuana. Tens of thousands of plots and fields would eventually be destroyed, hundreds of kilograms of drugs seized.

The DEA and the now Jimmy Carter White House (1977–1980) sang the praises of Mexico's "model program," and indeed Condor had severely restricted the amount of drugs crossing the United States border. By 1979, the amount of heroin entering the U.S. had been almost halved—an ambiguous victory, as suppliers responded to scarcity by jacking up prices (a milligram's street value rose from $1.26 in 1976 to $2.25 in 1979), which in turn hiked crime rates as junkies sought to feed their more expensive habit.[8]

---

8   In 1979, the Herrera Organization was targeted directly, but though thirty-nine kilograms of heroin were seized, and three Chicago-based bosses were captured, the top leadership and the organization itself sailed on into the 1980s, until 1988, when Operation Durango led to the capture of Jaime Herrera-Nevarez. By then, however, the

The unanticipated consequences ran deeper still. When Operation Condor smashed into Sinaloa, the top narco bosses—who had been left suspiciously untouched—simply relocated.[9] They moved their operations down from the mountains to Mexico's second-largest city, Guadalajara, in the state of Jalisco. There they bought splendid villas and continued their business on an even bigger scale. Condor inadvertently centralized the trade by winnowing out the small fry and strengthening those with the resources to buy protection from the police, the military, the DFS, and PRI politicians.

Perhaps the primary outcome of the latest Great Campaign was to solidify the "*plaza* system" that had been rudimentarily set in place during the 1940s, 1950s, and 1960s. Operation Condor had reminded the gangsters who was boss, and when the program slackened off in the late 1970s, and drug commerce attained its former levels, it was handled in a more orderly fashion. Government agencies (particularly the DFS, whose writ was *suppression* of the trade) established unofficially sanctioned trafficking corridors at strategic transit points through which drugs had to pass on their way to the United States. The *plazas* were not controlled by the criminals; they were, instead, checkpoints at which the traffickers were greeted by the federal police or the military, there to collect bribes, or to bust (and occasionally kill) anyone who was not paying up. This also allowed them to rack up drug seizures, and thus demonstrate they were ardently fighting the war on drugs. De facto state regulation kept the narcos under control, damping down their violence, while handsomely profiting the regulators.

In their protected terrains, drug entrepreneurs grew more ambitious. Some began organizing bigger than ever payloads. Instead of buying marijuana from small family farms, they built and maintained

---

organization's next generation had diversified into cocaine and methamphetamine, and soldiered on.

9   During Condor, owners of plantations that had received unofficial official approval flew flags on their fields to signal pilots not to fumigate but to spray water and fertilizers; drought conditions were prevalent, and some argued that it was the weather, and not the eradication campaign, that was responsible for much of the drop-off.

enormous plantations of their own. One of the boldest innovators was Rafael Caro Quintero, a trafficker from Badiraguato, in the heart of Sinaloan drug country. Born in 1952, Caro Quintero had worked in livestock grazing (as had his father), shifted to truck driving, then segued into working on a bean and corn plantation. In the mid-1970s he moved to the neighboring state of Chihuahua and started growing marijuana on his brother's ranch. Over the next five years he expanded his operation, buying up other local ranches, and amassing a fortune. By the early 1980s he was running the gigantic Rancho Búfalo—a 2,500-acre tract of desert land on which perhaps seven thousand campesinos labored, under conditions of virtual slavery, raising immense marijuana crops that were dried in twenty-five football field–size sheds. Yearly production—valued at $8 billion—was big enough to supply the U.S. its entire annual demand. By 1981, Caro Quintero was quite capable of making fabulous payoffs to police commanders in the state of Chihuahua, to regional politicians, to the military, and above all to Miguel Nazar Haro. A nasty piece of work, infamous for his role in the 1968 Tlatelolco massacre and for the part his "White Brigade" death squad played in the Dirty War, Nazar Haro was appointed chief of the DFS in 1978. By the early 1980s, following the new trend toward concentration, Caro Quintero had allied himself with two other kingpins who had been industriously opening up a whole new drug front, once again thanks to their northern neighbors.

◆ ◆ ◆

In the 1970s and 1980s, cocaine wildfired across the U.S.A. While grass had been associated with political dissent, the counterculture, peace, love, and mellow, the disco drug conjured up glamour, speed, sex, business, and money. *Lots* of money, as its markup was spectacularly higher than pot, and generated billions upon billions of dollars. At first the profits flowed not to Mexicans but to the Colombians whose country's climate was ideal for coca leaf cultivation. Colombians not only manufactured their product, they delivered it. Mobsters in Medellín flew most of their cocaine directly to Florida, a nine-hundred-mile straight shot, airdropping their parcels at sea, from where they were retrieved and rushed ashore in speedboats—as during Prohibition booze was smuggled in from cargo ships parked on Rum Row, just outside the three mile limit.

Presciently, the Colombians launched something of a pilot project in the early 1970s devoted to developing a supplementary route through Mexico. At first they relied on two non-Mexicans to develop the prototype operation. Their direct contact was a Honduran, Juan Ramón Matta Ballesteros, who got the cocaine to Mexico and there turned it over to Cuban-American Alberto Sicilia Falcón, a Tijuana-based gangster, who moved the product across the border. Sicilia Falcón was no ordinary gangbanger. He had quit Cuba for Miami after Castro's arrival in 1959, and was trained there by the CIA to participate in raids and weapons-delivery runs to his former homeland. According to Scott and Marshall, he relocated to Mexico in 1972 and with help from his DFS connections—the DFS and CIA having a close working relationship—he established an operation that unloaded Matta's Colombia product in California. At the same time that presidents Echeverría and Nixon were ratcheting up their anti-marijuana and opium efforts, a $5 billion–per-year cocaine enterprise sprang into being, along with a collateral money-laundering operation provided by Mexican and U.S. banks. Indeed, Sicilia Falcón's Tijuana fortified base of operations, "The Roundhouse," was protected by a coterie of DFS agents armed with AK-47s.

Sicilia Falcón's luck ran out in 1976 after DEA agents penetrated his operation, flipped some of his traffickers, and got the Mexicans to arrest him. (This was not the first time, nor would it be the last, that the DEA and CIA worked at cross-purposes.) Convicted, and dispatched to rot in jail, Sicilia Falcón became the first drug kingpin to be taken down; he was, after all, a foreigner.

With Sicilia Falcón now history, Matta cultivated relations with the rising stars among Sinaloan gangsters. Among them were Rafael Caro Quintero (the maestro of marijuana), Ernesto Fonseca Carrillo, and primus inter pares, Miguel Ángel Félix Gallardo. A Culiacán native born in 1946, Félix Gallardo had joined the Sinaloan judicial police, served as bodyguard to the governor, then sidled into the drug business, departing Sinaloa for Guadalajara after Operation Condor. Once the Matta connection was established in the mid-1970s, he and his associates became the premier couriers in Mexico of Colombian cocaine. Still, up to the early 1980s, their transshipments accounted for only 30 percent of the coke consumed in the United States. What sent them into hyperdrive was the election in 1980 of Ronald Reagan.

CHAPTER FOUR
1980s

Reagan cast himself as a law and order man, ready to reverse the wimpy policies of Jimmy Carter, who indeed had pulled back from Nixonian fanaticism. In this Carter was responding to the growing disinclination of middle-class parents to have their children locked up for marijuana use, which few still believed to be a menace, unlike Reagan who, channeling Anslinger, declared it "probably the most dangerous drug in America." Unluckily for Carter, cocaine use had exploded on his watch, allowing Reagan to run successfully as a reincarnation of Nixon. Once in office he relaunched the war on drugs. In January 1982 he created the South Florida Task Force to go nose-to-nose with the cocaine barons. Headed by Vice President George H. W. Bush, the task force brought in the army and navy, and put Miami vice in its crosshairs.

It worked. Surveillance planes and helicopter gunships throttled the hitherto wide-open Colombia-Florida connection. Seizures cost Medillín drug lords hundreds of millions of dollars. But there was a fix ready to hand: the Colombians simply abandoned their direct shuttle service and increased the flow through their Mexican pipeline. At first the benefits were chiefly channeled back to South America; *Forbes* magazine would estimate the personal fortune of Pablo Escobar, the number one Medellín smuggler, at $9 billion, making him the richest criminal in history. But increasingly the Mexicans shifted from being simply a well-paid smuggling service to demanding and getting full partnership status. Soon Félix Gallardo, Fonseca Carrillo, and Caro

Quintero were providing 90 percent of the cocaine pouring into the ever-expanding U.S. market, and laundering back an estimated $5 billion a year. Twenty million dollars flowed through a branch of the Bank of America in San Diego in just one month.

It was in 1984 that the DEA began referring to the triumvirate as the Guadalajara Cartel, echoing the by then common reference to the Medellín and Cali Cartels. Though the term evoked the tremendous wealth and power of these entities, it was somewhat misleading. The conventional meaning is a consortium of established corporations or states aimed at eliminating competition and its unwelcome handmaidens, price wars and shrinking profits. OPEC (Organization of the Petroleum Exporting Countries) was the era's premier example of such a price-fixing federation. It is true that the Guadalajarans had effected a coalition—indeed, they had established a monopoly—but it had conjoined individual gangsters, or cliques of gangsters, not giant political or economic institutions. Still, the name stuck, though the participants themselves never embraced it.

"Cartel" was misleading in another sense, in that it left out the centrality of the Mexican state. The Guadalajara Cartel prospered largely because it enjoyed the protection of the DFS, under its chief Miguel Nazar Haro (1978–1982), and his successor José Antonio Zorrilla Pérez (1982–1985). The DFS provided bodyguards for the capos; ensured drug-laden trucks safe passage over the border by using the Mexican police radio system to intercept U.S. police surveillance messages; and handed out DFS badges with abandon. (DEA agents could not help but notice that every time they arrested a high-level trafficker he was carrying DFS credentials.) Nazar Haro did yeoman's service for the Guadalajarans until he was tripped up by his own greed. In 1981 the FBI arrested him in San Diego, having caught him smuggling autos into the U.S., a collateral business his drug profits rendered unnecessary. True, the CIA got him sprung—insisting he was an "essential, repeat, essential contact for the CIA station in Mexico City"—but Nazar Haro was now blatantly tarnished goods and axed accordingly. His replacement proved a more than adequate successor, though

Zorrilla Pérez would later prove an embarrassment and be sentenced to the slammer for thirty-five years, having been found guilty of ordering the murder of a prominent journalist.

◆ ◆ ◆

As it turns out, the Guadalajarans received further crucial support from yet another state—the government of Ronald Reagan—this time not inadvertently (as with the unanticipated consequence of shutting down the Miami corridor) but done on deadly purpose.

From 1982 on, CIA and White House apparatchiks (like Oliver North and Elliott Abrams) were looking for ways to circumvent a U.S. Congressional ban on further assistance to the Contras, the U.S.-supported paramilitary movement seeking to topple Nicaragua's Sandinista government. One idea they hit upon was to covertly ferry arms to the Contras via Mexican drug dealers. Félix Gallardo, at that point running four tons of cocaine into the United States every month, provided "humanitarian aid" to the Contras in the form of high-powered weaponry, hard cash, planes, and pilots. Indeed a Caro Quintero ranch became a training facility, run by the DFS—the CIA's faithful Mexican affiliate. In return, Washington looked the other way as enormous amounts of Mexican-processed crack cocaine flooded the streets of U.S. cities, the super-addictive, mass-marketed drug wreaking havoc in poor communities, and triggering an Uzi-driven competition for market share that sent crime rates spiking..

The DEA was becoming increasingly frustrated by DFS and CIA closeness to the drug cartel, which was growing daily in strength and power. DEA agent Enrique "Kiki" Camarena, who had been working out of Guadalajara since 1980, had been barraging Washington with complaints about the gangsters' protective cocoon. In November 1984 he was able to prevail upon a DFS rival, the Federal Judicial Police (PJF), to raid Rancho Búfalo. When 450 men backed by helicopters destroyed the fields and burned ten thousand tons of marijuana, the cartel leaders—enraged—kidnapped, tortured, and killed Camarena. His body was eventually found in a shallow grave on a Michoacán pig farm.

The DEA went ballistic. First they tracked the killers. Caro Quintero had escaped arrest at the Guadalajara airport by waving his DFS badge—Zorrilla Pérez was cashiered for giving it to him—but was eventually captured in Costa Rica, tried, sentenced, and jailed. So was Fonseca Carrillo, but for the moment Félix Gallardo remained in hiding. Then the DEA went to the media with the truth about the DFS and its symbiotic relation with the crooks it was supposed to be suppressing. The American agency had known this all along, of course, but had sat on the story because, in Reagan's administration, the CIA's anti-communist card trumped the DEA's anti-drug hand. More, they made public the corrupt involvement of senior PRI politicians, a blow to the party's image and credibility. In response the Miguel de la Madrid government (1982–1988) dissolved the entire DFS. Some agents and police commanders were sent to jail, but many simply changed uniforms and joined other federal agencies, either the old established PJF or the new CIA clone, CISEN (*Centro de Investigación y Seguridad Nacional* or Center for Research and National Security).

The scandal of Camarena's murder boosted the DEA's political clout in the States. Not only did it win an expansion of the agency's bureaucratic empire, it propelled passage of the 1986 Anti-Drug Abuse Act, which required the executive branch to annually certify that any country receiving U.S. assistance was cooperating fully with U.S. anti-narcotics efforts, or taking steps deemed sufficient on its own. (Thus did the U.S., the world's largest consumer of illegal drugs, set itself up as judge of *other* countries' progress on solving a problem the U.S. could not.) If the country in question failed to measure up—and Mexico was an obvious target—it would be struck off from all foreign aid programs. Worse (particularly for Mexico), the U.S. would oppose any loan requests that country might make to multilateral development banks (like the International Monetary Fund [IMF]), such opposition of course being a guaranteed kiss of death.

Also in 1986, with the crack epidemic at full throttle, with the Iran-Contra scandal about to splash into public view, and with the midterm elections approaching, Reagan turned up the volume of his drug war rhetoric. "My generation will remember how Americans swung into action when we were attacked in World War II," he cried. "Now we're in another war for our freedom." He signed a National Security Decision Directive declaring drug trafficking a threat to national security. This permitted the U.S. Department of Defense to get involved in a wide variety of anti-drug activities, especially on the Mexico-U.S.A. border.

President de la Madrid dutifully followed suit, declaring drug trafficking a threat to Mexico's national security, and authorizing an expanded military presence in anti-narcotics efforts. He had little choice. Mexico had tumbled into a full-blown economic crisis. Certification, hence access to credit, had now become essential. In the course of wrestling with it, de la Madrid would begin to engineer a profound transformation in the country's economy and polity, a transformation that would have major consequences for the organization of the drug business.

◆ ◆ ◆

Since the Cárdenas administration of the 1930s the PRI had been following an interventionist development policy, seeking to boost industrialization and achieve greater national self-sufficiency by imposing tariffs, limiting foreign ownership, investing in energy and transportation infrastructure, subsidizing farmers, and providing substantial social programs. On the whole they had not done badly: from 1940 to 1970 Gross Domestic Product had increased sixfold. In his 1970–1976 sexenio, President Echeverría had dramatically expanded state-driven development by nationalizing more than six hundred enterprises—movie studios, bus manufacturers, hotels, publishing houses—and underwriting major public works (highways, sewer systems), particularly in Mexico City. Much of this nationalization was financed by borrowing from the IMF or World Bank, and it tripled the national debt. Echeverría was encouraged in this spending bender by the 1972 discovery of huge reservoirs of oil under the savannahs of Tabasco—soon dubbed "Little Kuwait"—and then even larger ones offshore in the Bay of Campeche. These holdings were dramatically increased in potential value after 1973 when OPEC succeeded in jacking up global oil prices.

The country could not, however, escape fallout from the global recession that struck in the mid-1970s, leading to a drop in demand for Mexico's industrial exports. In 1976 Echeverría was forced to devalue the peso. It lost half its value, inflation soared, and capital flew away in search of safer climes. Salvation arrived during López Portillo's sexenio in the form of the oil gushers that now came on line; by 1979 one Campeche field alone was filling 1.5 million barrels a day. PEMEX, the state-owned oil monopoly, was able to stop importing and start exporting. Revenues climbed from $500 million in 1976 to $13 billion in 1981, the latter figure boosted by yet another rise in oil prices when in 1979 the Iranian Revolution temporarily subtracted its output from the market.

This windfall produced another one when U.S. bankers began arriving in Mexico City, their suitcases stuffed with petrodollars they were eager to lend such an oil-rich country. By 1981 its proven reserves were estimated at two hundred billion barrels. (One *Fortune* article was entitled: "Why the Bankers Suddenly Love Mexico.")[10] López Portillo was delighted to leverage Mexico's future prospects into cash on the barrelhead, and he doubled down on the PRI's state-driven development strategy.

Some of the massive flow of public spending went into productive enterprise, notably PEMEX itself. Between 1977 and 1980, the oil

---

10 Petrodollars were the swollen sums harvested by OPEC oil-producing members, which they turned over to U.S. and European bankers to invest on their behalf. In Mexico, First National City Bank's Walter Wriston led the money-shoveling pack—reaping whopping profits on the spread and huge fees—arguing that the dangerously insecure loans were perfectly safe since countries couldn't go bankrupt.

company received \$12.6 billion in international credits, representing 37 percent of Mexico's total foreign debt, which it used to construct and operate offshore drilling platforms, build onshore processing facilities, enlarge its refineries, engage in further exploration, and purchase capital goods and technical expertise from abroad. These investments helped increase petroleum output from four hundred million barrels in 1977 to 1.9 billion barrels by 1980. Other investments in railroad, highways, and manufacturing helped grow the Mexican economy at an annual rate of 8 percent.

But much of the spending was squandered on ill-advised projects; on current rather than capital expenditures; and on a self-serving expansion of the bureaucracy (and its salaries). Some of the outlays were blatantly nepotistic or corrupt. This kind of rot, like that of the proverbial fish, began at the head, partly because the PRI system vested virtually limitless power in its Pharaonic president. López Portillo stuffed his relations (wife, sister, son) into high government positions, made a mistress the secretary of tourism, and boasted of it all: "My son is the pride of my nepotism," he declared fondly.

An engineer and old López Portillo confidante, Jorge Díaz Serrano, got the top spot at PEMEX. While successfully expanding development of the new oil finds, Díaz Serrano also cupped his hands in the flow of profits, as did many other PEMEX executives in these years. He later served a five-year prison sentence for doing so. An old López Portillo school chum, Arturo "El Negro" Durazo, was appointed Mexico City's chief of police. Durazo had served in the previous sexenio as police commander of the capital's Benito Juárez International Airport, helping make it a key transshipment point for Colombian cocaine. Now he transformed the city's twenty-eight-thousand-man police force into a drug distribution network, handing out coke packages to brigade commanders to sell to underlings for personal consumption and resale to the public. During Durazo's 1978 to 1982 tenure, policemen had carte blanche to rape women, who soon learned never to ask the police for assistance, indeed to run in the opposite direction when they saw a cop approaching.

The foreign debt rose steadily—from $20 billion in 1976 to almost $59 billion by 1982—but it seemed Mexico could handle it. And then it could not, chiefly due to events beyond its control. In the mid-1970s the United States had added to its woes of recession those of inflation, due in considerable measure to OPEC's success in raising oil prices. To "whip inflation now" as President Ford (1974–1977) urged, the Federal Reserve Bank helmed by Chairman Paul Volcker began (in 1979) to raise interest rates, eventually driving the prime rate from 12 percent to 21 percent. By 1980 this had precipitated a far deeper downturn, which did lower inflation, but only by driving up unemployment to levels not seen since the Great Depression of the 1930s.

The recession Volcker engineered in the U.S. had an even more devastating impact on Mexico, as the interest rate on rolling over its short term loans nearly doubled. By 1982, simply meeting interest payments would have required more than $8 billion per year. Worse, just as expenses soared, income declined. Oil prices sagged because the global recession diminished demand and Iranian oil came back online, expanding the supply. Between 1981 and 1982 the price fetched by Mexican oil dropped from $78 to $32 a barrel. Meanwhile, Mexican capital was fleeing the overvalued peso for the U.S. dollar. Between January and June 1982, $12 billion left the country, forcing repeated devaluations, from 20-1, to 70-1, to 150-1.

Mexico made clear it could no longer make its interest payments. U.S. banks were terrified. Thirteen of the biggest stood to collectively lose $60 billion if Mexico went under—48 percent of their combined capital. And if Mexico fell, most of Latin America would come tumbling down behind it, likely triggering a collapse of the entire international financial system. The United States, accordingly, put together a multi-billion-dollar package of loans and credits, and worked out an unofficial debt moratorium. The World Bank and IMF were wheeled in to provide Mexico with emergency loans with which to resume paying the U.S. banks, rescuing them from their own recklessness. These institutions in turn—following the model first worked out in the so-called fiscal crisis of New York

City in 1975—now imposed "structural adjustment" on Mexico. The creditors demanded privatization of public services, cuts in government social programs, a wider opening to foreign investment, and a ruthless concentration on paying back loans and interest. This arm-twisting was given an ideological gloss, reviving hoary shibboleths about the inherent superiority of market over state, repackaged as "neoliberalism."

Executing these demands fell to President Miguel de la Madrid (1982–1988), who had been López Portillo's secretary of planning and budget. A member in good standing of the PRI's technocratic wing, de la Madrid had not emerged from the party's mass political organizations, but had risen through the financial and oil bureaucracies. He did not need to be coerced into following the neoliberal path, having absorbed its tenets at Harvard's Kennedy School of Government. He believed the state apparatus was a burden upon Mexican business that should be thrown off, along with much else in the PRI's inherited project and ideology. But he had no interest in jettisoning the one-party state. Indeed he would use the PRI to engineer the volte-face. De la Madrid privatized many of the smaller state-run industries, cut investment in infrastructure, reduced tariffs, refrained from taxing the elite, and encouraged foreign investment. He also slashed government subsidies to the agrarian sector, which was instructed to adopt an export-oriented model and start growing crops, not to feed Mexicans, but to pay foreign creditors.

This first round of shock treatment exacted a terrible price. The economy, knocked flat, remained on the mat for a decade. Many industries collapsed, with the loss of at least eight hundred thousand jobs. Farmers deserted the ravaged countryside and piled into Mexico City, where unemployment soared. Real wages plummeted as inflation climbed to 100 percent. By 1987, the Mexican government estimated that over half the population was malnourished. Meanwhile, the debt doubled from 30 percent of GDP in 1982 to 60 percent by 1987. The 1980s became known as *La Década Perdida*—the Lost Decade—and millions of lives were ruined.

The troubles came not singly but in battalions. In 1985 perhaps ten thousand lives were snuffed out in a magnitude 8.1 earthquake that devastated Mexico City. In an early sign of the state's weakened condition, partly due to ideological paralysis, the government failed to respond to the catastrophe other than to foolishly spurn proffered help from the U.S. and elsewhere, and indeed did its best to undercount the fatalities. The civilian population—especially youths and women—took up the burden of rescue, providing food and rudimentary shelter to survivors. Then they began demanding urban reconstruction. Popular organizations sprang up along a broader front, forging social movements aimed at contesting the austerity project itself. Citizens resisted evictions, mounted land invasions, demanded provision of public goods. The long extant discontent with PRI authoritarianism was now exacerbated by fury at its inefficiency and ideological reversals. Soon these energies would be channeled into political movements aimed at removing the PRI from power.

CHAPTER FIVE
1988

In 1987, de la Madrid chose as his successor Carlos Salinas de Gortari, who as secretary of planning and budget had been a principal architect of the president's neoliberal assault on the social contract inherited from the Revolution. A member of the PRI's quasi-hereditary leadership class—his father, a Harvard graduate, had been a secretary of commerce in the 1960s—Salinas finished his Harvard PhD in political science in 1978, and in 1982 joined the de la Madrid cabinet as its youngest member. The man who had been instrumental in cutting real wages in half and sending unemployment soaring to nearly 18 percent was convinced there was more to be done. Mexico's bloated government should be downsized, and the economy deregulated, making it more accommodating to foreign banks and investors.

The capture of the PRI high command by neoliberal technocrats did not go uncontested. A group of party members emerged who protested the dismantling of the Revolution's social achievements, and the abandonment of rights inscribed in the Constitution. They also decried the lack of internal party democracy, and proposed changing the focus from liberalizing the economy to liberalizing the polity; a project which, had they been consistent, the neoliberal PRIstas should have welcomed, but which, being the power holders, they decidedly did not.

The leader of this faction was Cuauhtémoc Cárdenas, the son of Lázaro Cárdenas and thus a scion of the party's most pedigreed family.

He had, moreover, served in important party positions as a federal senator and governor of Michoacán. Nevertheless it was he who launched a campaign for democratic reform of the PRI's presidential nomination process, a thrust at the neoliberal elite's vitals.

Though named for an Aztec emperor, Cárdenas seemed an unlikely candidate for such a task. Bookish and reserved, he nevertheless led an exodus of the disaffected PRIstas, joined forces with several small existing left parties, cobbled together a National Democratic Front (NDF), and entered the presidential lists as its candidate. His cause rapidly attracted support from the civil society activists who had emerged in the wake of the earthquake, and from organizations of workers and farmers furious at the collapse of their living standards, and what they considered to be the PRI's undermining of national sovereignty at the bidding of international capital.

Despite having virtually no funds or paid staff, being denied access to the mass media, and finding its rallies impeded by police, in February 1988 the NDF campaign began to click. In a tour of a northern agricultural region where his father had carried out a massive land-reform in 1936, Cárdenas was cheered and borne aloft by thousands of wildly enthusiastic campesinos at every stop. (When PRI candidate Salinas toured the region, he was jeered and doused with water.) In March, on the fiftieth anniversary of his father's nationalization of the oil fields, one hundred thousand supporters fêted Cárdenas in the Zócalo. In June the Mexican Socialist Party withdrew its presidential candidate and endorsed Cárdenas, and a Zócalo rally drew an unheard of two hundred thousand, including members of cooperative farms, urban barrio organizations, and student, labor, feminist, environmental, and indigenous organizations. He also drew huge crowds in Tijuana, Oaxaca, Acapulco, and Veracruz. (To compete, the PRI bussed in state employees who had been granted days off with full pay, and paid poor families to attend.)

A few weeks before the July 6 election, with Cárdenas surging in the polls, PRI bullyboys were unleashed, and worse. Four days before the election, Cárdenas' chief campaign assistant and long-time friend

Francisco Ovando, who had been in charge of blocking the election-day dirty tricks for which the PRI was notorious, was murdered, shot four times at close range, along with an assistant. Supporters massed at the Department of the Interior, screaming "Murderers!" Cárdenas denounced the "political crime" but restrained his followers.

On election day, with the PRI in control of the electoral machinery, the government began tallying ballots and entering them into the Federal Election Commission's computer system, supplied by UNISYS. At this point, as Miguel de la Madrid confessed in his 2004 autobiography, he received reports that initial results were running heavily against the PRI, and the public was demanding word on the returns.

"I became afraid that the results were similar across the country," he admitted, "and that the PRI would lose the presidency." So the public was told that the system had crashed, and results would be delayed. A week later, Salinas was declared the victor with 52 percent of the vote, compared with the PRD's 31 percent, and the PAN's 17 percent. Three years later the ballots were burned, and the only hard evidence of the fraud went up in smoke.

A huge crowd, estimated at over 250,000, the largest voluntary demonstration in the country's history, descended on the Zócalo. Holding aloft effigies of the balding and big-eared Salinas, they shouted, "You're a liar, baldy, you lost the election!" They sang, "We'll pull him out by the ears," and acclaimed their candidate with cries of *"Viva el Presidente Cárdenas!"* The demonstrations went on for months.

But on September 10, the slim PRI majority in Congress ratified Salinas as president. Eight months later, on May 5, 1989, most of the parties and social organizations that had formed the National Democratic Front established the Party of the Democratic Revolution (PRD), with Cuauhtémoc Cárdenas as their president.

CHAPTER SIX
1990s

The administration of Carlos Salinas (1988–1994), building upon the neoliberal policies introduced by de la Madrid, now put into effect a rolling counter-Revolution. In this round it was the larger public enterprises that were sold off at bargain basement prices: among the eighty or so he privatized were the telecommunications company, the two airlines, the national steel company, the fertilizer and sugar companies, the railways, and the commercial banks that had been nationalized in 1982. The process created a new class of Mexican tycoons. In 1987 there was one Mexican on the *Forbes* billionaire list. When Salinas left office in 1994 there were twenty-four.

Labor, conversely, was battered. When public enterprises were privatized their collective agreements were scrapped, benefits were removed, and "flexible" work rules were imposed. Salinas also distanced the party from its long-affiliated labor unions, and ordered a series of attacks on more militant entities. At the same time, state subsidies that had kept the price of basic foodstuffs low were suddenly removed. The price of milk, tortillas, petrol, electricity, and public transport shot up at the same time wages were being slashed. The provision of basic social services, long a feature of post-Revolutionary governments, was similarly cut so that fewer people had access to free health care and education.

The neoliberal offensive was particularly devastating to farm labor, partly as a consequence of the establishment of the North American Free Trade Agreement (NAFTA), which Salinas negotiated with

George H. W. Bush (1989–1992) and which went into effect under Bill Clinton (1993–2000). A principal U.S. condition for entering the agreement was that Mexico undo the agrarian reforms embedded in Article 27 of the Constitution, a principal legacy of the Revolution. Communal (*ejido*) land could now be divided and converted into private property. Price regulation of staple crops was scrapped. Tariffs and quotas on agricultural imports were removed. Subsidies that had supported small-scale farmers were deleted. All this enabled U.S. agribusiness (which, having zero qualms about ideological inconsistency, remained heavily subsidized) to export corn and other grains below cost. Rural Mexican farmers could not compete. This did not escape the attention of the farmers themselves, especially the Indians in Chiapas who, fearing the loss of their communal lands, formed a Zapatista Army of National Liberation. On January 1, 1994, the day NAFTA came into force, they declared war on the Mexican state.

The results of establishing a putatively equal trade between grossly unequal partners was that U.S. agribusiness pushed thousands of Mexican farmers out of their own markets. The price of corn dropped by around 50 percent following the NAFTA agreement, and the number of farmers living in poverty rose by a third. In the six years following the introduction of NAFTA, two million farmers abandoned their land. They flocked from country shacks to the burgeoning barrios of Mexico City; to the spreading slums of Tijuana and Ciudad Juárez to work in assembly plants on the border; and to the United States. (In anticipation of the arrival of a displaced peasantry—a migration NAFTA was supposed to have precluded by providing new jobs in the industrial export sector—the U.S. in 1994 launched the forthrightly named Operation Gatekeeper and beefed up the Border Patrol).

Worse was yet to come. Salinas had pegged the peso to the U.S. dollar, which did reduce inflation, a major accomplishment, though given all the other "reforms" the net result was lower real wages. Over the sexenio, the peso's real value declined, but Salinas propped it up to reassure U.S. investors and facilitate his NAFTA negotiations. After

Salinas left, however, his successor Ernesto Zedillo (1994–2000) was left holding the bag. When Zedillo let the peso float, it promptly sank, losing half its value, triggering double-digit inflation and a whopping recession. Many companies went out of business. In 1995 alone, one million jobs were lost. By the end of 1996, there were eight million unemployed and five million working within the informal economy, out of a total labor force of 35.7 million. Foreign investment melted away, Mexican capital decamped to Miami, and the middle class found its life savings wiped out. The Mexican government responded by adopting another austerity plan—raising the value-added tax, cutting the budget, and increasing electricity and gasoline prices.

◆ ◆ ◆

The crisis sparked a surge in crime. Despite the steady rise of drug trafficking, modern Mexico had not been an especially dangerous country. Now mugging, carjacking, and kidnapping rates shot up, especially in the capital. Police failed to respond to this crime wave, creating an atmosphere of impunity. Their foot-dragging was not surprising. It was estimated in 1995 that 70 percent of kidnappings were being committed by the police themselves.

The crisis also transformed the narcotics industry. Indeed it is impossible to understand the tremendous changes in the drug business during the combined sexenios of Salinas and Zedillo (1989–2000) without taking into account the massive political, economic, and ideological transformations wrought during that decade and the previous one by the PRI-governed state.

Much of the impact was indirect.

Farmers, unable to sustain themselves due to the removal of subsidies and the arrival of competition from U.S. agri-corporations, found the burgeoning market for marijuana and poppies their only avenue to surviving on the land.

The army of the urban unemployed gave the cartels a deep pool from which to recruit foot soldiers, and the miserably paid (and eminently corruptible) police and military provided the muscle with which to protect their interests.

The spread of everyday crime—aided by the rapid declension and corruption of local police forces—demoralized civil society, and provided a climate within which grander forms of criminality would flourish.

The adoption of free trade, and the deeper integration of the Mexican economy with that of the United States, dramatically increased cross-border traffic, making it far easier to insert narcotics into the stream of northward-bound commodities. Some NAFTA rules were of particular help: because *maquiladoras*—assembly plants just across the border—were exempt from tariffs and subject to only minimal inspections, Mexican smugglers began buying up such factories to use as fronts for shipping cocaine.

Narcotrafficking had formerly been integrated into the PRI corporatist state, an under-the-table equivalent of labor, peasant, and business organizations. As such it was subject to a certain degree of regulatory control, and to unofficial taxation, in return for the de facto licensing of smuggling (the *plaza* system). The state's abandonment of this form of corporatist inclusion contributed to the independent growth and power of organized crime syndicates.

The glorification of wealth and entrepreneurialism provided a cultural environment that boosted the social standing of narco businessmen. As in the former Soviet Union and other post-communist regimes, a neoliberal shock treatment simultaneously produced millionaires and gangsters, a twinning that *Forbes* registered by including them on the same list.

The weakening of the state and the glorification of "free enterprise" conferred authority and legitimacy on the private sector in which drug traffickers were now key players. As Watt and Zepeda point out, neoliberals prioritized accumulation of profit over social welfare, ruthless competition over cooperation, and the sanctification of private property and wealth over community and civic responsibility. These propositions—the cornerstones and guiding principles of free-market ideology—also formed the dominant ideology of crime syndicates.

◆ ◆ ◆

Not all the consequences of PRI initiatives were indirect. Presidents Salinas and Zedillo undertook a series of direct actions that would have major (though massively unanticipated) consequences for the narcotics industry.

Salinas was well aware of rising insistence in the U.S., in the aftermath of the Camarena torture-murder, that Mexico commit to a stepped-up war on drugs. This had been made clear with the establishment of the certification process in 1986, which threatened to punish non-compliance by throttling IMF loans. Salinas was also aware that bringing NAFTA negotiations to a successful conclusion depended on winning the good will of George H. W. Bush, an old anti-narco hand from his days running Reagan's South Florida Task Force.

Seven months after taking office, Bush declared in his first televised address to the nation that "All of us agree that the gravest domestic threat facing our nation today is drugs." He proposed spending billions on a militarized response. Salinas signed on. He approved a binational Northern Border Response Force to monitor the border, created the National Institute to Combat Drugs (INCD) modeled on the DEA, and permitted U.S. Airborne Warning and Control System (AWACS) planes to fly over Mexican airspace to track drug-trafficking activity. (Furious protests led him to terminate the AWACS program, but satellite surveillance was approved.) By tripling the resources available to the attorney general's office, and increasing the participation of the Mexican military, he produced an increase in the quantity of confiscated drugs and won plaudits from U.S. authorities.

Bush had a specific request as well: Salinas was to (metaphorically) bring him the head of Miguel Ángel Félix Gallardo, chief of the Guadalajara Cartel. Rafael Caro Quintero and Ernesto Fonseca

Carrillo, Félix Gallardo's accomplices in the murder of Camarena, had been apprehended but the boss of bosses himself, protected by the governor of Sinaloa, remained at large. In 1989, the task was assigned to Guillermo González Calderoni, a powerful commander in the Mexican Federal Judicial Police (the rough equivalent of the FBI), whose brief was combating narcos.

González Calderoni was told, he later avowed, that President Salinas wanted to reel in the master of the Guadalajara Cartel to ensure U.S. re-certification. According to González Calderoni, his super detective work tracked the gangster to his lair in Guadalajara. According to Félix Gallardo, the cop was an old friend who had invited him to dinner at a restaurant, then betrayed and arrested him. In 1990, President Bush certified that Mexico had cooperated fully in drug control efforts, praising in particular the arrest of Félix Gallardo.

The decapitation of the Guadalajara Cartel—a centralized regulatory gangster regime supported by the PRI state—gave the "free market" its head. The consequences for the criminal sector would be even more disastrous than the havoc wrought in the legitimate economy by the larger neoliberal project.

At first, the lieutenants of the original cartel attempted to establish some ground rules. Following Félix Gallardo's arrest in 1989, the subcapos held a gangster summit in the resort city of Acapulco. Some say the meeting was convened by Félix Gallardo himself via mobile phone from prison, others (including Félix Gallardo) denied this and identified none other than González Calderoni as the proposer. Whoever initiated the gathering, the attendees were almost all members of the old Sinaloan narco tribe, long intertwined by ties of marriage, friendship, or business. They proceeded to amicably parcel out production territories and smuggling routes to the U.S. market, awarding themselves the *plazas* that had once been assigned by the now-defunct DFS.[11]

---

11   In thus assuming responsibility for self-regulation, the Acapulco meeting was in the vein of the legendary sit-down held in Atlantic City in 1929, at which mafiosi from around the country divvied up market share and established protocols for settling disputes, including laying out rules for ordering approved executions and assigning the tasks to a covey of contract killers known as Murder, Incorporated.

The resulting organizations were called cartels, misleadingly, as they were in fact fragments of an exploded cartel—the byproducts of *de-cartelization*—and most were manned by descendants or associates of the original Guadalajaran trio.

Three were situated in the *west* of the Mexican borderland. The Tijuana Cartel went to members of the Arellano Félix clan—Félix Gallardo's nephews and nieces. The Sinaloa Cartel would be run by Félix Gallardo's professional lieutenants, most prominently Ismael Zambada, a.k.a. "El Mayo," and Joaquín Guzmán Loera, a.k.a. "El Chapo" ("Shorty") for his five-foot-six stature. Command of the Sonora corridor would be assumed by Miguel Caro Quintero, the brother of the incarcerated Rafael.

In the *center* of the borderlands, the Ciudad Juárez route went to the family of the jailed Ernesto Fonseca Carrillo, winding up eventually in the hands of his nephew, Amado Carrillo Fuentes.

Control of the *eastern* borderlands, including the transit points of Nuevo Laredo and Matamoros, remained the province of the Gulf Cartel, the only outfit whose roots did not run back to the Sinaloa seedbed. Its origins dated to the early 1930s when Juan Nepomuceno Guerra smuggled alcohol from Matamoros to the Prohibition-parched north, then diversified (after Repeal) into gambling, car theft, prostitution, and the smuggling of other items. In the 1970s he brought his nephew Juan García Ábrego into the business, and it was the nephew who in the 1980s moved the organization into cocaine, dealing directly with the Cali Cartel.

As the 1990s unfolded, all these Mexican traffickers flourished. Moving tons of narcotics north and pumping billions of dollars back, they steadily replaced the Colombians as the dominant partners in their conjoint cocaine trade, a peaceful takeover solidified after the 1993 death of Pablo Escobar at the hands of the Colombian police.

This new generation of traffickers pursued innovative strategies. In Ciudad Juárez, Amado Carrillo Fuentes of the Juárez Cartel had a fleet of cocaine-packed Boeing 727s making regular runs between Colombia and Mexican airports, earning him the sobriquet "El Señor de los Cielos" ("Lord of the Skies"). In the east, García Ábrego's sophisticated land-based system was able to smuggle over three hundred metric tons per year across the border, garnering him (the DEA estimated in 1994) $10 billion a year.

How were their expanded operations able to flourish in the early 1990s if Salinas, in cooperation with the U.S., was beefing up law enforcement agencies? In the short term, the old collusionary *plaza* system remained effective, thanks in part to the efforts and stature of one holdover from the old regime, Guillermo González Calderoni. With the DFS dismantled, the attorney general's Federal Judicial Police (PJF) had primary responsibility for manning the law and order ramparts, and the man in charge of anti-narcotic work was González Calderoni, who had had lengthy, amicable, and mutually profitable relations with most of the organizations.

The Juárez Cartel operation of Carrillo Fuentes, in particular, enjoyed his badly needed protection—all those airplanes and landing fields were spectacularly visible. In a nice touch, González Calderoni served simultaneously as Chief of Security for the Lord of the Skies and, among other official titles, the PJF's Chief of Aerial Interception. His services went beyond seeing and speaking no evil; the DEA believed that Carrillo Fuentes had once paid González Calderoni a million dollars to assassinate a rival drug lord.

At the same time, he was also on the payroll of the Gulf Cartel's García Ábrego, with whose family he had long had close personal relations. He had been known to be helpful to the Sinaloa Cartel as well. Comandante González Calderoni was thus in the good graces of government and gangsters, and able to extend the shelf life of their old relationship, though the government side was no longer in as commanding a position as in the old days. González Calderoni's protection did not come cheap, and the amount of funds that flowed to him personally was stupendous, valued by the DEA at $400 million.

In 1993, however, the comandante fell off the tightrope when the attorney general fired and indicted him for drug trafficking, torturing prisoners, and taking bribes from García Ábrego. González Calderoni escaped across the border to Texas, and when the Salinas government sought to extradite him, he successfully defended his U.S. residency by claiming, very publicly, that his friend García Ábrego had told him that President Salinas had employed him to murder the two top Cuauhtémoc Cárdenas campaign advisers in the 1988 election—a fate he did not wish to share. He also announced that Carlos' brother Raúl was a frequent guest at García Ábrego social events , and suggested Raúl was himself a narco protector. (Both assertions were stoutly denied by the brothers.) In 2003, González Calderoni was gunned down by parties unknown, shot in the head as he entered his silver Mercedes parked outside his lawyer's office in McAllen, Texas.

After González Calderoni's fall it would not be possible to resurrect the old relationship between crook and state. Governments (or pieces of governments) would certainly continue to protect narco operations, but the initiative would increasingly come from the gangsters' side, for the simplest of reasons. With the ascendancy of the cocaine trade, cartel profits had soared into the empyrean, and the amount of money they could now budget for bribery allowed them to make irresistible offers—unrefusable ones too when accompanied by threats of violence, as in the formulation *plomo o plata* ("lead or silver"), i.e., take the money or die. According to a 1994 study by the National Autonomous University of Mexico, overall trafficker payouts rose from perhaps $3.2 million in 1983 to $460 million in 1993, larger than the Mexican attorney general's entire budget. In 1995, the Department of the Interior estimated that 30 to 50 percent of the one-hundred-thousand-strong Federal Judicial Police (PJF) had been captured by drug money.

The conquest of hundreds of local municipal police forces was even more thorough, corruption producing an all-but-wholesale desertion of police into the ranks of criminality, where they served as escorts and adjutants. The terms of the relationship had been reversed. Previously criminals had been forced to pay up, or face sanctions from state agents. Now criminals chose to pay, and it was they who would punish noncompliance. State regulation had been thrown off, as neoliberal doctrine dictated, and replaced by a privatized regime, in which public officials were suborned on a piecemeal basis.

It may be simply coincidence but the departure of González Calderoni overlapped with the first fissuring of the confederation of cartels. Competition erupted—as it will in an unconstrained marketplace—between the Arellano Félix brothers and the Sinaloans Ismael Zambada and El Chapo Guzmán, over access routes into California. Likely more was involved than commercial considerations. The two outfits had different lines of descent from the mother organization—one familial, one professional—and they were also (as Ioan Grillo notes in *El Narco*) clannish, given to vendettas as well as strictly business-based rivalries. Violence was a natural concomitant. In feuds between gangsters, competition was not a matter of price-cutting but of throat cutting. Nor was violence employed in only a utilitarian way; it was a matter of performance as well. Power flowed to those able to demonstrate a greater ferocity than their opponents.

The Arellano Félix boys took an early lead in the violence sweepstakes. Not only did they put together a notorious regiment of killers—recruiting Chicano gangbangers from San Diego and sons from Tijuana's wealthy families—but Ramón Arellano Félix took pains to construct a terrifying public image. He became infamous for allegedly throwing a victim's corpse onto a fire, grilling up some steaks over it, and standing around with his *compadres* while enjoying beef, beer, and cocaine. Whether this was true or not mattered less than that rivals believed it to be so; a street rep for cruelty was itself a powerful competitive asset. Ramón also introduced a new and bloody tactic, with a new word to describe it: an *encobijado* ("an en-blanketed one"), meaning a corpse wrapped up in a blanket and dumped in a public place, often with a threatening note attached. Again, these were performances with a public purpose, that of displaying their kill-willingness for all to see.[12]

---

12 There was another element in this mix, the growth of a local market in drugs. In the 1990s, meaningful numbers of Mexicans started taking hard drugs, partly a matter of increased distribution due to lapsed regulation. Mexican capos started paying their lieutenants with bricks of cocaine and bags of heroin as well as cash (a practice pioneered by

In 1993, a spectacular instance of violence, made so by its victim rather than its method, put the growing inter-gang warfare on the national public's radar screen. In May, Cardinal Juan Jesús Posadas Ocampo went to the Guadalajara airport to meet the arriving papal nuncio when (according to the official story) he drove into the middle of a firefight between the Tijuana Cartel's Arellano Félix brothers and the Sinaloa Cartel's El Chapo Guzmán and his thugs. Posadas' murder generated many alternative explanations, most of which assumed the cardinal was an intended and not an accidental victim. But whatever the cause, the consequence was that drug war battles now had the capacity to impact the highest levels of Mexican society. The resulting media firestorm put terrific pressure on the federal government to do something decisive, and within two weeks police in Guatemala had nabbed El Chapo Guzmán and deported him to Mexico, where he was locked up in a maximum-security prison.

Drug-related violence now touched secular as well as ecclesiastical elites. In March 1994, the PRI candidate fingered to succeed Salinas— Luis Donaldo Colosio, previously president of the party—was assassinated at a campaign rally in Tijuana. Again rumors swirled, and the truth remains elusive, but most contending explanations revolved around Colosio's relations (or refusal of relations) with narcos. The same was true with another murder that followed hard upon Colosio's, that of José Francisco Ruiz Massieu, brother-in-law of Carlos Salinas and secretary general of the PRI, who had been pushing for further investigation into the death of his close friend Colosio. The assassination in broad daylight of the PRI's two most powerful officials suggested murky dealings between the party and the cartels, and revealed that the commanding heights of political authority were no longer so commanding.

Arturo Durazo, chief of the Mexico City police force). Mid-level hoods unloaded their products on local streets, nowhere more so than in Tijuana, which developed the highest level of drug use in the country. Arellano Félix affiliates set up hundreds of *tienditas*, "little drug shops," especially in the center and eastside slums. Fighting over street corners drove violence to new heights. Toward the end of the nineties there were some three hundred homicides per year in Tijuana, and a similar number in Juárez.

This latest blow to its legitimacy might have cost the PRI the presidency, and indeed the election returns in August 1994, as certified by the new and quasi-independent IFE (*Instituto Federal Electoral* or Federal Electoral Institute), demonstrated the growing strength of both old established and newly created rivals. The PRI's replacement candidate Ernesto Zedillo received 50.18 percent of the vote; the PAN candidate Diego Fernández de Cevallos Ramos, 26.69 percent; and Cuauhtémoc Cárdenas, choice of the new PRD (the leftist *Partido de la Revolución Democrática* or Party of the Democratic Revolution), 17.08 percent. Conventional wisdom held that the combination of assassinations with the Chiapas uprising led many to opt for stability, but that the single party chokehold on the political system had been all but broken.

President Ernesto Zedillo, only too aware of the party's peril, opted during his sexenio (1994–2000) for some efforts at reform.

In 1995 Raúl Salinas, the brother of former president Carlos Salinas, was arrested. Swiss banking authorities had discovered he had 289 bank accounts, containing an estimated $500 million, which they charged were profits from working with drug dealers. Salinas denied this and the case was never proven. Instead he was arrested, convicted, and jailed for allegedly masterminding the murder of his ex-brother-in-law, José Francisco Ruiz Massieu, but after serving ten years he was acquitted. Whatever Raúl Salinas did or did not do, the furor further chipped away at the legitimacy of the ruling party.

In 1996, Gulf Cartel kingpin García Ábrego was arrested and extradited to the United States. Tried and convicted with $350 million of his assets seized, he was sentenced to eleven consecutive life terms and dispatched to a maximum-security prison in Colorado, where he remains to this day. The removal of García Ábrego would prove rife with unanticipated consequences.

Also in 1996, Zedillo, deciding the PJF was hopelessly corrupt, began dismantling it—the equivalent of disbanding the FBI in disgrace. Some 1,800 agents were dismissed on grounds of corruption or incompetence, and the remainder transferred in 1999 to a newly minted *Policía Federal Preventiva* (Federal Preventive Police [PFP]).

The deflating of the police was accompanied by an inflating of the role of the military, a policy strongly promoted by Bill Clinton's appointed drug czar, Barry McCaffrey, a recently retired four-star general whose previous position had been as head of the United States Southern Command. Given the rising drug war violence in the north, the crisis of the political system, the disintegration of police credibility, the collapse of the currency, and the attendant need to stay in U.S. good graces, Zedillo acquiesced. He established a five-year plan (the National Program for the Control of Drugs) that significantly widened the involvement of the (reluctant) armed forces beyond their sporadic participation in eradication programs. By 1996, almost a thousand soldiers had received special training in counter-narcotics tactics in the U.S.A.

In addition, in December 1996, a very high-ranking military man, indeed the likeliest candidate to become Mexico's next secretary of defense—General Jesús Gutiérrez Rebollo—was chosen by the attorney general to head up the INCD, Mexico's national anti-drug agency. General Gutiérrez Rebollo would become the counterpart of drug czar General McCaffrey, who hailed his new colleague as a man of "impeccable integrity." Two months later, in February 1997, the current secretary of defense grimly announced that General Gutiérrez Rebollo had long been protecting (and profiting from) Amado Carrillo Fuentes, El Señor de los Cielos, to whom he had almost certainly handed over a mountain of classified information. The barbarians, it turned out, were already inside the military gates. By August 1997, 402 military officers had been taken into custody, fifteen of whom ranked between lieutenant colonel and general. The breaking of Gutiérrez Rebollo and a significant portion of the officer class short-circuited further resistance by the Mexican military to its new number-one mission. It would bow to U.S. counter-narcotics priorities, just as its presumed moral invulnerability was so dramatically shown to be a fantasy.

Worse, just as the PRI state was opting for militarization, so was the Gulf Cartel, which had supposedly been defanged by the arrest of its capo García Ábrego. In 1998, after a period of intra-cartel battling, one Osiel Cárdenas Guillén, a García Ábrego lieutenant, had murdered his way to the top. But given ongoing confrontations with rivals, and the likely deployment of military force against him, Cárdenas Guillén set out to create a Praetorian Guard. He turned for assistance to Arturo Guzmán Decena, a commander in the army's elite *Grupo Aeromóvil de Fuerzas Especiales* (GAFE), Mexico's equivalent of the Green Berets.

The special forces had been given counter-insurgency training at Fort Bragg, North Carolina, and dispatched by President Salinas to crush the Zapatistas. Guzmán Decena had been sent to Tamaulipas to clamp down on drug gangs but had been amenable to bribes from Cárdenas Guillén to allow safe passage to Gulf Cartel drug shipments. This was not atypical for soldiers; skimming the profits of traffickers seemed a perk of the job. But Guzmán Decena left the barracks altogether, and signed up with Cárdenas Guillén. (Grillo speculates that his defection may have been triggered by General Gutiérrez Rebollo being sentenced to thirty-two years in prison, and the growing calls by families of the disappeared to investigate human rights abuses in the Dirty War in which Guzmán Decena had been a player.) Guzmán Decena brought with him to the dark side thirty or so GAFE colleagues, crack soldiers all, and an arsenal of the army's most sophisticated weaponry and surveillance equipment. Soon they had expanded beyond bodyguard duties to become the Gulf Cartel's mercenary military arm, and dubbed themselves: Los Zetas.

◆ ◆ ◆

Meanwhile, back in the west, the loss of Gutiérrez Rebollo's protection had proven a setback for the Lord of the Skies. Deciding he needed to alter his profile, Amado Carrillo Fuentes went to Mexico City in July 1997 for a rendezvous with plastic surgeons. He apparently died there on the operating table, from the effects of an anesthetic. His death served as flypaper for theorists of assassination conspiracies who attributed his demise to a variety of proposed perpetrators. But whatever its cause may have been, his passing unleashed a tempest. As his brother Vicente struggled to take command of the Juárez Cartel, the Arellano Félix brothers, sensing an opportunity, tried to move in on their Ciudad Juárez *plaza*.

The Sinaloa Cartel, which was already at war with the Tijuana crowd, joined forces with the Juárez Cartel, on the enemy-of-my-enemy-is-my-friend basis, and launched a counter-assault on their Tijuana stronghold. Now the streets ran red, with hundreds killed, tortured, and disappeared. At first Ciudad Juárez and Tijuana were the principal battlegrounds, but then the fighting expanded to adjoining states.

At the very same time that a centralized regulatory regime gave way to chaotic competition in the criminal underworld, the centralized one-party regime gave way to a competitive party system in the world of politics.

In 2000, having teetered since the late eighties, the PRI was toppled in that year's presidential election. Its candidate Francisco Labastida Ochoa was an experienced politician, having been a senator, cabinet member, and governor of Sinaloa, but he bore the burden of the PRI's deep unpopularity.

Cuauhtémoc Cárdenas again took to the hustings for the PRD, now more than ever identified with the democratization movement. In 1997, responding to popular demand, Zedillo had opened the mayoralty of Mexico City, hitherto an appointed position, to electoral contest, and Cárdenas had won.[13] But Cárdenas was also identified with the PRI, of which he had been a longtime member (and his father a founding father) and he brought that baggage with him. He was also a man of the left, and there was a sizable block of voters who, while disaffected from the PRI, would prefer the devil they knew, if there was no other choice.

But most of all, voters were looking for a fresh face, and it was the PAN that provided one. Vicente Fox seemed a brilliant choice, perfectly suited to the moment. He was put forward by a right-wing party, but he was not a hardline ideologue or a Catholic militant. Raised

---

13 Zedillo had also strengthened the IFE's autonomy by dissociating it completely from the executive branch and any existing party, making it ever harder for the PRI to fix elections as it had so often in the past. And indeed in 1997, for the first time, the PRI lost control of the lower legislative chamber.

on the family ranch, he had earned a BA in business administration, buffed his credentials at Harvard Business School, worked his way up to the presidency of Coca-Cola for Mexico and Latin America, and segued into politics by becoming governor of Guanajuato in 1995. Fox was forthright and folksy. He wore cowboy boots and jeans; even his name was refreshingly different. His personality promised change.

Still, he might have lost, had not a center-left coalition of public figures—calculating that Cárdenas had no chance of winning but could split the anti-PRI vote—decided to ensure a regime change by supporting Fox. On July 2, 2000, he won the presidency with 43 percent of the vote to Labastida's 36 percent and Cárdenas' 17 percent. For the first time in seventy-one years, an opposition candidate had won the presidency of Mexico.

♦ ♦ ♦

President Fox's administration began on December 1, 2000. Three weeks later, on December 22, he went to Tijuana and declared war on the Arellano Félix Organization. He intended, he said, to recruit twelve thousand to fifteen thousand new federal police officers and dispatch them to Tijuana, the gateway to the rich California drug market, where he would "eradicate" organized crime. "We will beat them," he boasted, and do so in six months flat.

Fox put the Arellano Félix brothers at the top of his hit list because they were the drug lords "most wanted" by the U.S.A. Eight months earlier, on April 10, 2000, the Tijuana capos had captured Pepe Patiño, one of the handful of honest and effective Mexican anti-drug prosecutors. Patiño had been working closely with the DEA and the FBI in San Diego and was entrusted with sensitive intelligence information. When he crossed the border to Tijuana, however, the Arellano Félix brothers, alerted by a corrupt colleague, seized him and tortured him by breaking virtually every bone in his body, before slowly finishing him off by crushing his skull in a pneumatic vise. This galvanized U.S. law enforcement. Not only was the Arellano Félix group considered Latin America's most important criminal organization, having shipped tons and tons of drugs across the border; and not only was Ramón on the FBI Ten Most Wanted Fugitives list, having killed (as the gang's enforcer) hundreds and hundreds of people; but now, as with Kiki Camarena, it was personal with the Americans.

Fox was eager to oblige. Especially since his old friend George W. Bush—another cowboy-booted, plainspoken, rich rancher and former governor—had agreed to make the first foreign trip of his presidency (2001–2009) to Mexico. He would be meeting Fox in San Cristóbal, in the state of Chiapas, on February 16, 2001. Fox had an agenda stuffed with asks—notably opening up the border, and winning legal status for the 3.5 million undocumented Mexicans working in the States—and he wanted to have his anti-crime credentials in order.

Then, embarrassingly, on January 19, 2001, El Chapo Guzmán escaped from jail. Having bribed his way into a comfortable-going-on-luxurious prison life, he now bribed his way out altogether, and rejoined his colleagues in the Sinaloa Cartel. This was bad news for Fox, coming as it did on the eve of his presidential tête-à-tête with Bush.

His response came one week later, on January 25, when he went to Culiacán, heart of El Chapo's Sinaloan domain, and repeated his Tijuana in-your-face challenge, escalating it to countrywide status. Announcing a *"Cruzada Nacional contra el Narcotráfico y el Crimen Organizado,"* he declared "a war without quarter against the drug traffickers and the pernicious criminal mafias." The tough talk was enough to meet the immediate need. When Bush arrived in February, he expressed confidence that Fox was committed to fighting traffickers, and even admitted, with an unusual degree of candor, the obvious but uncomfortable fact that Mexicans were selling drugs north of the border because Americans were buying them.

◆ ◆ ◆

But when Fox visited the White House in September 2001—Bush's first state visit—he was welcomed with open arms but empty hands.

The dot.com bubble had burst, and the U.S. had sunk into a recession that dragged Mexico's NAFTA-manacled economy down with it. Fox had promised to add 1.4 million new jobs, but instead lost nearly half a million. Bush had earlier talked of a guest worker plan but as U.S. unemployment surged, so did conservative opposition, and the idea was put back on the shelf. Then, five days after Fox addressed a joint session of Congress, the Twin Towers came down, and his plea for a more open border became an instant nonstarter. Worse, as Fox loyally pledged support for Bush's global war on terror, a crackdown ensued on illegal crossings along the two-thousand-mile-long frontier. This in turn exacerbated the crisis of the Mexican countryside, making it ever harder to get a cross-border job and send south the remittances that were the life-support on which many devastated communities so depended.

Cooperation in the war on drugs became ever more central to Mexican-U.S. relations. On November 1, 2001, Fox replaced the notoriously corrupt Federal Judicial Police (*Policía Judicial Federal* [PJF]), with the Federal Investigations Agency (*Agencia Federal de Investigación* [AFI]), modeling the new organization on the U.S.A.'s FBI. He also backed off a preelection vow to withdraw the military from the drug war in order to avoid deepening the corruption of its general staff, and to comply with Mexico's constitutional prohibition on using the military for anything but national defense. The U.S. made clear it considered Mexico's army its most reliable force, despite Fox's 2001 arrest of generals who had been protecting gangsters. Fox also reneged on a campaign promise to investigate the military's role in the Dirty War, as he was now unwilling to alienate those on whom he would be forced to rely.

Fox's U.S.-backed strategy seemed to produce rapid results. On February 10, 2002, Ramón Arellano Félix was killed, but apparently luck had played a major role. He had been traveling aboard a Volkswagen sedan when he was pulled over by state agents, who did not recognize him. Arellano Félix fatally shot one officer twice in the chest before the officer fired a fatal shot of his own. But Ramón's "John Doe" corpse was swiftly seized from the mortuary in Mazatlán, raising doubts about belated claims that Arellano Félix had been deleted.

These doubts were allayed a month later, on March 9, 2002, when Benjamín Arellano Félix was captured in Puebla—in this case the result of a months-long manhunt by GAFE (the Mexican Army Special Forces team that had spawned Los Zetas), working in conjunction with DEA agents in the San Diego office. The capture was perhaps facilitated by the loss of protection from corrupt state officials, booted from their jobs after the PRI's defeat. In any event, by the spring of 2002, it looked like the Arellano Félix Organization was on the ropes. Fox seemed on the verge of making good his vow to vanquish the Tijuana Cartel.

But he had also opened a deadly can of worms. The Tijuanos' distress was duly noted by other drug lords, particularly the Sinaloans. In October 2001 they had held a summit meeting in Cuernavaca, devoted to pooling their separate local efforts, thereby (hopefully) putting back together again the Humpty Dumpty fragments of the old Guadalajara Cartel. In effect they were out to re-cartelize the drug trade. Present in addition to the recently self-sprung-from-jail El Chapo Guzmán were Ismael Zambada, an old Sinoalese hand in the business since the 1970s who had first grown marijuana and poppies, then entered the coke trade. Also at the sit-down was Juan José "El Azul" Esparragoza, a former federal police officer turned drug trafficker, who had also been part of the old Guadalajara Cartel. As had the Beltrán Leyva brothers, whose careers had paralleled El Chapo's since they had been dirt-poor neighbors in Sinaloa. Ignacio "Nacho" Coronel represented the drugs of the future, ephedrine and methamphetamine, which his crew manufactured in clandestine labs in Jalisco.[14]

---

14   Amphetamine was isolated from the ephedra plant in 1887 in Germany, and meth-amphetamine, a more potent and easy-to-make variant, was synthesized in Japan in 1893; a crystallized version followed in1919. Marketed in the 1930s as a decongestant for sinus sufferers, meth was widely used by all sides in World War II to keep pilots and troops at peak efficiency. In the fifties, speed was used as a performance enhancer by night owls (college students, truck drivers) and athletes, and from the sixties on as a euphoriant and aphrodisiac. In 1970, Nixon's Controlled Substance Act outlawed most uses, creating the demand that Nacho supplied.

These allies, who now styled themselves The Federation, debated plans for expansion. There was considerable sentiment for attacking the weakened Arellano Félix crowd on the western end of the U.S.-Mexican border, but they held off on that approach. There was equal interest in taking over the central border *plaza* of Ciudad Juárez, stronghold of the Juárez Cartel, but instead the Federation reluctantly struck up an alliance with Vicente Carrillo Fuentes, who had formally taken over the position of his departed brother, Amado Carrillo Fuentes, the Lord of the Skies. What really attracted the Federation's attention, however, was the far eastern *plaza*, centered in Nuevo Laredo (in the state of Tamaulipas), an incredibly lucrative and newly vulnerable border crossing, theretofore the exclusive domain of the Gulf Cartel. Here the major routes from Mexico's southern border with Guatemala arrived at the northern border with Texas, spanning the Río Bravo over Nuevo Laredo's one railroad and four vehicular bridges. The daily, NAFTA-supercharged flow of freight cars and cargo trucks provided great cover for funneling narcotics into the U.S. rail network and onto Interstate 35, the highway to San Antonio and points north.

No western or central outfit had ever before thought of attacking the far-eastern Gulf gang, but a series of high-profile arrests by Fox's forces seemed to provide an opening.

On March 28, 2002, Mexican troops nabbed Adán Madrano Rodríguez, the number two guy in the Gulf Cartel, first lieutenant to chieftain Osiel Cárdenas Guillén. Once again, United States pressure and participation proved crucial. Back in 1999, in Matamoros, Madrano Rodríguez had confronted and nearly killed two U.S. agents, one FBI, the other DEA, backing off only when reminded of the fate of Kiki Camarena's assassins. Once again, the professional had become personal, and the U.S. slapped a $2 million price tag on Madrano's head, which helped lead to his capture.

The second takedown came in November 2002, when Mexican soldiers, again with U.S. assistance, cornered and killed in a Matamoros restaurant Arturo Guzmán Decenas, the ex-Mexican military man whom Cárdenas Guillén had recruited to establish and run his bodyguard outfit, the Zetas.

The third and biggest blow came in March 2003 with the capture of the big boss himself, Osiel Cárdenas Guillén, who had incautiously attended a birthday party for one of his daughters. He had been indicted in the U.S.; been put on the FBI Ten Most Wanted Fugitives list (backed by a $2 million reward); and the Bush regime had been pressuring the Fox regime to bring him in.

To El Chapo and company, Nuevo Laredo now seemed up for grabs. True, Los Zetas—still only a rib of the Gulf Cartel—had come up with new leadership, another GAFE defector, Heriberto Lazcano Lazcano (a.k.a. "El Verdugo," or "The Executioner," for his gory predilections). Like Guzmán Decenas, Lazcano had been trained by the U.S. in combat and covert operations, partly at Fort Benning in Georgia. Still, it seemed a propitious moment and the Federation decided to invade.

Arturo Beltrán Leyva (a.k.a. "El Barbas" or "The Beard") was put in charge of organizing the attack. Beltrán Leyva in turn recruited as chief *sicario* (assassin) the Texas-born Edgar Valdez Villarreal, known as "La Barbie" for his blue-eyed Ken Doll good looks, though he was every bit as bloodthirsty as the Zetas' new leader, Lazcano. Together Barbas and Barbie established Los Negros, the heavily armed strike force of the Federation, recruiting, among others, members of the notoriously cruel Salvadoran-American Mara Salvatrucha gang. This was an effort to build up an effective counter to the militarily sophisticated Zetas, who themselves had brought in as post-graduate instructors Guatemalan Kaibiles, the elite counter-insurgency commandos who were notorious for having committed horrific massacres in the 1980s, and for their sanguinary taste for beheading and dismembering victims.

From the first skirmishes in 2003, the firefights on the streets of Nuevo Laredo grew steadily until by 2005 spectacular battles, deploying ever more sophisticated and deadly weaponry, had become commonplace. In July, after the rivals had wheeled out machine guns and rocket-propelled grenade launchers, American officials shut down the U.S. Consulate.

The new levels of lethality appalled the Americans, but should not have surprised them as the "iron river" of armaments had been flowing more briskly, courtesy of the U.S. arms industry and the Republican Party's powerful right wing. There had always been a vigorous and legal cross-border transfer of arms—some by sale or transfer from the U.S. federal government to the Mexican federal government, some by sale from arms dealers and licensed brokers direct to local governments and police forces—and some of both had been subsequently diverted by corrupt officials to cartel arsenals. There had also been a significant quasi-legal flow with drug gangs recruiting groups of "straw" buyers to purchase up to twenty weapons at a time from the 6,700 licensed gun dealers along the Mexican-U.S. border. Phoenix, a favorite shopping center for Sinaloan traffickers, had 853 of them, and Arizona was strong on the production end as well: in 2004, eleven companies produced more than one hundred thousand weapons. The straw buyer's purchases were then smuggled across the border.

Back during the Clinton administration, an impediment to the southward flow had been put in place when in 1994 Congress slapped a ban on the manufacture of semiautomatic assault weapons. Though it was scheduled to sunset in 2004, two-thirds of Americans (among them President Bush) supported extending the ban. Fierce opposition by the National Rifle Association (NRA) and right-wing Texas Congressman Tom DeLay blocked this renewal. A grateful NRA invited DeLay to keynote its annual meeting in 2005 and, as he took the podium, he choked up slightly as he proclaimed the tribute "the highlight of my career."[15]

---

15 The annual average of 88,000 firearms sent south during 1997–1999, during the assault weapons ban, rose to 253,000 during 2010–2012.

In1997 Clinton had signed CIFTA, the Inter-American Convention Against the Illicit Manufacturing of and Trafficking in Firearms, Ammunition, Explosives, and Other Related Materials. The treaty required signatory countries to: reduce the illegal manufacture and trade in guns, ammunition and explosives; adopt strict licensing

Lifting the ban facilitated a growing cascade of powerful weaponry south, just at the time powerful weaponry began showing up in Nuevo Laredo—including such narco favorites as the AK-47 Kalashnikov assault rifle (known affectionately as the *cuerno de chivo* or "goat horn" rifle), the AR-15 assault rifle (a civilian version of the M16, built by Colt), and the Barrett .50-caliber armor-piercing sniper rifle preferred by all the best professional assassins, along with machine guns, fragmentation grenades, shotguns, cop-killer pistols, and the like. Not only did the ability to shoot a massive number of bullets lead to hundreds of civilian bystander deaths, but the massive buildup of firepower—rivaling that of the Mexican Army—fostered an increasing willingness to tackle state authorities. In 2005, seven police commanders were ambushed and killed, seriatim, in Nuevo Laredo. The position remained vacant until a printing-shop owner accepted the post on the morning of June 8, 2005. Within six hours, Zetas toting AR-15 assault rifles had riddled him with bullets.

This latest slaying, coupled with pressure from the U.S. ambassador who was worried about murders and kidnapping of American citizens, spurred countermeasures from the Fox regime, despite some

---

requirements; mark firearms when they are made and imported to make them easier to trace; and establish a process for sharing information between national law enforcement agencies investigating smuggling. Thirty-three members of the Organization of American States ratified the treaty. Three did not, one of them being the U.S., where the gun lobby successfully blocked Senate ratification.

The National Rifle Association had once promoted itself as defender of the little man's right to protect his home and family, if need be against Big Government itself, and had prided itself for not being "affiliated with any firearm or ammunition manufacturers." But over time, though it retained a politically significant base of support among gun owners, the bulk of its income switched to coming from gun makers. Corporate contributions (via "Ring of Freedom" sponsorships or ads in NRA publications) poured in from the likes of Arsenal, Inc. (of Las Vegas), Beretta, Browning, Smith & Wesson, and Sturm, Ruger & Co. It was well worth it, as whenever a shooting massacre took place in the U.S., the NRA's hunters and collectors could be trotted out to take the heat, sparing arms industry CEOs from the annoying demonstrations that had troubled tobacco executives. And whatever the merit of the gun lobby's appeal to the Second Amendment might be in the U.S., it has zero applicability to foreign countries. Every assessment of weaponry confiscated from cartel killers in Mexico has found that between 75 and 90 percent of their arsenals come from the U.S.A.

internal grumbling about "external meddling." Fox decided to create a combined military and police strike force, the muscle behind a program entitled *México Seguro* (Safe Mexico). On June 11, 2005, three days after the latest police chief was gunned down, Fox sent six hundred members of the Federal Investigations Agency and the Federal Preventive Police, together with members of GAFE (the special forces of the Mexican Army), parading into Nuevo Laredo. They were met with gunfire from local police officers in the pay of the Gulf Cartel. Federal authorities removed almost one-third of the municipal police officers for failing drug tests or having alleged ties to drug traffickers, and suspended the rest, replacing them with federal police and troops. This was widely perceived as having all but no effect on the ongoing slugfest.

On August 3, 2005, a few weeks after the launch of President Fox's Seguro program, two bodies appeared in Nuevo Laredo. The Zetas had left a written message on the corpses—a *narcomensaje*—a novel method of communicating with their opponents: "DAMN YOU BARBIE AND ARTURO BELTRÁN, YOU WON'T GET IN HERE NOT EVEN WITH THE SUPPORT OF THE SPECIAL FORCES OR BY KILLING INNOCENT PEOPLE."

And they did not. The Federation invasion was held at bay in the east. But now other fronts were opened, in the west, with the Federation butting heads with the Zetas in one state after another. As the war spread, violence went viral.

Tasked with invading new territories and taking over old *plazas* (or opening up new ones), the Beltrán Leyva brothers and their henchman "La Barbie" headed for Acapulco, the popular tourist city (and a major entry point for South American cocaine) in the state of Guerrero. There fighting broke out with the Zetas, still acting on behalf of the Gulf Cartel, but increasingly toying with the idea of striking out on their own. The ensuing bloodshed soon brought intervention by state authorities, to which the Zetas registered their emphatic objection by taking a leaf from the Kaibiles' book. Decapitating the leading official of the police strike force and one of his men, they impaled their severed heads on a fence in front of police headquarters one morning in late April 2006. Extending their practice of making their narcomensajes hyper-explicit, a note was found alongside the victims, with words scrawled on a piece of cardboard reading: "So that you learn respect."[16]

◆ ◆ ◆

Inter-gang warfare got wilder, and more complicated, in the adjoining state of Michoacán, farther up the Pacific coast. A resource-rich territory, with rugged mountains and lush valleys, Michoacán's extensive agricultural sector (limes, avocados, etc.) had been hard hit by NAFTA and successive recessions, driving many farmers into growing pot and poppies, which they sold to an organization of home-grown drug traffickers who styled themselves "La Empresa" ("The Enterprise"). Led by one Carlos Rosales Mendoza, it plowed some of its profits into manufacturing methamphetamine in labs hidden up in the hills.

In 2001 Rosales Mendoza had called on his ally Osiel Cárdenas Guillén to help him drive out some local competitors, and the Gulf Cartel chieftain obligingly dispatched a number of his fearsome Zetas. For several years La Empresa and Los Zetas collaborated, but in 2006 war broke out between them. Los Zetas, edging ever closer to independence from the Gulf Cartel (especially with Cárdenas Guillén now in jail), had turned their attention to seizing control of the Pacific port of Lázaro Cárdenas. It had been made newly and spectacularly profitable, thanks to the United States Congress, which in 2005 restricted bulk purchasing of pseudoephedrine, driving methamphetamine-makers to underworld suppliers. Legitimate shipping into Lázaro Cárdenas had grown dramatically, and along with the licit trade came a flood of contraband. Precursor chemicals from India, China, and Thailand were shuttled to dry land by fast launches that rendezvoused with ships anchored offshore.

---

16   Some analysts claim these first beheadings copycatted al-Qaeda killings that had been recorded on video and posted on the Internet.

Los Zetas applied their now usual tactics of beheading those who resisted them, whether commercial rivals or agents of the state. Those tactics were soon embraced by competitors.

La Empresa, now under the control of Nazario Moreno González (a.k.a. "El Más Loco" or "The Craziest One"), allied itself with local vigilantes who resented the Zetas' power grab and brutalizing of the populace, and proclaimed itself the defender of Michoacánians against the foreign invaders. The enterprise rebranded itself in 2006, adopting the more homespun-sounding name of La Familia Michoacana, and spoke of siding with the poor, supporting family values, and fighting drug use (by locals; gringos were of course fair game). Moreno González also insisted on his rebel credentials, hailing Zapata and Che Guevara, and arguing that drug trafficking was a result of Mexico's unequal system that gave the poor no opportunities. "They say that each society has the government it deserves," he wrote. "I would also say that each society and government have the criminals that they deserve."

La Familia presented a spiritual as well as a patriotic and revolutionary face. The Craziest One had lived in the States during the 1990s and become a follower of one John Eldredge, a self-proclaimed apostle who had forged a self-help, he-man, evangelical Christian sect. El Más Loco redeployed some of Eldredge's tenets, added a few epigrams of his own, and came up with his own bible, *Mis Pensamientos* (*My Thoughts*), which was required reading for new recruits. Youngsters drawn from the abundant ranks of the unemployed were commanded to spurn drugs and alcohol and undergo months of motivational training, upon completing which they could do the Lord's work.

The first inkling of what that entailed came on September 6, 2006, when a group of armed men rolled five heads—freshly hacked off low-level Zetas while still alive, using Bowie knives—onto a disco dance floor in Uruapan, Michoacán. Picking up on another Zeta practice, they left behind a written message describing the action as "divine justice," retribution for what was believed locally to have been the rape and murder of a waitress/prostitute who had worked in the bar: "The Family doesn't kill for money; it doesn't kill women; it doesn't kill innocent people; only those who deserve to die, die." The Lord's work also included, for narco-evangelicals who showed an aptitude for violence, being trained as professional assassins and backbone cadre for the methamphetamine business.

La Familia's peculiar mix of motivations proved a potent one, and the organization succeeded in limiting Zeta incursions. And as its booming methamphetamine exports to the U.S. increasingly demanded the negotiation of passage rights with powers to the north, the Michoacánians began to cast their lot, at least tactically, with El Chapo and the Sinaloese.

♦ ♦ ♦

Faced with the expansion of hyper-violent cartel conflicts beyond their crucible in the northeastern state of Tamaulipas, President Fox beefed up his México Seguro program. Hundreds of federal agents and troops were dispatched to the states of Michoacán, Guerrero, Baja California, and Sinaloa, among others. Local police—more often than not in cahoots with the cartels—were purged and replaced with a combination of PFP federal police, AFI federal agents, and army units. These established military checkpoints, searched for drugs, and arrested addicts or street-level dealers. It was widely believed that México Seguro was having no impact on the big cartels.

More to the point, the big cartels were having a big impact on the federal forces sent against them. Fox's shiny new (in 2001) Federal Investigations Agency (AFI) was badly tarnished by 2005. Fifteen hundred of the seven thousand AFI agents—nearly 25 percent of the force—were under investigation for suspected criminal activity. Some were believed to be actively working as enforcers for the Sinaloa Cartel and 457 were already facing charges.

The army itself was disintegrating. Some soldiers were walking off out of fear, others were lured away by better offers. The success of Los Zetas underscored the benefits that awaited those who took their military skills over to the dark side, especially given the notoriously poor salaries, harsh living conditions, and humiliation by officers that were their daily fare in the barracks. Between 2000 and 2006, 123,218 had deserted, two-thirds of the 185,143 Fox had started with. And it was in these dispiriting circumstances that the Fox sexenio sputtered to an end.

CHAPTER EIGHT
2006

In the campaign to replace Fox, two candidates quickly moved to the fore.

The PAN, much to most people's surprise (including Fox), nominated a little-known wonkish lawyer, Felipe Calderón, who had been born into the National Action Party and spent most of his life advancing its cause. His father, Luis Calderón Vega, was one of the PAN's founders, and an advocate both of democracy (he fought PRI authoritarianism) and a Catholic version of Christian Socialism. The elder Calderón resigned from the party in 1981, believing it had become a right-wing organization serving only the rich. Felipe stayed on, as despite sharing his father's democratic leanings, he was much more conservative in his economics. In the 1980s he moved from his home town of Morelia, in Michoacán, to Mexico City, where he studied law and got an MA in economics. He then added a degree in public administration from Harvard's Kennedy School of Government (2000), imbibing neoliberal ideology while rising through the party's ranks. He served in the Fox administration as secretary of energy, but resigned in 2004 to protest Fox's support for a rival cabinet minister as his successor. When he pulled off his surprise victory, Mexico's wealthy minority threw their hats in his ring. However, Calderón tailored his platform to appeal to those in the middle class who had benefited from specific Fox programs, like loans that enabled them to buy their own homes, and from the very modest but very timely uptick in the economy during Fox's last two years (driven in part by an unexpected windfall from a jump in oil prices).

His chief opponent was not the PRI's Roberto Madrazo, who was weighed down by the opprobrium barnacled to his party, but Andrés Manuel López Obrador (often referred to as AMLO). López Obrador hailed from the southern state of Tabasco, where he joined the PRI in 1976, and studied political science at a public university. In 1984, he relocated to Mexico City, where in 1988 he joined the dissenting left wing of the PRI led by Cuauhtémoc Cárdenas, and after the stolen election, shifted to the new PRD. A party stalwart and social activist, López Obrador was elected mayor of Mexico City in 2000. There he further developed existing social welfare programs, and initiated one that provided cash subsidies to single mothers and the elderly. He left office in 2005 with an unprecedented 84 percent approval rating, and a highly visible national profile. As the PRD candidate, his campaign slogan was "For the Good of Everyone, the Poor First," referring to his advocacy of increasing taxes on the rich and extending resources to the poor. Such policy proposals, together with an austere lifestyle and a record of support for indigenous Mexicans, alienated many in the upper class and business community who viewed him as an uncultured (read: not quite white) Robin Hood figure. But his appeal to the poor and working class, together with his name recognition, helped propel him to an early double-digit lead in the polls.

Calderón struck back with television attack ads, accusing López Obrador of being a "Danger to Mexico," claiming that his domestic cash transfer policies would derail the economy, and comparing him to Venezuela's Hugo Chávez. These ads were well below the belt, according to Mexico's enlightened and very strict campaign rules against negative campaigning, and they were eventually banned, but not before they had helped (together with some AMLO tactical errors) close the gap between the two front-runners.

In the end, two different but overlapping Mexicos faced off, one more socially conservative, the other more socially liberal; one more rooted in the industrial north, the other strongest in the central and southern states where most of the country's poor lived; one favoring state action, the other preferring to let the market work its magic. As Ginger Thompson reported in the *New York Times*, the contest would come down to how the middle class would vote. And the single biggest line of division within that sector—as demonstrated by post-election analyses—was what a voter thought about NAFTA. Those who believed they had benefited from it (and from closer ties to the U.S.) tended to back Calderón, those who felt damaged by it (and by the enhanced U.S. links) leaned toward López Obrador.

What the 2006 election was *not* about was the drug-related blood-letting—the battles between the state and the cartels, and between one cartel and another—that had broken out big time during the Fox sexenio.

Nor was it about crime in general, in part because Mexico as a whole had been experiencing a decided *drop* in crime of all sorts. Since its peak in 1992, the national homicide rate had declined steadily from 19.72 per 100,000 citizens, to 8.04 in 2007. Other crimes had plummeted as well, leaving Mexico's criminal indices near the average of other industrialized nations, and lower than those of England, Holland, and Ireland. The Mexican "crime crash" paralleled with uncanny precision the one underway in many U.S. cities, with violent crime in New York peaking in 1991, and hitting a record low in 2005.

All the candidates were remarkably circumspect in their rhetoric, making no mention of particular cartels, lest they call down gangster wrath. (The death of candidate Colosio had not been forgotten.) Calderón talked vaguely about freeing "cities like Tijuana, Nuevo Laredo, or Acapulco from this cancer before it eats away our society," and advanced a series of specific reforms—changing the judicial system, centralizing the police forces, extraditing captured drug lords to the United States, and imposing life sentences on convicted kidnappers. López Obrador argued that creating jobs and reducing poverty was the only real way to fight crime—"I don't think you can make much progress with prisons or threats of heavy-handed approaches and tougher laws," he said, though he also broke with the left's anti-military tradition by suggesting a bigger role for the army in fighting the drug trade, given how well armed were the cartels.

On election day, July 2, the contending forces proved to be as sharply divided in votes as they were in views. Calderón received 35.89 percent of the vote. López Obrador got 35.33 percent. Madrazo of the PRI trailed in third place with 22.26 percent. The 0.56 percent separating the two Mexican front-runners in 2006 was a trifle larger than the 0.51 percent gap in the USA contest of 2000, though of course Al Gore had *won* the popular vote, and only the existence of an Electoral College allowed the Supreme Court to overturn the popular decision, generating a firestorm of claims by furious Democrats that the election had been hijacked, that Bush was an illegitimate president.

In Mexico, where there was no Electoral College, the López Obrador forces, pointing to a variety of irregularities, claimed that Calderón's popular vote margin had been obtained by straight-out fraud—hearkening back to the great theft of 1988—and that López Obrador was the rightful president. But where Gore eventually backed down and accepted the outcome, López Obrador refused to acquiesce. His supporters declared Calderón's looming presidency illegitimate, and took to the streets to abort it. During July and August, López Obrador's followers had been blocking major thoroughfares like Avenida Reforma (a Champs-Élysées lookalike) and had set up a giant encampment in the Zócalo, Mexico City's enormous central plaza, roughly equal in size to eleven football fields.[17] But after undertaking a partial recount of the ballots (not the full one AMLO was demanding), the Federal Electoral Tribunal declared Calderón the winner. The protests continued.

---

17 This was a highly symbolic occupation, as the Zócalo was (and is) the city's symbolic, cultural, and political center. Around it are grouped major Mexican institutions: the baroque sixteenth-century Metropolitan Cathedral; the National Palace (constructed in the sixteenth century on the site of, and redeploying materials from, the Palace of Moctezuma), which housed the federal executive branch, a White House without the living quarters; the Palace of Government of the City (City Hall); and the ruins of the Aztecs' Templo Mayor.

On November 20 (not coincidentally, the anniversary of the Mexican Revolution), an ocean of Obradordistas—they claimed to be a million strong—massed in the vast Zócalo and bulged out into surrounding streets. They had come to "install" their man as president. At the center was a huge stage, on which was placed a replica of the podium in the Legislative Palace. Behind it was a gigantic backdrop featuring an eagle-topped cactus (the symbol of the nation) drawn by a renowned cartoonist, pen-named "El Fisgon" or "Mr. Snoop." And it was at that podium, to the strains of patriotic music and thunderous applause from the immense assemblage (and on-stage dignitaries, including several governors and senators), that Rosario Ibarra de Piedra, an iconic Mother of the Disappeared whose son had been spirited away in Mexico's Dirty War of the 1970s, draped a reproduction of the green presidential sash around him and knotted it in place. López Obrador, the crowd-sourced president of Mexico, then delivered his inaugural address, and named the members of his cabinet (oddly including PRI people who had helped engineer the 1988 fraud).

Eleven days later, on December 1, when Calderón arrived at the Legislative Palace of San Lázaro to take the oath of office before a joint session of Congress, all was bedlam. Outside, hundreds of thousands paraded through the center of the city, hoisting red banners, Mexican tricolor flags, and placards emblazoned "No to Fraud," all the while chanting over and over: "Obrador! Obrador! Obrador!" Inside, shouting and jostling representatives from the two leading parties struggled to dominate the scene. López Obrador's people tried to block the entrances to prevent those of Calderón's party from getting in, hoping to short-circuit the proceedings by precluding a quorum. This would not be a mere inconvenience; the Constitution provided that if the elected president did *not* take the oath on the appointed day in the appointed place, the presidency would be declared vacant and a new election called.

A flying wedge of PANistas outflanked the PRD stalwarts and hustled Calderón into the chamber through a back door. Bulling their way to the podium, skipping all the traditional ritual, forgoing the shaking of hands, throwing protocol to the winds, they slapped on the sash of office. Calderón swore a hasty allegiance to Mexico, his voice drowned out by boos and cheers. The new (if precariously perched) president of the republic was whisked away and out the door. The whole business was over in three minutes flat.

In all the hubbub, less attention was paid to a press conference Calderón had just held, hours before his dash to the sash. In addition to announcing the members of his security cabinet, Calderón tossed a bombshell into the roiling national conversation. He was declaring, he said, a war on drugs, a "battle against drug trafficking and organized crime, which will take time, money, and even lives."

Organized crime, he explained, had been allowed to grow exponentially due to corruption and sloth, and it had become so powerful that it now exercised control over significant parts of the country. "Mexicans cannot and should not allow de facto powers to defy the authority of the state on a daily basis," Calderón said, nor should they accept the attendant flouting of the law, the explosion of crime, the violence that, he argued, was spinning out of control. His war would protect the citizenry, diminish corruption, and reduce the bloodshed. It was a matter of great urgency, a matter of national security. It required and would receive immediate action.

Ten days later, on December 11, 2006, 5,300 armed troops, assembled chiefly from various federal forces (the army, navy, and federal police), rolled into the State of Michoacán, due west of Mexico City—an initiative presumably worked up in closed-door consultations sometime between July and December. The latest iteration of the War on Drugs was underway.

Many Mexicans were stunned by this development. Calderón had not provided the slightest hint during the campaign that he intended any such military undertaking. Not surprisingly, many believed this conjured-up war was a desperate bid by Calderón to save his presidency. It looked like an effort to change the conversation, to distract attention from the throngs in the streets, to establish his legitimacy by rallying the country behind its commander-in-chief and his heroic stand against a quasi-external foe.

There is a lot to be said for this theory, and one day the smoking gun that proves it may turn up. But even if eventually it can be shown conclusively that such self-serving motivations dominated Calderón's decision, it is still too facile an explanation of how and why the war was launched. The burgeoning lawlessness and horrific violence of the Fox era were legitimate causes for alarm. With heads rolling—and in his home state of Michoacán, no less—it was not prima facie unreasonable for Calderón to argue that the federal state needed to recapture territory that had been effectively seized by organized crime.

The question was how best to go about doing so. In his campaign Calderón had talked about (once again) reorganizing the rotted-out federal police force and reforming the judiciary. He had made passing mention of establishing yet another law enforcement agency modeled on the DEA. He had spoken about raising military salaries, which might have been seen as portending his next move. But still, in all his campaign rhetoric, there had been nary a whiff of war. If anything, he had depicted the greatest menace facing Mexico as coming not from drug lords, but from López Obrador.

Nor had he talked publicly of war during the electoral crisis, when he was president-elect. What he did do, in the months between the voting in July and his rocky inauguration in December, was to consult with Antonio Garza, the U.S. ambassador, and then with President George W. Bush, about a fully militarized war on drugs. In September, at a private dinner with Garza in Mexico City, Calderón said he planned to make attending to the narcos a key pillar of his administration. Garza offered a hearty concurrence. Indeed he warned that if Calderón wanted to attract the investments needed to jump-start Mexico's economy, "foreigners and Mexicans alike had to be reassured that the rule of law would prevail." Calderón stressed his strong desire to improve cooperation with the U.S. on security matters.

In November, at the White House, in his first face-to-face meeting with Bush, the president-elect pleaded for a major commitment of guns and money.[18] He received the president's energetic blessing—perhaps no surprise given that three years earlier Bush had initiated his own "war of choice." Four months later, at a March 2007 presidential meeting in Merida, Mexico, the leaders finalized the terms of a billion-plus dollar U.S. commitment to providing weapons, intelligence-gathering equipment, and training.[19]

But while Calderón had taken steps to arrange for backup, he had not fully grappled with the weakness of the Mexican armed forces under his command, nor had he fully assayed the strengths of his enemy.

The spectacular desertion rates in the military under Fox called for measures beyond a modest raise in pay.[20] And sending the army to deal with criminal disorder in the middle of Mexico's cities would require a lengthy training period, for which his blitzkrieg war plan made no provision. Perhaps here Calderón was unduly influenced by U.S. Secretary of Defense Donald Rumsfeld, who, when responding in December 2004 to complaints from front-line soldiers in Iraq about a dangerous lack of preparation, issued his famous dictum: "you go to war with the army you have—not the army you might want or wish to have at a later time."

Conceivably Calderón's proposed centralizing of the national police forces—bringing the Federal Preventive Police and the Federal Investigation Agency under a single command—might mitigate corruption. But

---

18   The timing of the meeting was a bit awkward as two weeks before the Oval Office get-together Bush had signed into law the Secure Fence Act of 2006, which called for erecting 698 miles of fence on the boundary between the two nations. Calderón criticized the plan in a meeting with Hispanic groups, saying he wanted to see "the U.S.-Mexico border not covered in walls and barbed wire, but as an area of opportunity and prosperity for Mexicans and Americans both."

19   Lucrative contracts for arming the Mexican state went to, among others, Bell Helicopter, Northrup Grumman, Sikorsky, and United Technologies Corporation.

20   Though this was a promise on which he delivered: soldiers who received 4,300 pesos ($316) a month in 2006 got 10,800 pesos ($795) a month by 2012.

the fantastic amounts of money gangsters could bring to bear might have given a more prudent man pause. Nor was significant attention paid to the nation's roughly two thousand local police forces—which were at best useless, and more often than not active adjutants of the cartels—other than a willingness to evict them from office wholesale, or, if need be, have federal forces shoot them down.

An even weaker reed than the means of violence was the means of justice. The criminal justice system was a bad joke, corrupt beyond belief, wildly inefficient, its conviction rates infinitesimal, its prisons porous or controlled by inmates.

And for all Calderón's sweeping references to "the state" regaining control of cartel-dominated territory, there was no longer a "state" in the old unitary sense. The days of one-party rule were over, for ill as well as good. The defeated PRI, licking its wounds and looking for a comeback, was not inclined to join a coalition government. López Obrador's PRD supporters were still in the streets contesting Calderón's right to be president. Congress was effectively gridlocked. And key state governorships were in the hands of rival parties. All this may have influenced his decision to skip any effort to cultivate support and instead just spring his war on the citizenry—staging not a coup but a *coup de théâtre* that he hoped would carry the day. But even Bush had taken pains to put together a "Coalition of the Willing."

Then there was the strength of the enemy, which might have been better assessed. It was not just the cartels' gringo-derived firepower— Calderón was very alive to that issue and would call on the U.S., repeatedly, publicly, and fruitlessly, to restore the assault-weapons ban, to sign CIFTA, to stem the flow of Kalashnikovs. Rather, it was that Calderón seemed not to comprehend that the drug business had taken deep root, with hundreds of thousands of campesinos having become dependent, for lack of better alternatives, on the narco economy. Perhaps it was hard for him to reckon with this silent support, because that would have required confronting the profound crisis of the countryside, and reconsidering the role of NAFTA and the whole neoliberal project in creating it.

Calderón and his party had run on a pro-NAFTA platform, aiming at and receiving the support of the substantial number of Mexicans who were benefiting from the new order. Analysis of the 2006 voting statistics showed PAN's support had come disproportionately from the industrial and service sectors of the north, from the middle- and upper-middle classes, and from self-identified Catholics. AMLO had done better with agrarian, southern, and poorer voters, though the PRI's Madrazo had done better still in those sectors. Calderón had talked of fighting poverty, but he believed the way to do so was by pressing ahead with the neoliberal project, opening the country still further to international capital, and expanding the industrial sector so it could absorb the growing number of farmers being driven from the land by unequal competition with U.S. agribusiness. A New Mexico would thus peaceably replace the Old. He did not quite get that the drug business, whose illicit cargoes rolled north from Nuevo Laredo and Ciudad Juárez alongside the trucks conveying automobiles and electronics, was *itself* part of the New Mexico. The impoverished peasants pouring into the narcoeconomy—getting jobs as growers, gunmen, packagers, drivers, guards, and peddlers—and the many rural villages being "modernized" through profits from the drug trade, had a stake in this new status quo, and would fight to defend it.

Nor was Calderón quite prepared to tackle the interdependency between Mexico's narcoeconomy and the country's financial, commercial, and industrial infrastructures. Though he did win passage of some (extremely modest and feebly enforced) money-laundering legislation, he never fully confronted the degree to which the banking system benefited from the billions of dollars repatriated each year from sales in Gringolandia, monies that in turn helped fertilize a host of "modern" sectors like transportation, hotels, security, cattle ranches, record labels, and movie companies. In 2009, midway through his sexenio, the roughly $30 billion that annually flowed to Mexican gangsters ran a close second to profits from oil exports ($36.1 billion), and exceeded remittances from migrant Mexican maids and agricultural laborers ($21.1 billion), and foreign tourism ($11.3 billion). He did not quite grasp the degree to which *his own constituents* might be complicit in per-petuating the established narco-order he was now setting out to topple.

He might also have given some attention to the cultural appeal of the narco-enemy among an indeterminate but sizeable percentage of Mexico's youth, especially the popularity of *narcocorridos*. These songs, which cast drug dealers as heroic rebels, had evolved (or devolved) from a 200-year-old tradition of peripatetic balladry. Back in the day, wandering minstrels would bring the latest news, set to music, to the hinterlands of northern Mexico. During the War of Independence in the 1810s and 1820s, the lyrics took on a rebellious cast. This emphasis was still in place a century later during the Revolutionary wars when (as Grillo notes in *El Narco*) they were sung around the firesides of militia camps.

In the 1930s, balladeers began singing about bandits and boot-leggers, celebrating outlawry much as popular culture did in the con-temporary U.S.A. In the 1970s the outlaws being limned became drug dealers, the bootleggers' latter-day incarnation. With the huge success in 1974 of "Contraband and Treason," a ditty by the group Los Tigres del Norte, the format went mass market. The tale of drug runners driv-ing over the border to San Diego with pounds of marijuana stuffed into their car tires—probably the first recorded narcocorrido—was a sensation in Sinaloa, and among Chicano gangs in California. Soon hundreds of imitators from both sides of the border were churning out hardcore narcocorridos, with obvious interlinks in the 1980s and 1990s to U.S. gangsta rap.

Despite songster claims to have inherited the mantle of a sub-versive tradition, and for all their heroizing of young hoods as fearless machos with Robin Hood inclinations, they were in fact bulwarks of the system. The songs were paeans to consumerism and misogyny, cele-brating fast cars and snappy clothes and sexy subservient women—the enjoyment of wealth not its redistribution. Their depiction of narcos as successful self-made men, entrepreneurs with Uzis, was equally obfus-catory, as the drug trade was a quasi-corporate machine that relied on active complicity of the forces of order.

Their essential congruity with the status quo was one reason that the songs were popular not just with the gangsters themselves, not just to many of the disaffected masses of the unemployed and semi-employed of the Old Mexico, but were taken up as well by affluent children of the New Mexico. These private-school graduates and scions of rich ranching families striking hip-hop gangsta poses in the manner of suburban U.S. youth, thought it cool to dress up like hoodlums or hang out with the sons of capos. While no more likely than their U.S. counterparts to pick up AR-15s, their susceptibility to the allure of gangster culture complicated Calderón's notion that he could rally a unified "us" against a marginalized "them."

Of one thing the new president was certain: it would be a bad idea to reverse macroeconomic policy (as the left advised) by refurbishing the safety net, reestablishing subsidies the PRI had long promoted, slowing or reversing the privatization of public services (of education and day care, for instance, which only appealed to voters who could afford to pay for them), or restoring price controls on basic commodities. (Though on the latter issue he proved pragmatic, backing down when resistance to his proposed cutbacks in tortilla subsidies threatened to become explosive.)

Instead, Calderón defined what he was up against in purely military terms. And in this he was egged on by the United States. This was, after all, Bush Time, when terrorism was treated not as a crime against humanity but an as act of war requiring in response a "global war on terrorism," albeit a war with no clear definition of "victory." It is possible that Calderón had Operation Condor in mind as a model—a quick campaign to beat hell out of the narcos for a year or so, reminding them of who was boss, after which the bad guys would fall back in line. But given that the old PRI apparatus of corrupt federal oversight of the drug trade had been largely dismantled, there was no obvious line to fall back to, even if he had wanted (which he did not) to replace the PRI's de facto organization of the industry with one run by the PAN.

He might have been better advised to take Bush's war in Iraq as a *negative* role model. By 2006 Iraq had long since turned into a

Vietnam-style quagmire, and in the November 2006 elections it had just cost the Republicans control of the House and Senate. But just as Calderón was assuming power, Bush, who had been sidling away from his "stay the course" rhetoric, now changed course again—prodded by the right—and threw another twenty thousand troops into the Middle-Eastern morass. ("The surge" would buy him a little more time, at the cost of many more American and Iraqi lives, but in the end would lead only to his party's being booted from the White House by an anti-war Democrat in 2008.)

Like Bush, Calderón charged heedlessly ahead, with equally disastrous results.

CHAPTER NINE
2006–2012

The first strike came on December 11, 2006, ten days after he assumed office, when Calderón sent 6,500 ground troops and masked federal police snaking up mountain roads into the heart of Michoacán's drug country, where Los Zetas and La Familia, former allies, had been locked in murderous combat. Weeks later, Calderón flew into a military base to salute the troops, donning a soldier's cap and army jacket—a drastic break with the strict separation between civilian and military leadership in effect since the 1940s. "New pages of glory will be written," he told them. "I instruct you to persevere until victory is achieved.... We will give no truce or quarter to the enemies of Mexico."

Calderón rapidly spread the offensive, opening up one front after another. Seven thousand troops rolled into Acapulco, 3,300 federal police and soldiers marched into Tijuana—numbers far greater than Fox had committed—and soon roughly 50,000 men were in the field, including almost the entire federal police force and much of the military.

The offensive achieved some quick results. Federal agents stormed a Mexico City safe house and confiscated $207 million of meth money, the biggest cash bust in history. Mexican marines seized more than 23.5 metric tons of cocaine, the biggest coke bust in history. Calderón's men also arrested thousands of suspected traffickers. Most were low-level hoods, but some kingpins were taken off the board as well. Several of these, to the great satisfaction of the northern neighbor, were extradited to the U.S., including top target Osiel Cárdenas Guillén, putting an end, it was hoped, to his running the Gulf Cartel from his Mexican jail cell. True, the confiscations added up to only a tiny fraction of cartel profits, and most of the arrested personnel were released without being prosecuted. But all in all, Calderón had come on like gangbusters. Yes, critics complained that, after his first half year in office, the violence on Mexico's streets still exceeded Fox-era levels. Then that changed too.

In August 2007, the Gulf Cartel and Sinaloa-Juárez Federation agreed to a ceasefire. Each had underestimated the other. Both had suffered heavy casualties. Warfare had been bad for business. Their respective contacts in Colombia were beginning to wonder about the Mexicans' reliability. With victory nowhere in sight, the Sinaloan high command (El Chapo & Company) and its field commanders El Barbas and La Barbie, reluctantly decided to call off their invasion and seek a rapprochement with the Gulf Cartel and its Zeta army. At a peace summit in Monterrey the two mafias agreed to stop massacring each other and to respect the facts on the ground. The Gulf Cartel would keep northeastern Mexico, including Nuevo Laredo, as well as the eastern state of Veracruz; the Sinaloa-Juárez Federation would keep their old western territories including Acapulco; and in other domains they agreed to co-exist. Arturo Beltrán Leyva was made the Sinaloan point man to keep the peace with the Zetas' Heriberto Lazcano. The killings began to subside in the ensuing months, and although 2007 finished with 2,500 drug-related murders, more than in 2006, the death rate was trending down. As Ioan Grillo notes, after Calderón's first year in office, his war looked "pretty damn good."

Then, at the beginning of 2008, Mexico exploded. For the remainder of Calderón's sexenio, the war he had started would expand and intensify, quantitatively and qualitatively, and become incredibly convoluted. There would be no trench warfare, no great set-piece battles between contending armies, no clear lines of demarcation between—or within—one side and the other. Instead, in a deadly dialectic, the war *on* narcos would exacerbate the war *between* narcos, which in turn would bring on an escalation of the war *on* narcos. The cartels fissured into fragments, which came together in new alignments; allies became enemies, foes mutated into friends. Government forces fought one another as furiously as they did the narcos. The lines between combatants and civilians blurred, disappeared. At times it seemed a war of all against all. It also grew steadily more monstrous. The mound of corpses and body parts rose to epochal proportions. The roughly seventy thousand who died—more often than not in grotesque and grisly ways—put the carnage level on a par with that of the Cristero War and the Mexican Revolution itself. Hell really had broken loose.

Sorting the geography of this nightmarish calamity into tidy theaters of war is all but impossible. Territorial borders became as mutable as the boundaries of combatants. Battlegrounds could shuttle abruptly from blood-drenched killing field to relatively pacific landscape. Yet a geographical approach—focusing on the trajectories of violence in the western, eastern, and central states of the northern borderland regions—provides a rudimentary way to get a grip on the main lines of conflict. What follows will be a fairly high-altitude flyover of the Boschian terrain below, though it also will descend to limn the horrors, drawing on the host of accounts eyewitnessed at ground level that were written by brave and resourceful reporters (those who lived to tell their tales).

From our elevated vantage point above the maelstrom of murder it seems clear that the major trigger of renewed warfare in 2008 was the truce that had terminated warfare in 2007. The peace treaty had given responsibility for keeping things peaceful to each cartel's military wing. So assiduously did they live up to their responsibilities that both the respective field commanders—Arturo Beltrán Leyva of Los Negros and Heriberto Lazcano of Los Zetas—decided to strike out on their own, cutting out their respective cartel bosses, and entering into a business arrangement with each other. The effect of these formerly mortal enemies reconstituting themselves as commercial accomplices was to redraw the map of Mexico's organized drug trafficking. Their respective cartel superiors, however, declined to accept this new state of affairs, and went to war with their respective former subordinates.

✦ ✦ ✦

Sinaloa Split

Hostilities broke out almost immediately in the west, driven as much by personal vendettas as by the underlying commercial logic.

Victory over the Zetas—or at least having battled the ferocious enforcers to a draw—went to Arturo Beltrán Leyva's head. El Barbas (the Beard), and even more so his brother Alfredo, were often seen and photographed with his top security man, Edgar "La Barbie" Valdez Villarreal, attending glamorous parties. Their flamboyant lifestyle seems to have grated on the more low-key El Chapo rather as, back in the 1980s, the flashy carryings-on in New York City of the publicity-hungry Mafia boss John Gotti had ruffled the elegant feathers of Big Paulie Castellano, a more conservative capo, who believed bosses should be neither seen nor heard. So when on January 21, 2008, Alfredo was arrested in Culiacán, it was commonly believed that El Chapo had tipped off federal authorities as to his whereabouts.

This conviction was strengthened when El Chapo failed to help Alfredo win his freedom, in marked contrast to Los Zetas' Lazcano, who immediately provided his new buddy Arturo with his most trusted attorney. El Chapo's unhelpfulness, some surmised, might also have been aimed at currying favor with the authorities, in order to win the release of one of his sons from a maximum-security prison in the State of Mexico. And, indeed, said son was sprung a few months later, on April 11. A few weeks after that, on May 9, the Beltrán Leyva clan—presumably having drawn their own conclusions about the timing of events—sent a fifteen-man hit squad to kill El Chapo's other son, Édgar, a twenty-two-year-old university student. He and two friends were riddled with five hundred bullets in the parking lot of a Culiacán mall.

Buoyed by their growing link with the Zetas, the Beltrán Leyva Organization (BLO), as the brothers styled themselves, now broke with The Federation and, accompanied by their trusty sidekick La Barbie, declared full-scale war on the Sinaloa Cartel. The ensuing battles were the more vicious for being fratricidal—the rivals having worked and fought alongside each together for decades—and for being centered in their common homeland, every inch of which was known to both sides. Massacre followed massacre, cut-up corpses piled high, and by year's end Sinaloa alone had tallied 1,162 homicides.

2009 proved to be more of the same until December, when DEA agents tracked Beltrán Leyva to a high-end apartment block in Cuernavaca, and then gave the address to Mexican marines, an elite force that had trained with the U.S. Northern Command. Two hundred marines surrounded and shot up the building while a helicopter hovered overhead, and Arturo and his band fired back and lobbed grenades. After two hours, the marines stormed the apartment and killed all the occupants. Then they stripped Beltrán Leyva's body, covered the corpse with his money and jewelry, and snapped away, creating a state-issued photographic version of the narcomensajes. Later the remains were entombed in a two-story mausoleum in the Humaya Gardens, a unique (not to say bizarre) cemetery on the southern edge of Culiacán, that had become Narcoland's favorite final resting place.[21]

No sooner was the Beltrán Leyva Organization decapitated than two rival factions sprang up in its place, one led by Arturo's former right-hand man La Barbie and the other by his brother, Héctor Beltrán Leyva. They now lit into one another. It was La Barbie and his Los Negros versus Héctor Beltrán Leyva assisted by Los Zetas. Bodies piled up, videotapes of torture sessions were exchanged, and in August 2010 four decapitated bodies were hung from a bridge in Cuernavaca, along with a message on a banner (a *narcomanta*) guaranteeing a similar fate to anyone who helped Valdez. It was just then that the DEA traced La Barbie (by tracking his cell phones) to a rural house near Mexico City, where on August 30, 2010, he was arrested by federal police. (Some say La Barbie gave himself up, feeling safer in the custody of the federal government than on the run from Héctor and his Zetas). With the

---

21   For more on Los Jardines del Humaya Cemetery, see Natalia Almada's 2011 documentary *El Velador* (*The Night Watchman*).

BLO bereft of both Beard and Barbie, local warlords began battling to seize control of its lucrative territories. The war in the west now spilled over from Mexico's northwest to its center and south, with bloodbaths breaking out in a dozen different states.

A similar trajectory played out in the east.

◆ ◆ ◆

Gulfos v. Zetas

The first cracks in the Gulf-Zeta partnership appeared in 2007, after the Gulf Cartel leaders made peace with their Sinaloan counterparts, a move the Zetas saw as a sellout. Over the next two years, the Zetas began expanding their own operations, spreading down the eastern coast, setting up loosely networked cells in small towns, villages, and barrios. Many Zetas had been born poor country boys, and now they recruited thousands more of their ilk. By 2010, the Zetas were estimated to have more than ten thousand soldiers adept at military-style strategizing and fond of sadistic violence.

Early in 2010, long-standing tensions escalated into open warfare. Zetas began attacking Gulf operatives wherever they found them and taking over their turf. The Gulf Cartel allied with their old Sinaloan rivals and fought back, engulfing the northeastern region in violence. The first clash between these partners-turned-combatants came in Reynosa in the state of Tamaulipas. Fighting expanded to Nuevo Laredo, Matamoros, and other municipalities along the Tamaulipas-Texas border, and then into neighboring states of Nuevo León and Veracruz. Calderón dispatched more troops, but Los Zetas fought off army units and rival cartel hit-squads alike, using heavy-caliber machine guns and rocket-propelled grenades. Some battles lasted for hours, paralyzing entire downtowns, leaving behind a war-ravaged cityscape of burned-out businesses. The body count soared. In 2009 the federal government had reported 90 drug-related murders in Tamaulipas; in 2010 the figure was 1,209, a substantial portion of the nationwide total of 15,000 dead.

The impact of all this mortality was greater than the simple numbers suggested, as it included the largest single instance of mass murder to date. San Fernando was a town in Tamaulipas, where the strategic north-south Federal Highway 101 intersected a network of dozens of local roads and trails that led off to various frontier cities, making it a critical node in the Zetas' drug-smuggling operation. (Zeta dominance of San Fernando included control of the local police force, nearly half of which was on the cartel's payroll.) Naturally such a strategic location was repeatedly targeted by Gulf Cartel forces, which after one foray "strung the bodies of fallen Zetas and their associates from light poles."

In what appears to have been a hyper-cautious (not to say paranoid) response, Los Zetas began not merely stopping trucks and buses heading north on 101—they had been doing that already as part of their expanded extortion and kidnapping initiatives, which preyed on Central and South American migrants heading north toward an illicit river crossing into the U.S.—but now they dragged off people whom they suspected had been sent by Los Golfos or by their allies in Michoacán and Durango (the La Familia and Sinaloa Cartels) to beef up the Gulf forces.

On August 22, 2010, seventy-two migrants (fifty-eight men and fourteen women) were taken from two vehicles, grilled as to their destination, their cell phones inspected for incriminating evidence. Though no signs of a Gulf connection were uncovered, it seemed better to be safe than sorry. The migrants were accordingly taken to a nearby abandoned farm shed, tied hand and foot, laid facedown on the ground, and mowed down en masse—except for one Ecuadorian who, having feigned death, was able to reach an army checkpoint on the highway.

This, it turned out, was only a dress rehearsal for a more macabre massacre committed less than a year later. In March 2011, several buses on 101 were stopped and their passengers (this time mostly Mexicans) were removed and murdered. By June, excavation of forty-seven mass graves in the San Fernando area had unearthed 193 corpses. Most had been dispatched by blunt force trauma to the head rather than by gunshot. Despite the capture and confessions of several self-professed

Zeta perpetrators, the cause and nature of the executions remain murky. Explanations range from the same justification offered for the 2010 killings (fear of Gulf reinforcements), to refusal to work for the Zetas as drug mules, to kidnapping (not particularly plausible given the immediate killings and lack of ransom demand), to a cinematic story told to a reputable Texas journalist by an at-large, anonymous, and self-proclaimed participant. He claimed the men were given weapons, including sledgehammers, and forced to battle one another to the death like "a gladiator fight from ancient Rome." The survivors were recruited as Zeta assassins and sent on suicide missions, like driving into a Gulf stronghold and shooting it up.[22]

With 566 people dead at Zeta hands, thousands of San Fernando citizens now picked up and fled to other parts of Mexico, or to the United States. Calderón flooded the area with soldiers, deposed the local police, and turned the territory into a military base. But the Gulf-Zeta conflict merely moved on to other venues, with the Zetas (in 2011) steadily pushing the parental cartel out of much of its traditional turf along the Texas border. They also expanded southward into the states of Oaxaca and Chiapas, and over the border into Guatemala, behaving less like gangsters (Grillo notes) than "like a paramilitary group controlling territory."

In 2012 Calderón proclaimed a major setback to this Zeta juggernaut when Mexican naval forces killed Heriberto Lazcano in the state

---

22 The second San Fernando slaughter was trumped when, also in March 2011, the Zetas exacted terrible retribution on the relatives, friends, and even present or past employees of two cadre who had stolen five million dollars and fled across the border into a witness protection program, disrupting the cartel's cocaine trafficking into Eagle Pass, Texas, which had been netting six million dollars a week, funds badly needed for the war with the Golfos. A small army of Zetas showed up in the two men's home town of Allende, in the state of Coahuila, equipped with grenades, sledgehammers, and heavy construction machinery and proceeded to totally demolish any buildings connected with the turncoats, and to kidnap and kill any resident even faintly associated with them, even if they just had the same last name. A minimum of three hundred people vanished, undoubtedly into one or another of the mass graves strewn across the barren landscape. The entire episode was hushed up until 2014. The survivors were terrified into silence—especially after one enterprising soul who began offering tours of the ruined buildings was found with a bullet in his head—and the authorities had no interest in spreading more bad news.

of Coahuila on October 7. Unfortunately the Hydra Principle—chop off one head and two or more spring back in its place—was as operative here as elsewhere. Lazcano's leadership role was taken over, in fact many Zeta-watchers believed his place had already been usurped, by his number two man, one Miguel Treviño Morales. While Lazcano ("The Executioner") was a hard man to top for cruelty, Treviño was an even more vicious piece of work, given, for instance, to "stewing" his victims—dumping them in fifty-five-gallon oil drums, dousing them with gasoline, and burning them alive. The "be careful what you wish for" maxim was all too appropriate in the case of Lazcano's demise and Treviño's rise. And so it proved to be with the similarly premature celebration by Calderón, across the country in Michoacán, of the excision of another kingpin, the "Más Loco" ruler of La Familia, a surgery that led only to deeper malignancy.

◆ ◆ ◆

Familias, Templarios
By late 2009, La Familia Michoacana, with help from the Sinaloa and Gulf Cartels, had succeeded in driving their now common enemy, Los Zetas, out of the state. Then, not satisfied with commanding the methamphetamine business—exporting about one hundred tons to the U.S. each year, with a street value of perhaps $10 billion—they expanded into the cocaine, heroin, and marijuana trades, and added sidelines such as smuggling people as well as drugs into the U.S. They also tightened their grip on local government, buying some politicians and murdering others, gaining the ability to name the police chiefs who were their purported pursuers. Nor were they shy about directly attacking the federal forces that Calderón poured into the state. When one Familia lieutenant was arrested in July 2009, his comrades retaliated by capturing, torturing, and murdering a dozen federal police, dumping their bodies by a mountain highway, and affixing a narco-mensaje reading: "So that you come for another. We will be waiting for you here." Calderón dispatched an additional thousand federal

police, but to no great effect. Until December 2010 when, thanks to intelligence information provided by ever more deeply involved U.S. agencies, the government announced they had killed the cartel's capo, Nazario "El Más Loco" Moreno González, in a firefight, though disappointingly the body had been spirited away before it could be definitively identified.

After the apparent death of its strategic and spiritual leader, La Familia retreated into its mountain fastness, where the leadership split in two, prompting triumphalist government assertions that Michoacán would soon be back under control. But while one of the factions began to fade away, the other mutated into an even more repellant descendant, *Los Caballeros Templarios*—"The Knights Templar"—named after the medieval Catholic crusaders. Claiming Moreno's mantle, the Knights were led by two Moreno lieutenants, Servando "La Tuta" ("The Teacher") Gómez Martínez, and Enrique "El Kike" Plancarte. They donned white cloaks blazoned with red crosses, erected statues of the departed drug lord decked out in medieval armor, and, decorating them with gold and diamonds, venerated El Más Loco as a saint.

As had La Familia, the Knights Templar professed a devotion to social justice and even to revolutionary politics. They also affected respect for the Roman Catholic Church, and when Pope Benedict XVI visited Mexico, they hung banners on bridges in seven cities proclaiming: "The Knights Templar Cartel will not partake in any warlike acts, we are not killers, welcome Pope." They too promised to protect Michoacán from outside evildoers. Soon after appearing on the scene they hung more than forty banners across the state proclaiming: "Our commitment is to safeguard order, avoid robberies, kidnapping, and extortion, and to shield the state from rival organizations." By which they meant the Zetas, against whom they invited other cartels to join in a countrywide anti-Zeta alliance.

It took the Knights far less time to turn super-malevolent than it had La Familia.

In addition to dominating the drug trade, the Templarios began terrorizing the local populace, committing all the crimes they had promised to "avoid." They extorted tribute from farmers by forcing growers of avocados and limes to pay a quota for every kilo, terrorized corn growers into selling their crops cheap, then resold them to tortilla makers at double the price. They raped women at will, kidnapped with abandon, and tortured and beheaded resisters in public. They also took control of much of Michoacán's political order, installing local politicians in office, controlling municipal budgets, and employing local police as assistants.

The Knights menaced not only local campesinos, but also corporate and multinational enterprises. Starting in 2010, they boldly began robbing iron mining companies of their ore, or seizing the mines outright. Then they sold the product to processors, distributors, and Chinese industrial firms—voracious consumers of iron ore—having established all but total control of the port of Lázaro Cárdenas, now the country's second largest. In 2010 they moved over a million tons of illegally extracted ore, a blow to the country's economy and international standing. The Templarios, now an eight-hundred-pound leech, had opened up a whole new field of endeavor for Mexico's organized crime.

But for all the setbacks Calderón's war experienced in the east and the west, it was the developments in the borderland's center that proved most disheartening.

◆ ◆ ◆

Ciudad Juárez, Murder Capital of the World
The nightmare that overwhelmed Ciudad Juárez cannot simply be explained by the battle between the drug trafficking syndicates vying to control this crucial corridor to the U.S. marketplace, though that was at the core of the story. The world-class catastrophe that befell the city stemmed from a concatenation of historical forces, some dating back to the Second World War, which came together with unfortunate simultaneity in 2008.

In 1942, the United States and Mexico had launched the Bracero Program, a series of bi-lateral agreements that allowed

Mexican agricultural laborers to work seasonally on United States farms. The resulting ebb and flow of hundreds of thousands of campesinos ended the perceived shortage of (low-waged) manpower north of the Río Bravo, in effect reversing the massive deportations that had been carried out back in the depressed thirties, when there had been a perceived surplus. In 1964 the program was ended, due partly to U.S. labor protests against the undercutting of farm worker wages. Mexicans found their access to northern jobs blocked. In response to the resulting rampant unemployment, the Mexican Government launched the Border Industrialization Program. In doing so they followed the lead of Hong Kong and Taiwan, which had established free trade zones, enclaves within which foreign corporations could build factories and hire local workers to assemble imported component parts into finished products, e.g., television sets. The corporations paid no tariffs on the "imported" parts, and were liable only to an export tax on the value added by the laborers, which, given the extremely low wages, was a modest increment. The Mexican government's maquiladora program—a term derived from the practice of millers charging a *maquila* or "miller's portion" for processing other people's grain—offered U.S. companies cheap labor, tax breaks, and a location that was steps (not oceans) away from American soil.

United States companies leapt at the offer, opening factories along the border throughout the 1970s and 1980s. The number of these plants grew from twelve (employing 3,000) in 1965, to 1,920 (employing 460,258) in 1990, by which time Mexican maquiladoras had outstripped their Asian rivals. Ciudad Juárez led the field, sucking in enormous numbers of migrants from the surrounding distressed rural areas to work in the industrial enclaves. Between 1950 and 1990, the city's overall population swelled from 122,600 to 800,000.

The maquiladora sector surged again in the 1990s, boosted by the signing of NAFTA in 1994, and the devaluation that year of the peso, which lost more than half its value. The resulting rise in the inflation rate from 7 percent in 1994 to 52 percent in 1995 drove down the price of dollar-denominated Mexican wages by almost 30 percent. United States firms raced to Mexico to profit from the super-cheapened labor which is why, even as the country's overall economic growth rate *contracted*, maquiladora employment shot up by an average of 11 percent per year between 1995 and 2001. In Ciudad Juárez, the 140,045 maquiladora workers of 1994 nearly doubled to 262,805 by 2000. And the city's overall population skyrocketed along with its labor force, rising from 800,000 at the beginning of the nineties to over 1,200,000 by its end.

The profits from this surge flew away north, but while the workers were in some respects better off than they had been in the countryside, the downward pressure on wages (from local and increasingly international competition) kept people impoverished. Living conditions in the spreading slums outside the factory gates were squalid. Some of the ramshackle housing was built out of pallets from the loading docks of the American factories. Vast numbers had limited or no access to running water, a functioning sewage system, paved streets, or electricity. Schools, hospitals, parks, public transport—public amenities in general—were in scarce supply. In some respects Ciudad Juárez, despite its name, was less a *city* than a holding pen for workers in the private-sector enclaves.

Social stress levels were high, particularly along the gender divide. The assembly plants, though originally intended to solve the male unemployment problem, opted instead to hire single young women, who were cheaper and deemed more pliable. This suited the needs of desperate rural households who, confronted with the agrarian crisis, needed to increase their number of income streams. Urban maquiladoras allowed them to place their daughters in the industrial labor force; indeed, young women came to constitute the great majority. The work, working conditions, and wages were grim. Maquiladora employers paid Mexican women roughly one-sixth the wage paid women just across the Río Bravo. Worse, the women faced hostility from males, many of whom were unemployed—not simply over access to jobs, but because the body of independent and mobile working women represented a challenge to a profoundly patriarchal gender order.

Starting around 1994, when poverty shot up as the peso declined, and maquiladora employment rose but females got the jobs, a plague of violence against women—overwhelmingly maquiladora workers—swept through the city. The number of rapes, beatings, tortures, and increasingly violent deaths (strangulation, stabbing, mutilation) began to climb, the killings abetted (sometimes perpetrated) by the police force, and facilitated by darkened streetscapes that enhanced women's vulnerability. More than 340 were killed between 1993 and 2003, by which time the "murdered women of Juárez" had been made an international byword by outraged protestors. While some of the killings were rooted in specific situations and prompted by personal motives, it seemed clear that the murder wave was more than just an agglomeration of individual incidents. It was something rooted in the city's social ecology.

The nineties were also the heyday of "El Señor de los Cielos," Amado Carrillo Fuentes, who in 1993 had ascended to overlordship of the Juárez Cartel. By 1995, his fleet of jets landing at Juárez airport, laden with Colombian cocaine, was generating over $12 billion a year. The northward flow of drugs, paralleling and piggybacking on the NAFTA-expanded flood of legitimate products, provided the profits that supported lavish lifestyles for Carrillo Fuentes and his fellow drug lords. It also furnished the payroll for an army of drug traffickers who moved the tons of product warehoused in the city—an army whose numbers, some believed, matched those working in the assembly plants. Until his untimely demise in 1997, El Señor de los Cielos maintained a reasonable degree of order in his sector. Murders were, of course, part of doing business in an illegal industry, one could not take such business disputes to the courts, but they were limited to a modest two hundred to three hundred a year.

As the twenty-first century dawned, additional stresses were added to a dangerously fraught situation. Competition from even lower-waged Chinese assembly plants tempted some corporations to relocate their operations to Asia. And in March 2000, the U.S. dotcom bubble popped, and the economy slid into recession. The Mexican economy promptly nose-dived: it had always been sensitive to America's financial perturbations, and now, more vulnerable than ever, it was dragged down by the chains of NAFTA. Nowhere were the consequences more devastating than in the border belt. Between 2000 and 2002, maquiladora employment in Ciudad Juárez lurched downward, as 529 plants were shuttered, taking with them roughly 49,000 jobs (out of 262,000).

The recession proved a brief one, and the roller-coaster economy headed up again. Employment rose. So did in-migration. By 2005 the population reached 1,464,100, leading some to worry that the underdeveloped city was simply not capable of sustaining such numbers.[23]

There were other things to worry about. The death of El Señor de los Cielos in 1997 had been followed by the customary succession crisis and attendant instability, but by the early 2000s Amado's brother Vicente Carrillo Fuentes had come out more or less on top. Now styling himself "El Viceroy," Vicente strengthened his position by entering into the Federation alliance with the Sinaloa Cartel of El Chapo Guzmán. But 2004 brought disturbing signs that this united front—directed against the Gulf-Zeta powerhouse—was coming unglued.

On September 11, 2004, Rodolfo Carrillo Fuentes, another brother of the departed Amado, was executed by sicarios believed to have been dispatched by El Chapo. This prompted the revenge killing three months later of Arturo Guzmán Loera, a brother of El Chapo. As the alliance crumbled—its complete breakup postponed only by the ongoing war with the Gulf Cartel and its Zeta army—factionalism deepened within the Juárez Cartel, undermining El Viceroy's shaky grip on power.

Once the east-west war was ended by the truce of 2007, the break between the Sinaloa and Juárez Cartels became complete, and

---

23   Of course such evaluations depended on the eye of the beholder. In 2008, Ciudad Juárez was designated as "The City of the Future" by the prestigious magazine *Foreign Direct Investment*, published by the influential *Financial Times* group. As the website *Global Direct Investment Solutions: Corporate Development for a Networked World* enthused: "Congratulations to Ciudad Juárez, Chihuahua, Mexico as the Winner of the Overall and Most Cost Effective rankings plus a Top Five ranking for Best Infrastructure in the 2007/2008 North American Cities of the Future competition by *fDi* magazine for the Large Cities category (five hundred thousand to two million population)."

full-scale war ensued. Violence spiked upward in January and February 2008, racking up a record one hundred murders in sixty days. In April, Calderón launched Operation Chihuahua (it was compared to Bush's "surge" in Iraq), which eventually sent thousands of soldiers and federal police to the city. It had the effect of spraying gasoline on a fire. By the end of 2008, 1,600 had died.

Another calamity landed on the city's head that year. On September 15, Lehman Brothers filed for bankruptcy. The subsequent downward plunge of the U.S. economy produced the sharpest drop in the Mexican economy in twenty years. Gross Domestic Product contracted by 6.6 percent in 2009, the biggest decline experienced by any Latin American country.

The Great Recession combined with the escalation of violence interrupted foreign investment flows, with devastating consequences for the maquiladora belt. Ciudad Juárez, the city with the highest concentration of export assembly jobs, took the biggest hit. Manufacturing employment, which had dropped by 50,000 earlier in the decade, now lost another nearly 50,000 jobs, cascading down from 214,272 in July 2007 to 168,011 in December 2009, a 22 percent decrease. Tijuana dropped 21 percent. Another blow: as Mexican-Americans in the U.S. were hammered by hard times, their ability to send remittances south diminished, and in 2009 Mexico experienced a 16 percent drop in this vital income stream. Countrywide, ten million people fell below the poverty line between 2006 and 2009.

Economists noted that, in partial compensation, the so-called informal economy grew by nearly a million jobs from 2008 to 2009, though few dwelt on the fact that a hefty number of these positions were not being created by plucky independent entrepreneurs, but by the biggest business sector left standing. The cartels hired the unemployed to serve as everything from mules to murderers, an appealing prospect (given the lack of alternatives) especially for youth, who tumbled out of schools and onto the streets. In Ciudad Juárez, one 2010 study found that 120,000 Juárez youngsters aged thirteen to twenty-four—45 percent of the total—were not enrolled in any educational institution, nor had they any formal employment. Instead many were wielding cartel-provided Kalashnikovs and AR-15s, having been transformed from high-school students into baby-faced sicarios, ready to kill for cash. (The going price per corpse in Juárez was $85, which covered a week's worth of beer and tacos.) Thousands from the city's sprawling slums were pulled into the conflict, recruited either directly by the Juárez or Sinaloa Cartels, or by their subordinate street gangs.

◆ ◆ ◆

By 2009 Calderón was being implored from many sides to respond to the economic crisis. The Mexican Catholic Church, speaking through the Archdiocese of Mexico's weekly newspaper *Desde la Fe* (*From the Faith*), declared that the U.S. financial crisis had proved that savage, speculative capitalism "had failed," and called for a return to a socially responsible economy. The PRD proposed that the Bank of Mexico set aside twenty-five billion dollars for the building of public works, to generate jobs and reactivate the economy. López Obrador also called on the government to cancel all increases in the prices of gasoline and electricity; provide educational stipends for all students; and create a food budget for older adults, beginning with the indigenous population and the urban and rural poor.

Calderón's response was to launch a crash program intended to reverse decades of neglect of Juárez's social fabric, but it amounted to putting a Band-Aid on the arm of a patient who had just been shot in the gut. He hailed his "TODOS SOMOS Juárez" program ("WE ARE ALL Juárez") as "a set of policy interventions" designed to address "not only the effects but also the causes of violence and crime." They included: seventy-one schools extending their hours; establishing a "Safe Schools" program that "promotes safe environments through addiction- and violence-prevention plans"; granting "soft loans" to 1,379 small and medium-size businesses; nineteen public spaces in poor urban areas being "rescued or improved," including sports facilities, parks, and community centers; signing up more people for

Seguro Popular, the federal government's free medical insurance program; doubling the number of households (to 21,808) covered by the federal anti-poverty program Oportunidades—which Calderón had inherited from Fox and Zedillo—that gave conditional cash grants to low-income families who enroll their children in school "and take them for regular medical check-ups." The pathetic inadequacy of these otherwise worthy initiatives was underscored by the first use for one of the new soccer fields—as a killing ground, on which seven people were murdered.

Nationally, the government's response to the crisis was to pass budget cuts for 2010, the austerity measures dedicated to "restoring investor confidence."

Ironically, one thing that did seem to buoy investors' spirits were the drug profits that continued to flow as copiously as ever. Analysts were surprised at how well Mexico's banking sector was doing, given the tanking economy. Calderón's government attributed this to financial reforms undertaken after the 1994 financial crisis. But according to Antonio Maria Costa, then head of the United Nations Office on Drugs and Crime, it appeared to be "drugs money worth billions [that] kept the financial system afloat at the height of the global crisis." The thirty billion dirty dollars that had been laundered south into Mexican bank vaults proved, the global drug czar believed, to be "the only liquid investment capital" available during the meltdown to institutions on the brink of collapse. The Mexican Treasury secretary assayed a more modest assessment of the bonanza's dimensions when he said, in a press conference on June 15, 2010, that the forty-one banks operating in Mexico had "ten billion dollars that cannot be explained within the proper dynamics of the country's economic activity."[24]

---

24   HSBC accepted at least $881 million in cash deposited by the Sinaloa Cartel, hundreds of thousands at a clip, using boxes designed to fit the precise dimension of their teller windows. In addition, the bank failed to monitor more than $670 billion in wire transfers, and more than $9.4 billion in purchases of U.S. currency from HSBC Mexico. Executives admitted they had failed to follow money laundering rules, and in 2012 the bank was fined $1.9 billion—about two months' worth of profits—but prosecutors refrained from

Calderón did try to remedy this situation. He decreed measures to clamp down on cash deposits, and won passage in October 2012 of a modest money-laundering bill that tightened regulations on banks, casinos, and credit-card companies, and limited cash transactions in certain real-estate operations or in the buying and selling of vehicles, jewelry, precious metals, watches, gemstones, and works of art. But prospects for efficient enforcement seemed bleak, with Mexico's Ministry of Finance reporting that only 2 percent of money laundering investigations in 2010 had ended with the accused being sentenced.

◆ ◆ ◆

Rather than confront the financial and systemic crises, Calderón doubled down on the military option. In Ciudad Juárez, approximately eight hundred officers were dismissed from the police department and replaced by troops and federal police. As of March 2009 at least 4,500 had arrived; by August there were more than 7,500. Further reinforcements followed in 2010, with Calderón insisting: "We won't back down against the enemies of Mexico."

In this he had the full backing of the United States government, which, despite a change of regime, stood foursquare behind the strategy of sending the military into the streets of Mexican cities. The Merida Initiative, which had authorized $1.4 billion worth of hardware and training to be disbursed over three years, had been signed in 2008 by President Bush, but its administration fell to President Barack Obama (2009–). On his first presidential visit to Mexico, in April 2009, Obama praised Calderón for taking on the drug cartels, and promised to expedite the shipment of Merida weaponry that had been slow to arrive in government hands.[25]

---

bringing criminal charges, lest they topple the bank and further destabilize the global financial system. "Too big to indict" was the consensus.

25   Weaponry destined for the *cartels*, however, had continued to flow at a brisk and profitable pace. Obama admitted this, noting (as had Bush) that more than 90 percent of the arms seized from Mexican gangsters had come from the United States. Obama

As the violence in Ciudad Juárez exploded, the Obama administration and the Pentagon's Joint Forces Command worried that Mexico might be verging on becoming a "failed state." They wondered if cartel violence might trigger a collapse of the government, sending the country spinning down into chaos, which in turn "would demand an American response based on the serious implications for homeland security alone." In April 2009, Homeland Security Secretary Janet Napolitano announced she would be sending hundreds more federal agents and other personnel to border areas.

As the Mexican death toll mounted, Calderón had asked Bush for armed drones, having been impressed with their results in Iraq and Afghanistan. The White House rejected this, fearing collateral damage (as in Iraq and Afghanistan). But after the July 2009 shooting death of a U.S. Border Patrol agent, Predator drones were okayed, for reconnaissance only, with U.S. pilots sitting at the controls in the States, and Mexican military or federal police commanders directing their flight path south of the Rio Grande. Obama also approved DEA and CIA training of Mexican counterparts to hunt down drug kingpins, using counter-terrorist "high-value target" strategies of the sort used against members of al-Qaeda and the Taliban. The Americans also tried to set up trustworthy Mexican units by polygraphing, drug-testing, and vetting candidates, but these operations were routinely penetrated by moles.

Anxiety levels mounted in 2010. In January (as a Wiki-leaked cable revealed) U.S. embassy officials saw Calderón as struggling with "spiraling rates of violence that have made him vulnerable to criticism that his anti-crime strategy has failed." In September, Secretary of State Hillary Clinton visited Mexico and declared that cartel violence might be "morphing into or making common cause with what we would call

promised action, saying he would push the U.S. Senate to ratify CIFTA, the inter-American arms-trafficking treaty. In this he failed. He also indicated that he favored reinstating the U.S. ban on assault weapons, but on this front he declined even to try, as, given NRA and Republican intransigence, he believed gun control, even for export to gangsters, was just not in the political cards.

an insurgency." In February 2011 the U.S. undersecretary of the army expressed concern about "the potential takeover of a government that's right on our border," a development that might possibly require America's "armed soldiers" to fight "an insurgency right on our border or just across our borders."

This hint of possible U.S. military action—evoking memories of Pershing's incursion of 1916 if not Polk's 1846 invasion—touched off an uproar in Mexico that won an immediate retraction. But days later, on February 15, 2011, U.S. Immigration and Customs Enforcement (ICE) agent Jaime Zapata was shot to death by Zetas using a weapon smuggled in from the United States. This was the first such murder since Kiki Camarena's in 1985, leading some to demand the growing number of U.S. agents in Mexico be allowed to carry weapons. In March 2011, Calderón flew to Washington for talks with Obama, which led to the latter praising the former for his "extraordinary courage" in fighting the drug cartels, and insisting that Calderón's war had in the United States a "full partner." To support Mexican operations in Ciudad Juárez, U.S. authorities arranged brainstorming sessions at nearby Fort Bliss in Texas, and U.S. liaison officers were placed inside the federal police war-room in Ciudad Juárez.

But on the ground in the beleaguered city, it quickly became apparent that the military, eyeing all locals as potential narco-assassins (which many were), had launched brutal attacks against suspect civilians and municipal police, becoming part of the problem rather than its solution. Worse, they and the federal police—as if infected by a greed virus—swung over to the dark side in great numbers, stealing, raping, robbing, and kidnapping at will. Though they had been welcomed at first by the citizenry, many of the latter soon changed their mind, and complaints about abuse poured in. A November 2011 report by Human Rights Watch (*Neither Rights Nor Security: Killings, Torture, and Disappearances in Mexico's "War on Drugs"*) asserted that: "Instead of reducing violence, Mexico's 'war on drugs' has resulted in a dramatic increase in killings, torture, and other appalling abuses by security forces, which only make the climate of lawlessness and fear worse in many parts of the country."[26] Major General Manuel de Jesús Moreno Aviña, commander of the Third Infantry Company, and in charge of operations in the entire state of Chihuahua, was soon relieved of duty and charged with torture, murder, and collaboration with traffickers. But the carnage continued.

A feeding frenzy of murder, kidnapping, extortion, robbery, gang clashes, revenge slayings, and sicario assassinations gripped the city. Bursts of machine gun fire became routine background noise, as prevalent as car alarms. Spent cartridges from AK-47 and AR-15 rifles, and .40-caliber and 9mm pistols, littered the streets. So did decapitated, burned, mutilated, or merely bullet-riddled cadavers.

In August 2009 the murder rate in Ciudad Juárez was declared the highest in the world, leaving second place Caracas in the dust. By year's end 2,660 had died, nearly doubling the 2008 total. In 2010, the body count reached 3,116.

Tens of thousands fled the city between 2007 and 2011, those with money and papers relocating across the border in El Paso and points north. A reported one hundred thousand homes were vacant, abandoned, or destroyed.

Inside the inferno, death seemed omnipresent, a war of all against all, beyond rational explanation. Journalist Charles Bowden, who lived in Juárez during those days, wrote in his harrowing account *Murder City* that it seemed as if "violence is now woven into the very fabric of the community, and has no single cause and no single motive and no on-off button." Violence was "like the dust in the air, part of life itself." Or no, Bowden reflected, "not a part of life, now it is life."

But the bloodletting was not pointless, nor inexplicable. Though inflamed by Calderón's intervention, it was ultimately a product of the struggle to control the *plaza*, and the tens of billions of dollars that would accrue to the victor. When in 2011 El Chapo and his Sinaloans significantly degraded El Viceroy's forces, and Calderón was pressured

---

26 Between 2006 and 2009, there was a 1,000 percent increase in complaints against SEDENA (the Department of National Defense) for alleged violations of human rights; a great leap upward from levels under Fox.

into withdrawing the inflammatory military in favor of reconstituted federal and local police forces, the violence began to subside, the body count dropping by year's end to 2,086. And in 2012, reflecting the clear (though not total) triumph of Sinaloan forces, it lurched downward to 750—still atrocious, but a quantitative change sufficiently significant to be reflected in qualitative experiences. Businesses reopened; citizens basked in the relative calm.

But the tamping down of the clash between goliaths, this time not through truce but through victory, did not bring countrywide relief. Quite the opposite: the war generated a vast expansion of collateral criminality, a rampage not of tyrannosaurs but of raptors, and one that wreaked havoc across the land.

◆ ◆ ◆

Collateral Criminality

Calderón had argued that his fundamental goal was not drug interdiction but beating back the narcos' de facto (verging on de jure) challenge to the authority of the state, thereby ending organized crime's undermining of public order and security. But the president chose to define victory as the dismantling of cartels by taking down kingpins—going mano a mano with the drug lords—in the belief that decapitating the organizations would degrade and hopefully destroy their ability to dominate great patches of Mexican territory. By this metric his sexenio was a great success, as Calderón's forces captured or killed twenty-five of the top thirty-seven bad guys. But the end result was not the desired one.

On the one hand, the five or so major organized crime organizations of 2006 were consolidated into the two gigantic super-cartels of 2012—the Sinaloans, who dominated the western half of the country, and the Zetas, who dominated the east. Calderón had inadvertently furthered the concentration of power in the industry (with the Gulf, Beltrán Leyva, Juárez, Tijuana, and Templario outfits reduced to secondary status).

On the other hand, there was an explosion of *disorganized crime*. The Hydra Principle was again in effect. Calderón's war, coupled with the fissionability of the criminal industry, spawned an estimated eighty smaller criminal organizations, restoring the free enterprise system and its murderous concomitant: competition. He argued that the resulting explosion of violence by ganglets, against one another and against civilians, was an indicator of success—in the way that a fever signals that a body is fighting off an infection. This disturbing level of abstraction allowed him to depict a horrifying breakdown of public order as merely the storm before the calm.

In truth, the wartime scramble for revenue streams was remaking the criminal landscape as the competitors broke open new markets. In the United States a somewhat similar situation had emerged after the repeal of Prohibition in 1933. When legitimate corporations regained control of the production and distribution of alcohol, the chieftains of organized crime—whom the liquor trade had empowered and enriched—were now forced to diversify into other entrepreneurial channels, like labor racketeering, extortion, gambling, and prostitution. In twenty-first century Mexico there was wrought, rather, a bifurcation. The big boys maintained their grip on the big international drug business, leaving the lesser hoods to do the diversifying, by moving into distinctly local rackets.

In this context, according to statistics compiled by the Instituto Nacional de Estadística Geografía e Informática (National Institute of Statistics, Geography, and Computing), crime skyrocketed, reversing the historic decline that had been underway since the 1990s. Leading the league were the kidnappers.

◆ ◆ ◆

The last time abductions had been abundant—during the economic crisis of the 1990s—they had mostly been carried out by freelance criminals, with no links of consequence to the organized drug traffickers of the day. Indeed it was, at times, rather the reverse: when independent gunslingers in Sinaloa began kidnapping wealthy ranchers and cutting off their fingers to hasten the arrival of ransom payments, drug bosses issued an edict prohibiting the practice in their territory, under penalty of death. Perhaps that's why the state had one of the lowest kidnap rates in the country.

Kidnapping surged again during Calderón's war years. One government study found the number of reported cases rose 317 percent between 2005 and 2010, spiking particularly in 2008 and hitting 1,350 in 2010. As the ratio of reported to actual instances was generally considered to be 1-to-10—given the fear that calling in the police (assuming they had not done the deed in the first place) would increase the chance of the kidnappers killing their victim—criminologists calculated that Mexico's kidnapping rate was arguably the highest on the planet.

Much of the dirty business was undertaken by the small-fry gangs, emerging out of the chaos of the war itself and fueled by the growing availability of ever younger recruits who, hammered by the economic crisis and the war's disruptions, were casting about for accessible avenues of profit. They were joined by cashiered cops from local police forces, evicted by the military who regarded them (not unreasonably) as being under cartel control. This had the double downside of diminishing such local policing as had existed, and creating a cadre of unemployed gunsels.

These newcomers tended to snatch not the rich and better protected but professionals and small businessmen, doctors and auto dealers, and even better-off employees like oil workers. And almost always they went after locals rather than Americans and Europeans.

This is not to say that the giant cartels passed up the opportunity. Indeed, the Zetas entered the business—it being an obvious and easy sideline for an armed and fearsome organization—but did so on an industrial scale, turning to a massive supply of potential victims, the migrants coming up from Central America, heading for the Río Bravo frontier.

From the 1970s into the 1990s, Guatemalans, Salvadorans, Hondurans, and Nicaraguans had been in flight from civil war and government-backed and U.S.-supported death squads that killed and disappeared hundreds of thousands. Two million more had made their way up to Mexico and the United States. Since 2000, the 180,000 murdered in the Northern Triangle (El Salvador, Guatemala, and Honduras) have sustained the region's position as the most impoverished in Latin America and the most violent on earth. Their murder rates swerved upward from about 2007—reaching (in Honduras) over 90 per 100,000 in 2012, far outstripping Mexico's 21.5 (and the 4.7 in the U.S.)—and partly in response to the arrival of Mexican cartels in their homelands, adding their own brand of savagery to the homicidal culture the citizenry had inherited.

The ongoing mayhem in turn sent an estimated four hundred thousand to five hundred thousand to seek refuge in the U.S. each year. Most chose to get to the border by clambering aboard the roofs of cargo trains, known collectively as *La Bestia* (The Beast), or if their families could scrape together the money, traveling by bus or truck. Organized criminals in close collusion with crooked cops feasted on the flow: robbing, raping, kidnapping, killing.[27] Zetas calculated there were huge potential profits in low-unit-price, high-volume ransoming. Aware that even the poorest migrant had relatives who, if they pooled what they had, could come up with $5,000 a head, on paper ten thousand kidnaps could fetch $20,000,000. And they had the organizational capacity to kidnap by the trainload. Such projections were not fanciful. In 2009, the country's National Commission on Human Rights documented 9,758 *reported* kidnappings in six months, from September 2008 to February 2009. And in 2010, between April and September, the Commission cited 214 mass kidnappings involving 11,333 people. Still, neither government nor media paid much attention to the roundups and ransoming until that year's San Fernando massacre of seventy-two migrants jolted the country into noticing the plight of the Central Americans passing through their midst.

---

27   Six to eight of every ten women, it is estimated, are raped or sexually assaulted during the trip north, by narcos, criminals, police, government officials, or other migrants; many, aware of what awaits, begin taking contraceptive pills before departing.

Those who made it to the U.S. border confronted another set of problems. The beefed-up wall did not cover all two thousand miles. It left a series of lacunae, usually adjacent to hostile environments, which had produced a fortified frontier punctuated by funnels, the only viable avenues of access for illegal migrants. But this left them vulnerable to the swarms of ski-masked bandits who, knowing precisely where the travelers must go, awaited them there to rob and rape. Still more dangerous were the narcos, who squeezed through the same spaces, and were enraged when mass movements of migrants attracted the attention of the Border Patrol. On one occasion, at a small town on the border between Mexico and Arizona, drug traffickers belonging to the Sinaloa Cartel seized almost three hundred migrants using one of "their" routes through the desert. Their ankles were broken with baseball bats—a symbolic punishment as well as effective deterrent. On other occasions they simply killed entire groups of Central American intruders. On others still, they kidnapped and held them for ransom. Or forced them to deliver drugs as the price of being allowed to move north. Alternatively, the cartels could act as coyotes, profiting handsomely by smuggling the migrants themselves across the border. Given that tighter enforcement had raised the price, they could charge more for their services.

◆ ◆ ◆

Kidnapping was a species of extortion directed at individuals. But the hungry new arrivals at the banquet table of criminal opportunites tackled businesses as well, demanding payoffs in exchange for not inflicting damage on the proprietors or their property. Until 2008 shakedowns by *organized* crime were relatively rare, but then the Zetas realized that given their control over great swatches of urban space, they could convert their territories into preying grounds, on a grand scale. And so they demanded protection payoffs from restaurants, bars, discos, brothels, car dealerships, taxi stands, pharmacies, and funeral parlors—the commercial infrastructure of city life. Enterprises that did not pay up were raked by gunfire or burned to the ground—as when Zetas set fire to an obstinate casino in Monterrey and barred the exit doors, killing more than fifty people.

The discovery of this form of taxation at gunpoint accelerated the cartel's expansion across Mexico, as the more territory it controlled, the more money rolled in. The Zetas even began franchising their name, allowing local extortionists (for a price) to claim they were Zetas, and use the brand's terrifying reputation to faciliate exaction of tribute.[28] Other cartels quickly jumped on the extortion bandwagon. La Familia Michoacana, and its successor the Caballeros Templarios, became masters of the form, expanding their leeching beyond small businesses into the agricultural and industrial sectors, shaking down growers of limes and diggers of mines.

The war accelerated this new practice. Extortion rackets took off in Ciudad Juárez after 2008, partly to compensate for the interruption of other business by turf wars and the government crackdown, and partly because police officers evicted from office provided a ready form of muscle. The Juárez Chamber of Commerce soon felt the bite: while it had never complained much about the tons of narcotics passing through the city, or the drug dollars washing back, it now indignantly called on the United Nations to send troops.

◆ ◆ ◆

In addition to kidnapping and extortion, robberies and burglaries of all sorts underwent a resurgence, sharply reversing indices that had been declining since the early 1990s. Some of these were old standbys, like auto thefts. Cattle rustling too made a comeback. In September 2010 at least eleven states showed an increase of 30 to 50 percent in

---

28 In a less organized way, this was the practice of the famed Black Hand "gang" that flourished in the U.S. in the early twentieth century: independent extortionists would affix a black-inked handprint to their letters demanding payoffs under threat of death, and people came to believe they were all members of a single fearsome criminal band; in fact the Black Hand was a modus operandi, not an organization.

the business of stealing cows and then selling them back on the open market, a practice that ranchers attributed to drug-trafficking cartels expanding their field of activities. Here, too, the cartels operated on a grander scale than garden-variety thieves were capable of doing. The Zetas again were pioneers. Between 2008 and the end of 2009, when federal attention was focused elsewhere, they (and copycat cartels) stole more than $1 billion worth of oil from PEMEX, the Mexican national oil company. They simply tapped directly into federal pipelines, siphoned the oil off to stolen tanker trucks, and sold the fuel to Texas-based oil companies.

◆ ◆ ◆

Virtually all this crime went unpunished. Calderón had believed he could fix the broken criminal justice system on the fly, in the midst of war, but he was proven wrong. He did win passage in 2008 of a judicial reform package, which among other things changed the trial system from a closed inquisitorial to an open adversarial model, similar to that used in the U.S., and specifically prohibited the use of torture.

But the problem was getting criminals into a courtroom in the first place, given massive corruption, inefficiency, and lack of public confidence. The Mexican Human Rights Commission found in 2012 that only eight of every one hundred crimes committed were even reported, and only 1 percent of these were investigated by prosecutors. Drug war murders rated a trifle more attention: 5 percent of them were investigated. Convictions, however, were virtually nonexistent. Criminals of all sorts had been guaranteed near total immunity. Murderers were in effect given a "007 license to kill." This impunity extended to the upper echelons, of course, with virtually no money launderers or corrupt politicians being arrested during Calderón's sexenio.

The military, too, had been granted de facto immunity. While its reputation had been repeatedly tarnished by the many charges of human rights abuse—murder, rape, torture—they virtually never led to punishment. According to a report by Amnesty International of the

7,164 complaints of torture filed between 2010 and 2013, exactly zero resulted in convictions.

The military was more severe in dealing with deserters. SEDENA (*Secretaría de la Defensa Nacional*, the Mexican Department of National Defense) reported that between December 2006 and April 2012, 56,886 soldiers deserted—over one quarter of the armed forces—of whom roughly one fifth were tracked down and punished. (Penalties could go as low as a month in jail, depending on rank.) On the other hand, most of the four-fifths simply vanished, and many feared they had sold their skills to the cartels. Calderón had raised salaries—perhaps why his desertions, though abysmal, were only half those of the Fox years—but wages still remained low, making soldiers susceptible to better offers.

◆ ◆ ◆

Language and Silence

During his war on the cartels Calderón focused, understandably enough, on recapturing physical control of territory, a goal for which he believed, rightly or wrongly, the application of military force was the appropriate method. But there was another dimension to the conflict, though seldom spelled out as such, which was a struggle over what could and could not be said (or read, or seen, or thought) about the war; a battle, that is, over public perception and discussion. On this front, too, he was challenged in ways he perhaps had not anticipated.

The power of Mexican presidents to shape national narratives through their command of the public podium had been dramatically weakened by the breakup of the PRI's monopoly of political power, and consequently its ability to dominate the national media. In the old days, the PRI presidency and the PRI state authorities spoke with something approaching a single voice, and both information and analyses dispensed from the top hewed fairly closely to the party line. PRI regimes moreover had had tremendous influence over messages disseminated by private channels of communication.

In the world of television, media barons and government officials forged close political, economic, social, and ideological ties. Tele-sistema Mexicano (which became Televisa in 1973) worked hand in hand with the reigning party. The company head, Emilio Azcárraga Milmo, was fond of calling himself "a soldier of the PRI." His channels notoriously censored coverage of the student movement and blacked out the 1968 massacre. In the print world, publishers and journalists were rewarded for fealty (with government subsidies and inside information), while those who wandered too far afield faced withdrawal of advertising patronage, denial of access to newsprint from the state-owned paper agency, and physical intimidation up to and including murder.

One of the most sensitive areas deemed to require information control was the *plaza* system of organized collusion between PRI officials and drug traffickers. Though corruption was widely understood to be all but omnipresent, silence was the tribute that vice demanded from virtue. During the cocaine boom of the 1980s, when the stakes for both partners rose significantly, extreme measures were taken to suppress unauthorized and unwanted reportage, especially when it also touched on Cold War concerns.

In 1984, Manuel Buendía was a well-known print reporter, very well connected in the halls of power, but also the author of investigative exposés of government corruption, law enforcement links to organized crime, and covert operations by the CIA. The unholy trinity of state, mob, and CIA, believing Buendía to be on the verge of exposing their financing of the contras in Nicaragua, had him assassinated, shot from behind as he left his office in Mexico City. The case remained "unsolved" until 1989, when José Antonio Zorrilla Pérez, former head of the by then disgraced and defunct Federal Security Directorate—Mexico's equivalent of J. Edgar Hoover—was arrested and jailed for having masterminded the murder.

In the 1990s, as the narcos' power grew, they began to share the work of silencing. In 1997 the Arellano Félix brothers ordered the assassination of Jesús Blancornelas, the Mexican journalist and publisher who had co-founded the Tijuana-based *Zeta* magazine, and was known for his reporting on corruption and drug trafficking. Blancornelas had enraged Ramón Arellano Félix by publishing his photograph. So a squad of sicarios fired 180 bullets into Blancornelas' car, killing his driver and bodyguard, but only wounding the reporter. Blancornelas would continue his work, but spend the rest of his life a virtual prisoner in his bricked-up home and fortified office, surrounded by a phalanx of bodyguards whenever he moved between them.

In the 2000s, especially during the Calderón sexenio, journalist assassinations became ever more overt, their intentions heavily underscored.

In 2009, Eliseo Barrón Hernández, crime reporter for a newspaper in the northern borderland state of Coahuila, published some articles about a police corruption scandal. His coverage helped secure the firing of some three hundred police officers. It also led to his death when eleven masked gunmen broke into his home, beat him in front of his horrified family, then took him away. Twenty-six hours later his body was found in a ditch with five bullet wounds and evidence of having been tortured.

During his funeral the following day, narcomantas were hung around town reading: "WE ARE HERE, JOURNALISTS. ASK ELISEO BARRÓN. EL CHAPO AND THE CARTEL DO NOT FORGIVE. BE CAREFUL, SOLDIERS AND JOURNALISTS." Clear enough, except that a few weeks later suspects detained in unrelated events supposedly confessed (under torture?) to murdering Barrón Hernández— but on orders from the Zetas, the enemies of El Chapo. Information? Disinformation? No one knew, no one knows, as nothing more was ever heard about the putative killers. There were no further arrests, no trial, nothing remained but a question mark and a dead journalist.

In 2010 in the northern city of Saltillo, Valentín Valdés Espinosa, a reporter for the local paper *Zócalo de Saltillo*, had recently published a story on the arrest of a Zeta leader at a local motel, along with a crooked cop who was being paid off by the cartel. Days later Valdés was kidnapped, tortured, shot five times, and his body (arms and legs bound) dumped outside the same motel, accompanied by a handwritten narcomensaje: "This is going to happen to everybody who doesn't understand, the message is for everybody."

◆ ◆ ◆

These were not isolated instances. Mexico has had a long history of murdering journalists. But it is important to understand the pattern of assassinations, their distribution over time. One scrupulous accounting listed a total of 289 verified killings between 1876 and 2012 (including a few disappearances that were almost certainly murders but the bodies were never found). From 1876 to 1935—a period covering the Porfiriato plus the Revolution and its aftermath—there were thirty-three killings, for an average rate of 2.3 annually. Between 1936 and 1982 there were thirty-three, averaging .48 annually. Between 1983 and 2000, when drug trafficking became big business, the number jumped to 92, an average rate of 5.1 per year. The Fox years saw only a slight increase, the thirty-five murders producing an annual figure of 5.8. But during Calderón's time in office, 106 deaths were recorded, and the yearly average leapt to 17.7. In 2012 the International Press Institute Death Watch not only labeled Mexico "the deadliest country in the world for journalists in 2011," but it found arrests and prosecutions of those responsible for such killings to be essentially nonexistent.

The intent of this surge of attacks on the press by drug cartels and corrupt officials was clear enough: they were seeking silence, hoping to throttle the flow of unwanted information. And in large measure they succeeded.

In 2010, the *Zócalo de Saltillo*, to demonstrate it had clearly understood the "message" delivered with the corpse of its reporter Valdés Espinosa, quickly announced that "As of today we will publish zero information related to drug trafficking to avoid situations like the one we went through today." In July 2012, *El Mañana*, a major regional newspaper based in Nuevo Laredo, declared it would stop reporting on "violent disputes," after its offices were attacked with grenades and rifle fire; it cited the "lack of adequate conditions for freely exercising professional journalism."[29] Others began limiting their coverage to information taken from official government press releases or police reports. And if a publication did not self-censor, its reporters might. As Javier Valdez Cárdenas of the Culiacán-based weekly *Ríodoce* put it: "When you write an article about the narcos you don't think about your editor....You don't think about your reader. You think about the narcos and whether they'll like it, whether they'll have a problem with it, whether they'll be waiting outside to take you away. The narcos control the newsroom."

This was something of an overstatement, given the ongoing involvement of corrupt law enforcement officials, primarily at the state and local level, who had their own interest in sustaining the official federal narrative—that the war on narcos was a clear cut struggle of a unified people and virtuous state ("us"), against a criminal class ("them"), a limpid story line that exposés of state collaboration with gangsters would muddy. Similarly, Calderón's triumphalist narrative—that the gangs were on the ropes, that "we" had "them" on the run—might be undermined if the TV networks and the national press paid undue attention to the horrific realities of daily life. War reporting dominated the national media—stories from various "fronts" led off the nightly news—but in general the mass media zoomed in on showpiece "victories," a kingpin capture or big drug seizure, rather than the grimy daily realities which reporters had risked their necks to capture.

♦ ♦ ♦

With information about sicario executions and military operations under-reported in mainstream information channels, people turned

---

29   As this suggests, attacks on the media went beyond murdering individual journalists. The offices of newspaper and TV stations were subject to assaults with car bombs, hand grenades, IEDs (improvised explosive devices being used extensively in Iraq in those years), volleys from gunmen, and on occasion the receipt of severed heads, left on their doorsteps in coolers.

to social media for more detailed information. The existence of this alternative communication network was itself a recent development. In 2000, fewer than three million Mexicans had access to the Internet; by 2006 it was twenty million; by 2012 it was forty million, more than one-third of the population. Cell phone use also exploded, up 600 percent between 2000 and 2012, by which time roughly 80 percent of the population owned one, despite the high cost of purchase and the need to pay tribute to Carlos Slim's monopoly in order to access networks, which largely precluded the use of mobiles by the poor.

Residents in dangerous parts of the country could therefore turn to Twitter to find out if there were any shootouts in progress which they should avoid on their way to work. Increasingly these posts were hashtagged together, creating an ad hoc news service, perhaps the first of which was developed in the deadly Tamaulipas town of Reynosa.

Bloggers emerged, who devoted their postings to covering local narco violence, though this could be a risky business. In September 2011, two bodies were found hanged from a Nuevo Laredo pedestrian bridge with a notice that read: "This is going to happen to all of those posting silly things on the Internet." Shortly thereafter, María Elizabeth Macías Castro, a well-known editor at a Nuevo Laredo newspaper who had also blogged about organized crime activities in the region, ignored this warning. Several days later her body was found next to her severed head and a computer keyboard, along with a note signed with the letter Z that read: "I am here because of my reports." The same fate soon befell a collaborator of hers, whose decapitated corpse bore the text: "This happened to me for failing to understand that I should not report things on social media websites."

◆ ◆ ◆

Narco injunctions to silence most definitely did not apply to themselves. Indeed, during Calderón's time the cartels unleashed a barrage of communiqués, a torrent of words and images that challenged the president's ability to dominate the public conversation.

To some degree they let their violence speak for itself. Hanging, shooting, burning, hacking, or decapitating rivals, journalists, police, and citizens—and then dumping the bodies in public places (highways, plazas, the front doors of government buildings)—commanded attention even if unaccompanied by text. The mute corpses testified to the criminals' ferocity and the government's incapacity. But often these communicative capos delivered their victims' cadavers with words attached: messages hand-scrawled on a piece of cardboard and ice-picked to the chest of the corpse; illiterate rants painted on bed sheets draped over the body; garrulous proclamations professionally printed on banners (narcomantas) hung from overpasses; signs posted on the sides of hijacked buses and trucks turned sideways to block roadways—*narcobloqueos*—thus bringing stalled motorists face to face with their message.

During the Calderón era the number and ubiquity of narcomantas soared, as the cartels verbally and visually muscled their way into the public sphere. The appearance of narcomantas became a weekly and sometimes daily occurrence in many Mexican states. The messages were addressed to rival gangs, to the general public, and to the state, sometimes all at once.

In September 2011, one Sinaloa sub-gang challenged Zeta control of Veracruz by presenting two messages at a roadblock, the first announcing that "the *plaza* now has a new owner," the second urging: "People of Veracruz, do not let [the Zetas] extort you, and do not pay their dues." The missives were reinforced by the presence of thirty-five corpses dumped at the scene and alleged to be Zetas. Later, the Zetas rejoined with a neatly printed appeal to "all the people of Veracruz," posted in the center of the city, imploring citizens to not "let themselves be tricked [into believing that the Zetas] are their enemies."

Another common theme was whining to the state about its being "unfair." One sign Juárez gangsters hung up in their city read: "This letter is for citizens so that they know that the federal government protects Chapo Guzmán, who is responsible for the massacre of innocent people.... Chapo Guzmán is protected by the National Action Party since Vicente

Fox, who came in and set him free." "Why do they not fight with us face-to-face?" they asked. "We invite the government to attack all the cartels."

The Zetas also deployed recruitment posters aimed at getting military men to desert. One such classified ad, on a blanket hung from bridges, declared: "The Zeta operations group wants you, soldier or ex-soldier," adding that "We offer a good salary, food, and attention for your family. Don't suffer hunger and abuse anymore."

None of these were propaganda pieces in the classic political sense. Mexico's narcos had nothing in common with the FARC in Colombia, or Sendero Luminoso in Peru. They had no ideology, evinced no interest in bidding for power, were not into winning hearts and minds—except for the fact that they did make extraordinary efforts to persuade the populace that their own brand of criminality was a superior one, from the public's point of view, at times even suggesting they were defenders of the public interest. In March 2012, El Chapo gunmen killed fourteen Zetas in Nuevo Laredo, dumped their bodies, and plastered the vicinity with banners announcing Guzmán's intention to liberate the city from Zeta control. Deriding Los Zetas as "a bunch of drunks and car-washers," the Sinaloan capo declared: "We are narcotics traffickers and we don't mess with honest working or business people.... I'm going to teach these scum to work Sinaloa style, without kidnapping, without payoffs, without extortion."

◆ ◆ ◆

The cartels did not limit themselves to print media; indeed they quickly inserted themselves into the new Internet world. One of their premier strategies was to post homemade videos, the most effective of which took the form of a live performance, before a digital camera, of the interrogation of a rival gang member, or a politician, or a crooked official, seated and bound hand and foot. When a confession of wrongdoing was elicited, his or her execution immediately followed, usually by shooting or decapitation. Again the gangsters sought to persuade viewers they were acting justly, that their sentencing and execution of the accused (presented as an enemy of the people rather than a business rival) was legitimate, indeed praiseworthy, something done on behalf of the citizenry, something the state had proved unable or unwilling to do. Thus in 2011 the Gulf Cartel staged a video in which eight of their members used an axe to lop off the limbs of a supposed Zeta sicario, one at a time. The nightmare went on for eight minutes and thirty-four seconds, ending with the narrator, holding up the now severed head, declaring the execution had been in retribution for the Zetas' second San Fernando massacre—"a bid," as Robert Gomez argues in his "Narco Warfare through Social Media," for claiming "legitimacy as a just power in Mexico." And even if their performance failed to erase from viewers' minds that the filmmakers were criminals every bit as vicious as those they were dispatching, the films constituted a raw demonstration of their power and freedom to kill at will.

These performances were then restaged, millions of times, courtesy of the websites that emerged during Calderón's sexenio devoted specifically to coverage of the war on and between the narcos. The most well-known of these is[30] the *Blog del Narco* (BDN), launched in March 2010, about whose beginnings and founder there are various origin stories. *BDN* has survived and thrived, partly because it opened its site to all comers. While it posts (and re-posts) stories written by real journalists at reputable institutions, it also solicits contributions from ordinary citizens: "Send photos, videos, notes, links, or information about your locality," requests its home page, "and it will be published anonymously." Its first posting concerned a small-town shootout, which police would not even confirm had happened, but which had been captured in an amateur video by a drive-by resident, uploaded to YouTube, then reproduced on *Blog del Narco*. But soon the site was airing extremely gruesome videos created by the cartels themselves—filmlets that recorded interrogations, decapitations, gunfights, and torture sessions—but also other footage depicting horrific crime scenes that were accessible only to the military or police.

---

30   See (extreme viewer caution is advised): http://www.elblogdelnarco.org.

The arrival of *Blog del Narco* (and its YouTube incarnation) precipitated controversy in the journalistic and wider civic communities. The producers claimed from early on that the *BDN* was a response to self-censorship adopted by the press to avoid narco retribution. They asserted, too, that they were presenting unfiltered, un-journalist-mediated, un-state-censored (and admittedly un-fact-checked) accounts as a public service. While horrible, these accounts were representations of Mexico's current reality, about which citizens were entitled to know. The claim of financial disinterest was dented somewhat by the site's running of advertisements, though there are no doubt costs to be covered. More troubling was the ambiguity of intention on the part of both producers and consumers—the latter numbering in the millions. Were these spectacles of brutality providing essential information that might facilitate self-defense, or mobilize citizen resistance? Or were they merely a form of pornography, like snuff films, akin to sites on which homemade erotica was posted? Were they a challenge to the bloodbath or a salacious repackaging of its most grotesque aspects?[31]

♦ ♦ ♦

A similar debate surrounded the narcocorridos—an old established form, as we have seen—that also went viral during the Calderón war, uploading into the culture a nihilistic (yet eminently danceable) music whose lyrics glorified the kingpins and the violence they unleashed. "With an AK-47 and a bazooka on my shoulder," ran one ditty among thousands, "Cross my path and I'll chop your head off. We're bloodthirsty, crazy, and we like to kill." They heroized the Chapos and

---

31   There are, it should be emphasized, sites devoted to covering Narcoiana that are not marred by such ambiguity. Borderland Beat, an English-language site in operation since 2009, is moderated (hence not unfiltered) but latitudinarian in its selection of over-the-transom items. It relies heavily on articles written by its own staff of regular contributors (albeit anonymous ones, given concerns about narco-retribution). Insight Crime, founded in April 2010 with financing from George Soros' Open Society Foundation, relays news reports, with commentary appended, and undertakes in-depth investigations.

Barbies, recounted their deeds, hailed them as rebels who had beaten the system, defied the military and the gringos, and become stinking rich doing so.

Corridos have often been subsidized by their subjects, with the capo sponsorship acknowledged in the lyrics. Rookie composers, as Ioan Grillo notes, asked for as little as $1,000 to write some verses about an up-and-coming thug, but accomplished musicians could get tens of thousands of dollars for a tune about a ranking cartel member. But it proved a risky business. As corridos became weapons in the ongoing wars—capos paying to belittle their enemies—their composers became casualties of the larger conflict. Valentín Elizalde, known as "The Golden Rooster," was shot full of holes when he was leaving a performance at the Reynosa Fair, killed by Zetas distressed that his songs—particularly "A Mis Enemigos" ("To My Enemies")—favored the Sinaloans. And La Quinta Banda was playing in a dance hall in the city of Chihuahua when a hooded gunman armed with an AK-47 opened fire on them, killing five of the musicians; it was believed they were murdered because their song "El Corrido de La Línea" praised La Línea, the armed division of the Juárez Cartel. In the vast majority of musician slayings, as with the murders of journalists, police named no suspects, made no arrests.

Critics said the corridos glorified drug traffickers and contributed to the violence. Some states heavily impacted by crime cartels, such as Sinaloa and Chihuahua, banned them from radio and TV, and prohibited live performance of the songs in bars and nightclubs. Such blackouts were readily evaded, and narcocorridos remained accessible on the web, and CDs with covers featuring men in ski masks wielding Kalashnikovs could be bought virtually anywhere. Culiacán alone boasted five labels producing corridos, each of which had about two hundred balladeers churning out product. Arguably the verdict on their impact should be reversed: rather than the songs spurring the war, the war enhanced the appeal of the songs (which despite their incendiary lyrics remained staunchly traditional in their polka-like melodies).

◆ ◆ ◆

In addition to the rapid diffusion of death-oriented narco texts, videos, and music through Mexico's commercial culture, Calderón's war years overlapped with a rapid expansion of death-oriented religious cults. The bandit saint Jesús Malverde, a mythicized Robin Hood purported to have lived during the reign of Porfirio Díaz, had long been venerated in Sinaloa, but devotion to the mustachioed man in the white suit moved out into the larger culture during Calderón's sexenio.

On a far grander scale, so did the cult of *Santa Muerte* (Saint Death), a figure of great antiquity in Europe and then Mexico, whom narcos have long accepted as their own goddess. Covered with tattoos of her image—an elaborately costumed and shrouded lady skeleton carrying a grim reaper scythe—they implore her help in ensuring safe delivery of their narcotic cargoes to the north, and her protection before embarking on murder. The walls of jail cells across the country are adorned with her image.

During the narco-war years her cult grew with meteoric speed, drawing the veneration of many poor and working class Mexicans with no connection to crime. Sales of her paraphernalia zoomed, and shrines and roadside altars popped up with increasing frequency, especially in states along the northern border. Estimates of the number of her devotees in Mexico (notes R. Andrew Chestnut in his *Devoted to Death: Santa Muerte, the Skeleton Saint*) run as high as five million (roughly 5 percent of the population), with many additional followers in other countries influenced by Mexico's narcoculture, including parts of the United States.

Calderón, seeing Santa Muerte as a supreme manifestation of narcoculture, warred on her as well, at one point dispatching the army to bulldoze shrines on the border (where they were rapidly replaced). The Catholic Church, already beleaguered by the growth of Protestant sects, also condemned the "Bony Lady," another reason why the pro-Catholic PANistas helped attack this rival of the Virgin of Guadalupe. But the fact that Calderón opposed the cult does not negate the likelihood, given the timing, that his war was a significant factor in its spread—yet another unanticipated consequence of his purpo-sive social action.

◆ ◆ ◆

Civil Society Stirs

Calderón's efforts to shape the narrative of events were confronted with major challenges from the narcos, but what of the voices of civil society? Was the great mass of the population able to get a word in edgewise? Did the omnipresence of high decibel messaging from state officials and criminal cartels dominate the public sphere's soundtrack?

There were, in fact, innumerable acts of courageous (or foolhardy) individual resistance to narco and/or military activities, but the sad truth is that most of these were crushed. The survival rate of more orga-nized opposition to the status quo, however, was considerably higher. Groups already established or newly created existed in virtually every corner of the country, many of them flying the flag of human rights. These were overwhelmingly citizens' organizations, autonomous and independent, or affiliated with churches and universities, dedicated to building a civil sector that could bypass the endemic corruption of the government and political parties. Hundreds of these were active during Calderón time.

Many were local entities that collected and promulgated infor-mation on state-initiated human rights abuses, monitored gang vio-lence in their territory, searched for the disappeared, litigated human rights cases, prepared legislative proposals, and/or defended particular constituencies like women, migrants, or journalists.[32] Others had a

---

32   These include: the Nuevo Laredo Human Rights Committee, the Human Rights Commission for the state of Chihuahua, Defense and Promotion of Human Rights—Emiliano Zapata (in Matamoros), the Center for Border Studies and Promotion of Human Rights (Reynosa), the Human Rights Center—Fray Bartolomé de las Casas (Chi-apas), the Binational Center for Human Rights (Tijuana), the Fray Francisco de Vitoria Center for Human Rights (Mexico City), Citizens in Support of Human Rights (Mon-terrey), the Center for Human Rights of Migrants (Ciudad Juárez), and Forces United for Our Missing and Disappeared in Coahuila.

broader nationwide remit.[33] And one step further up were coalitions of these local and national organizations,[34] which were in turn wired into international organizations.[35]

Human rights activism was also a risky business. Scores of activists were threatened, beaten, jailed, tortured, and killed—thirty-one were murdered in 2011 alone—the killings virtually always unsolved and unpunished. In 2010 an outfit called Urgent Action for Human Rights Defenders emerged to keep track of such attacks, and offer security training to activists.

In addition to all this citizen-driven activity, a sizeable agency—the National Commission for Human Rights (CNDH)—was created in 1989 as part of the interior ministry. It achieved a quasi-independent status, though it continued to be amply funded by the government. It has the authority to investigate charges brought against any branch of government other than the judiciary, and its president is the equivalent of a national ombudsman. It served as one of the few avenues open to victims seeking redress of past grievances, and it documented some systematic obstacles to human rights reforms. But as the Human Rights Watch found in 2008, when it came to "actually securing remedies and promoting reforms to improve Mexico's dismal human rights record, the CNDH's performance has been disappointing." Similar critiques were leveled in subsequent years, and in 2014 its then president, Raúl

---

33   These include: the Mexican Commission for the Defense and Promotion of Human Rights, the Mexican League for the Defense of Human Rights, ASILEGAL: Asistencia Legal por los Derechos Humanos, the Collective Against Torture and Impunity, the Casa de los Derechos de los Periodistas, and Journalists on Foot. Meta-organizations like the National Center for Social Communication were devoted to helping the NGOs develop a media strategy as an integral part of their work.

34   Like the REDTDT (National Network of Human Rights Civil Society Organizations), which was composed of seventy-one human rights NGOs, and another bundler operation, Nuestra Aparente Rendición.

35   These include: the International Federation of Human Rights, the Coalition for the International Criminal Court, Human Rights Watch, Amnesty International, the International Coalition of Organizations of Human Rights in the Americas, the Organization of American States' Inter-American Commission on Human Rights, the Washington Office on Latin America, the Latin American Working Group, the Committee to Protect Journalists, Reporters Without Borders, and Article 19.

Plascencia, came under fire not only for sins of omission but of commission, such as channeling funds—from its ample annual budget of 1.4 billion pesos (ninety-five million dollars)—into promoting his own reelection, an endeavor in which he failed.

◆ ◆ ◆

For all their valuable work most of these organizations did not consider mobilizing the masses to be within their bailiwick. But there were entities who took up that challenge. Most were launched by individuals who had lost family members to organized crime, the military, or the police. A host of victims' family groups sprang up to investigate disappearances, and track down key witnesses and persuade them to speak. A few turned to organizing marches and demonstrations to gain national attention for their cause.

The most prominent of these was a poet, Javier Sicilia, whose son was murdered in March 2011 in Cuernavaca, capital city of the state of Morelos, his death attributed to drug gangs. On April 4, Sicilia published a blistering public letter addressed "To Mexico's Politicians and Criminals."

"We have had it up to here," he told the former, with their "permitting our children to be murdered," with their "badly proposed, badly made, badly led war," with their corruption that "generates the complicity with crime and the impunity to commit it," with their "miserable screaming" and "struggle for power" that precludes the unity needed to confront the problem. "The citizenry has lost confidence in its governors, its police, its Army, and is afraid and in pain," he summarized, and then reminded state officials of "the phrase that José Martí directed at those who govern: 'If you can't, then resign.'"

"As for you, the criminals," he continued, "we have had it up to here with your violence, with your loss of honor, your cruelty and senselessness.... In days of old you had codes of honor. You were not so cruel in your paybacks and you did not touch the citizens nor their families. Now you do not distinguish.... You have become cowards like the miserable Nazi *sonderkommandos* who kill children, boys, girls, women men and elders without any human sense. We have had it up to here because your violence has become infrahuman—not animal, as animals do not do what you do—but subhuman, demonic, imbecilic."

But given "the thousands of anonymous and not anonymous cadavers that we have at our backs, which is to say, of so many innocents assassinated and debased," Sicilia argued, flinging words was not enough, rather they "must be accompanied by large citizen mobilizations." Therefore, he announced, "We will go out into the street," with the goal of forging a "national citizen unity that we must maintain alive to break the fear and isolation that the incapacity of you, 'señores' politicians, and the cruelty of you, 'señores' criminals want us to put in our bodies and souls."

Sicilia's call for marches in Morelos and cities across the country—"We must speak with our bodies, with our walk, with our cry of indignation"—touched a national nerve, and hundreds of thousands rallied in over forty cities, under banners proclaiming "¡Ya basta!" ("Enough is Enough!"), "No More Blood," and "Not One More." This was followed by a three day march in May 2011 from Cuernavaca to Mexico City (roughly sixty miles to the north) culminating in a giant demonstration in the Zócalo. Over the next days and weeks, as a grassroots Movement for Peace with Justice and Dignity took shape, more specific goals emerged. Protesters called for a phasing out of the drug war, the withdrawal of military forces from the streets (though not precipitously), the legalization of drugs, and the resignation of Calderón's Public Safety Secretary Genaro García Luna. Many called on Calderón himself to step down.

The poet suggested making a pact with the cartels, one that would begin with the premise that Mexicans should stop assassinating one another on behalf of the United States. "The weapons that are arming organized crime and are killing our kids, our soldiers, our police," he noted, "come from the U.S. and they are not doing anything to stop them." So "if the U.S. doesn't prosecute and put a stop to its arms industry—a legalized horror—why should we prosecute the producers of the drugs?" Consumption should be treated "as a public health matter," and if the U.S. refused to do so, "the problem of their consumption is theirs, not ours." The criminals should be left free to compete with one another to sell drugs to gringos, so long as there was an agreement "that the civilian population won't be touched, that innocents won't be assassinated, and that the prisoners of gangs in conflict must be treated according to human rights standards."

In June 2011, with Sicilia gaining international attention, Calderón agreed to have a public discussion with him at Chapultepec Castle, the conversation broadcast live on TV. Sicilia called for a moment of silence "for all the victims of this senseless war," and accused the president of being responsible for forty thousand deaths while ignoring job creation, education, and public health. He asked him to apologize to the nation and the relatives of those who died or were disappeared. Calderón stuck to his guns, regretting only that he had not sent the military and federal police into the streets earlier, though he did apologize for having been unable to protect the many victims. Here and elsewhere he would insist that reports of abuses and disappearances by soldiers and police were isolated cases; that the Mexican military was not equatable to the death squads deployed by authoritarian regimes; that he could not and should not have waited for law enforcement institutions to change before attacking insecurity; and that protestors should say *Basta!* to the criminals who kidnap and murder, as *they* were the enemy, not the soldiers who fought against them.[36]

---

36 After the Gulf Cartel was initially blamed for Sicilia's son's death, it quickly hung a series of narcomantas in Morelos that denied any involvement in the killing. Indeed they abducted a member of the South Pacific Cartel (an offshoot of the Beltrán Leyva Organization), left him beaten and tied up in an abandoned truck, and alerted authorities to his involvement in Sicilia's murder. When he allegedly confessed to federal police, the Beltrán Leyvas released a series of mantas disavowing the murder and promising that its members "do not kill innocent people." In June 2012 army troops captured one Raúl Díaz Roman, the reputed boss of the Beltrán Leyva Organization in Morelos state, who they claimed was responsible for young Sicilia's death. It seems that at the time Díaz Roman was a member of the Morelos police, overseeing the war on drug traffickers (i.e., himself) in Cuernavaca. When some cops tried to rob or extort Sicilia and his friends, and the

The two had another televised conversation in October 2011, and while each stood his ground, Calderón, who had become increasingly upset with the United States, tacked a bit in Sicilia's direction. Blaming American demand for drugs for fostering the violence, he called on the U.S. to reduce the flow of money coming from consumers. "How to do this," he added, "is their problem." Alternately, he suggested, if they opted for legalization, perhaps they "need to open cocaine trafficking [routes]," though if they did, "they should do it through Florida or somewhere else, but not through here." And if neither of those approaches worked, the U.S. should look for other solutions, adding, "This is a discussion that needs to be held internationally."

It was Sicilia, however, who carried the case across the border. After organizing additional in-country marches from Mexico City north to Ciudad Juárez, and south to the Guatemala border, the poet took his movement north. In August to September 2012, a 120-person Caravan for Peace with Justice and Dignity—led by the mothers, fathers, sisters, and brothers of Mexicans murdered and disappeared during the drug war—traversed the United States from San Diego to Washington, covering 5,700 miles, holding events in twenty-six cities, and generating extensive media coverage. But by then Calderón's sexenio was on the verge of expiration, his party had just been repudiated at the polls, and Mexico's political climate appeared to have changed abruptly.

---

kids said they would report them, the cop-cops called in Diaz and his gang-cops from the South Pacific Cartel, who had in fact done the deed, as originally thought.

CHAPTER TEN
2012

The July 1, 2012, presidential election would not be simply a referendum on the drug war, but the subject was clearly front and center given the bulletins clattering in from all quarters during the campaign's final weeks. Nuevo Laredo: fourteen heads left in coolers in a van outside city hall; nine people hanged from a bridge. Veracruz: a mayor kidnapped from his home, his bound, tortured corpse found days later. Monterrey: forty-nine corpses minus heads, hands, and feet dumped in a nearby small town. Mexico City: a shootout at the international airport between two groups of uniformed federal police, at least one of which was working for a drug gang, with three officers left dead in a food court.

Calderón could not run again but whoever was chosen as the PAN candidate would have to run on his record, the evaluation of which would hinge on judgements of his war. Rather than leaving this to others, Calderón offered his own assessment, claiming it had been a success. At the end of November 2012, he argued that the war had turned a corner. Homicides attributable to organized criminal activity had finally fallen for the first time since he had taken office; there had not been a dramatic mass killing for several months; regions popular with tourists were relatively tranquil. In close-of-term speeches he asserted that "history will be the judge" of his time in office, and exuded confidence that the verdict would be a favorable one. But if winning a reduction of violence was Calderón's marker of success—as he himself stressed in his final days in office—then it was hard to accept a claim of "mission accomplished" without reckoning with the impact of his initial escalation of the violence.

People turned to counting bodies. There was a wide range of estimates of how many "drug war–related" murders were committed during his term in office, and a collateral conversation about how to prove any particular killing was "drug war–related."[37] But there was general agreement that many, many people unambiguously met their end in ways that met the legal criteria of "drug war–related." These included killings accompanied by a message relating to organized crime (as were 3,268 of the murders); accomplished with heavy caliber weapons (or another signature drug- gang method); captured (and boasted of) on a cartel video; evidently preceded by torture (as was clear from examining the bodies of 4,645 people); or committed by decapitation (as in the case of 1,892 individuals).[38]

Deaths meeting these criteria were scrupulously totaled by the Calderón administration itself and made public, partly because it was believed that almost all the casualties were themselves gangsters. This position, which implies that the gangs were being weeded out of the national garden, either by the state or one another, was occasionally voiced directly. Take the case of a Mexican general, who told the press they should stop saying the state had killed one person more, and instead rejoice there was one criminal less. But this argument became harder to sustain as the war dragged on, and outcries against the slaughter of civilians grew along with human rights violation complaints against the military and police, which is perhaps one reason why the regime stopped counting during its final year. While much of the violence was certainly internecine, as cartels or factions battled for market share, human rights analysts like Nik Steinberg concluded

---

37 For a lucid investigation of the statistical (and political) issues involved in the gruesome business of body counting, see Heinle, Rodríguez, and Shirk, *Drug Violence in Mexico* (2014).

38 These figures come from the respected newspaper *Reforma*'s running tally, as published in its "executonometer."

that the great majority of victims were not criminals, but young, working-class men with families. And even those who had irrefutably signed on as sicarios were not "born to kill," but had often been swept willy-nilly into the only game in town.

In any event, the official list sets a floor under the total—an unimpeachable floor, as it was constructed by Calderón's own administration. In January 2012 the government acknowledged that at least 47,515 people had been killed in "drug war–related" incidents between December 2006 and September 2011 (when it announced it would no longer update and release official figures). Multiple sources suggest that a conservative estimate for the additional deaths on his watch between October 2011 to December 2012 would hover around ten thousand, providing a mortality baseline of roughly sixty thousand souls.[39]

To this number must be added some percentage of those who "disappeared"—or who "*were* disappeared." Calderón's people maintained a list of these as well—though this one was kept under wraps throughout his sexenio, and only leaked (by a government analyst) to the *Washington Post* two days before he left office. It contained over twenty-five thousand names of people who had gone missing, for whatever reason, during Calderón's time. While some entries were accompanied by notes of chilling clarity ("Her daughter was forced into a car"; "The father was arrested by men wearing uniforms and never seen again") the list also included those who might have migrated illegally to the States, or simply run away from home. The next administration would release a pruned version suggesting that, after having checked with families to see if the relative reported missing had perhaps reappeared, roughly eight thousand were still missing, an unknown percentage of which were drug-war related. This number—later revised to twelve thousand—was hotly contested. It had not taken into account the ongoing recovery of hundreds of unidentified corpses, exhumed from unmarked mass graves, which the state had not examined,

---

39 *Reforma* reported that in 2012 there were 9,577 organized crime–style homicides while the equally respected *Milenio* reported there were 12,390 for that year.

despite promises to construct a DNA database that would allow comparison with information supplied by relatives of the disappeared. Nor had the state established the kind of Truth Commission investigation mounted in Chile, Argentina, and South Africa.

Accepting a figure of roughly ten thousand missing and presumed dead brings the conservatively estimated total to roughly seventy thousand over the six year period, but this number is also contested. Patient examination by responsible journalists, academics, activists, and human rights advocates, who plowed through news reports, legal documents, hospital records, and many other sources, produced higher figures. One careful accounting by *Zeta*, a weekly magazine published in Tijuana, placed the count at 109,000. But no one argues for *fewer* than the baseline constructed from the government's own numbers. Given such bloody statistics, it is hard to credit a claim of success based on reduction of violence. Had Calderón not lifted a finger, the mortality count would almost certainly have been but a fraction of that generated by his own intervention, obviating the need for lowering the violence level that he himself had raised.

Nor had some goal been achieved, some victory that might have afforded the PAN candidate grounds for claiming that these dead had not died in vain. Perhaps the interdiction of the flow of drugs to gringo consumers could—according to some bizarre species of cost-effective moral calculus—be held to have warranted the slaughter?

But the record offered no comfort on this ground either, as a wide variety of indicators made clear that, for all the inter-cartel mayhem, the drug lords had managed to keep their eye on business. Whether measured by price, quantity, or quality, there was no diminution whatever in the flow of illegal substances. Mexican marijuana, methamphetamine, and heroin remained cheap and more plentiful than ever in the United States. United Nations surveys indicated that the per-gram price of cocaine on American streets was roughly the same in 2012 as it had been a decade earlier, and with undiminished purity. A report that year from Bruce Bagley and the Woodrow Wilson Center argued that drug trafficking organizations were better than ever at what they did, and that all indicators suggested a generalized failure of the strategies used to contain them.

Some of the cartels' professionalism on Calderón's watch involved new high-tech tactics: more capacious tunnels, complete with railway line, electricity, and ventilation; submarines—the average sixty-foot narco-sub carried several tons of cocaine; and drones—airborne drug mules that border-hopped below the radar screen. But cartels still deployed old low-tech devices. A former chief of operations for the DEA noted that a few days after the U.S. erected a high-tech fence along a stretch of border in Arizona, the cartels showed up with a catapult and began flinging hundred-pound bales of marijuana over to the other side. "We've got the best fence money can buy," he observed ruefully, "and they counter us with a 2,500-year-old technology."

But the primary narco way was the highway. Thanks to NAFTA, the flow of legal commerce was tremendous. In 2011, according to U.S. Bureau of Transportation statistics, nearly 4.9 million trucks and sixty-one million personal vehicles crossed the U.S.-Mexican border. It was impossible for inspectors to check more than a small sample of vehicles. For all the occasional dramatic seizures—the record-breaking drug busts Calderón touted as metrics of his success—the truth is that the river of drugs just kept on rollin' along.

Worse: if reduction of drug consumption had been Calderón's goal, he seemed to have made matters worse. Drug use in Mexico itself had increased somewhat, which in turn had upped the violence level as gangs of small-time dealers vied for control—not of the big international *plazas*, but of local street corners, where they now did their vying, courtesy of the NRA, with big-time weaponry.

Perhaps the greatest burden Calderón bequeathed to his would-be successor was fear.

The criminals' ability to carve out new career paths—notably kidnapping and extortion—had in turn been facilitated by the war-engendered breakdown of public order, the spectacular increase in police corruptibility, the utter impunity afforded by a virtually defunct criminal justice system, and a state that, in many areas, was approaching the status of "failed"—precisely the nightmare scenario Calderón had set out to avoid. As the gangs had competed to establish their brand, their violence had grown increasingly grotesque, producing a paralyzing fear at all levels of society, leading to a weakening of social life, an abandonment of public space, an increase in distrust among neighbors, and a generalized sense of helplessness. In one 2011 national poll, two-thirds of Mexicans said they greatly feared being kidnapped, one-third had been a victim of crime in the previous three months, 43 percent had stopped letting their children play in the street, and 45 percent had stopped going out at night. 74.3 percent considered it "somewhat" or "very" dangerous to turn to the police (84.6 percent of those in the north). And when the drug struggle was presented as a "war," 58 percent (across all social classes) believed that organized crime was winning it, while only 18 percent thought the government was.

◆ ◆ ◆

In the end, the burden of Calderón's legacy would be assumed by Josefina Vázquez Mota, the PAN's candidate in the 2012 presidential sweepstakes. Vázquez Mota—the first woman candidate from a major political entity—had been trained as an economist, worked for business organizations, wrote a pop self-help book for wives, and then segued into a political and administrative career. She served in the Chamber of Deputies; was secretary of social development; and then was secretary of public education. She ran Calderón's campaign in 2006, and nabbed the nomination in 2012 despite *not* being Calderón's choice. As the PAN's person, there was no way she could distance herself from Calderón's war, no matter how unpopular it might be. So she did the opposite. She promised to continue his aggressive militarized campaign to break the cartels, arguing as had Calderón that it was his hard line policy, not El Chapo's victory, that had diminished the Juárez murder rate. She also suggested she would work even more closely with U.S. law enforcement.

López Obrador, speaking again for the PRD, firmly criticized the militarized approach, stressing its violation of human rights, and promised more aid to war casualties. He called, as had Calderón, for establishing a unified police command that would gradually take over security operations from the army; the training of its recruits, he stressed, should inculcate moral and civic values, as well as policing expertise. He would halt the activities of CIA operatives and DEA agents; reconsider the continuance of military aid under the Merida Initiative; and refocus intelligence activities on cracking criminal financial networks.

But the candidate who, immediately upon being nominated, leapt to first place in the polls and stayed there until he won was the youthful, telegenic, pompadoured governor of the state of Mexico, Enrique Peña Nieto, who would shrewdly pull off a comeback for the PRI, twelve years after it had been shown the door. Peña Nieto had deep roots in the state—which surrounds the autonomous Federal District (Mexico City proper)—and in the state's PRI, which had remained impervious to PAN victories at a national level. Wired into state politics through family connections since he was a teenager, he got a BA in law and an MA in business administration. In a break with recent presidential practice, neither degree was from a U.S. university. He worked in business and law and then entered government, occupying a series of offices of escalating importance, forging relationships as he climbed with top PRI politicians and wealthy state businessmen. (Peña Nieto's upward path was smoothed by his mentor and uncle, who was the notoriously corrupt governor of the state of Mexico from 1999 to 2005.) After winning a two-year term in 2003 in the state legislature, he was elected to the governorship (2005–2011). Generally accounted as a competent administrator, he was noted for infrastructure projects (state highways tripled during his term). However, his anti-crime record was mixed. Peña Nieto and his Attorney General Alfredo Castillo made inroads against a gang that had taken to leaving decapitated heads around the region, and managed to avoid the massive increase in murders suffered by much of the rest of the country. But violent attacks on women soared, reported robberies increased by almost 50 percent, and kidnappings quadrupled in his first four years. He also violently crushed protests by peasants incensed with a plan to expropriate their lands for a new international airport. His snaring of the nomination in 2012 was helped along by his marriage to a pop star, his mastery of TV self-presentation, and, student protestors charged, biased reporting from Televisa, whose news programs were the country's predominant information source. Marchers chanted: "Peña, the TV is yours, the streets are ours."

EPN—as Enrique Peña Nieto was often shorthanded—fashioned a canny strategy on the drug-war front. He would continue Calderón's struggle but shift its focus away from capturing kingpins and making drug busts, towards diminishing the violence his predecessor's approach had fostered. He would concentrate on domestic rather than international criminality—kidnapping and extortion rather than the flow of blow—prioritizing the safety and security of Mexico's people rather than striving to please the DEA and U.S. Congress. The unstated nationalist subtext suggested that the gringos should defend their own border, rather than asking tens of thousands of Mexicans to die on their behalf.

He never quite said how he planned to accomplish this, apart from establishing a national police force, similar to the ones his rivals were calling for. He would create a "national gendarmerie," an autonomous, forty-thousand-strong special force that would gradually replace army units, who would be returned to barracks. The gendarmes would be a hybrid force; its rank and file would be "of military origin"—a term never explained, but which was assumed to mean battle-hardened veterans of Calderón's war—while the leadership would be civilian, trained in using police tactics rather than overwhelming military force. On paper it was an inspired straddle, though critics did wonder how the new forty thousand would differ from the old forty thousand, and how it would be made and kept corruption free.

What EPN had going for him that López Obrador and Vázquez Mota did not was, ironically, precisely the PRI's legacy of corruption, which meant its proven ability to strike bargains with organized crime. This former negative now seemed a positive. Sicilia and others had called for cutting a deal with the cartels. It was politically impossible for the PRI to go along with this officially. But a portion of the electorate was convinced that, if elected, the PRI would revert to its old ways, allowing the cartels to operate freely as long as they played by certain rules and gave the government its cut. Here EPN's opponents unwittingly helped him out. Calderón warned that the PRI might negotiate with the cartels in order to keep the peace. American officials privately feared the same thing. Peña Nieto stoutly denied he would ever do any such thing. This reassured those who wanted the war to continue, while those who hoped for a violence-reduction strategy simply assumed that of course he was lying. In truth, the old Humpty Dumpty, PRI-dominated *plaza* system was far too thoroughly broken for its pieces to be put back together again. There were too many new gangs out there to cut deals with unless a wave of re-cartelization took place. And the presidency had lost its ability to command a secret state, given the opposition parties and a nosy press. Nevertheless, many believed the PRI could and would reach an accord with the cartels; they had done it before, they could do it again.

Peña Nieto was also creatively ambiguous in his approach to Mexican-U.S. relations. Where the PAN would accelerate the anti-drug collaboration, and the PRD would throttle it back, the PRI did both, setting new limits while simultaneously promising "an intense, close relationship of effective collaboration." There would, EPN insisted, be no armed American agents in Mexico, no armed joint counter-narcotics operations as in Colombia and Central America. Surveillance drones over Mexico to gather intelligence on drug trafficking were okay, if run by Mexico with the U.S. providing assistance and technology. He also favored U.S. military and police training their Mexican counterparts—a position, according to polls, supported by 75 percent of the population.

EPN could have argued, but preferred not to spell it out, that relations between the White House and the Mexican presidency might well *improve*, given that Calderón had become a strident critic of America's failure to crack down on the southbound flow of arms or to diminish U.S. demand for illegal drugs. Indeed it was the PRI's rather than the PAN's position that was gaining favor in Washington. A 2012 report by the Senate Foreign Relations Committee, ordered up by its chairman John Kerry, concluded that "military deployments to combat organized crime have achieved limited success and, in some cases, have led to human rights violations." The U.S., accordingly, should "encourage the reduction of the Mexican military's role in the provision of domestic security," and provide Mexico with trainers for police academies rather than more Black Hawk helicopters. Noting also that Calderón's core strategy of taking down top cartel leadership "has been widely criticized for de-emphasizing the daily security needs of average Mexicans," the committee tacked toward Peña Nieto's approach, fearing that if Mexicans did not see a reduction in violence, they might back a deal with the cartels.

◆ ◆ ◆

Peña Nieto won with 38.15 percent of the vote. López Obrador received 31.64 percent and Vázquez Mota trailed with 25.4 percent. EPN had won by a whisker, but a big enough whisker to keep post-election protests to a minimum.[40]

---

40 Calderón soon decamped for Harvard, where he taught classes at the John F. Kennedy School of Government, and worked on his memoirs, which were published in 2014.

CHAPTER ELEVEN
2012–

The PRI failed to muster a majority in either the Chamber of Deputies or the Senate, and would therefore have to forge alliances to get anything done. Which Peña Nieto did, cajoling representatives of the other parties into joining a "Pact for Mexico." This backroom agreement finessed public debate and cleared the way to passage of legislation that accomplished several key neoliberal goals. Notably, changing the Constitution to allow foreign investment in Mexico's oil sector; along with passing laws dealing with telecommunications monopolies, money laundering, tax policy, and the educational system (a domain in which EPN also established his anti-graft credentials when, in February 2013, his government arrested the flagrantly corrupt head of Mexico's teachers union).[41]

Vis-à-vis the drug war, EPN's initial tactic was to take the conflict off the front burner by simply talking about it less. Not only did he *not*

---

41 It has been suggested that Peña Nieto was "reaching out" in another way, by using the judicial system to extend peace offerings to particular interests. Thus in a possible bow to the military, he arranged the freeing and rehabilitation of General Tomás Ángeles Dauahare, whom Calderón had fired on flimsy or trumped-up charges of corruption, though he was likely guilty only of PRI leanings. Peña Nieto returned a favor to former president Salinas, who had backed Peña Nieto's PRI bid, by freeing his brother Raúl. And, conceivably, he sent a message to the cartel world by springing none other than Rafael Caro Quintero. Still doing time for the murder of Camarena, he promptly vanished upon release. The official story that he was freed on a suddenly discovered technicality strained credulity and enraged the DEA and the U.S. Justice Department. But what influence the godfather (by now the grandfather) of Mexican crime might have in the new era was difficult to discern. Still, the cluster of releases hinted at a commonality of purpose.

dress up in military uniform and rally the troops, he minimized mentions of bloodshed and narcos—turning down the volume, changing the subject, shifting the attention to his economic agenda. The U.S. was informed that the new president would not be as directly involved in counter-drug efforts as the former had been, and indeed would delegate to his interior minister the handling of ongoing relations between Mexican and U.S. crime-fighting agencies.

The switch in style quickly influenced media coverage: in the first three months of his sexenio, one study found that the use of terms like "organized crime" and "drug trafficking" dropped by 50 percent. Perp walks were cut back. The horrifying videotaped confessions of captured cartel assassins vanished. One early payoff was a resurgence of tourism at the country's top resorts, including Puerto Vallarta, Los Cabos, and Cancun, which one official attributed to the new strategy: "When the president talks less about drugs and violence, the national newspapers write less about it and so the international media report less on it. Perception becomes reality."

Peña Nieto also switched his rhetorical emphasis from fighting crime to preventing it. Two weeks into his term, he told state governors, military men, and security chiefs at a public meeting of the national security council that "We are going to focus institutional efforts on attending to the [social] causes of the criminal phenomenon and not only its consequences." Two months later, on February 12, 2013, he announced a $9.2 billion crime prevention program that would invest in social programs (job creation and improved health and social services) targeted to the country's most violent towns and neighborhoods. "We must put special emphasis on prevention," the president said, "because we can't only keep employing more sophisticated weapons, better equipment, more police, a higher presence of the armed forces in the country as the only form of combating organized crime."

The new emphasis on the economy was picked up and amplified by U.S. media and business. There was much talk of a newly aroused Aztec Tiger, whose surging growth in GDP suggested a great leap forward on the order of that attained by Asian Tigers like South

Korea and Taiwan. Foreign reporting on Mexico brightened up, with pundits such as the *New York Times'* Thomas Friedman highlighting the nation's potential rather than its problems. In a February 23, 2013 valentine, "How Mexico Got Back in the Game," Friedman confided that: "In India, people ask you about China, and, in China, people ask you about India: Which country will become the more dominant economic power in the twenty-first century? I now have the answer: Mexico." True, "drug cartels, crime syndicates, government corruption and weak rule of law" continued to "hobble the nation," as did stifling monopolies in energy, telecom, and media, and a weak K-12 education system. But "Something happened here," he observed, reporting from Monterrey: "It is as if Mexicans subconsciously decided that their drug-related violence is a condition to be lived with and combated but not something to define them any longer." He urged greater attention be paid to the country's new tech startups, multiple free trade agreements, cheap natural gas finds, and especially the fact that Mexico, given rising wage costs in China, was "taking manufacturing market share back from Asia and attracting more global investment than ever in autos, aerospace and household goods."

Others joined the chorus. A *Foreign Affairs* article by Shannon O'Neill, "Mexico Makes It," announced that "modern Mexico is a middle-class country," citing a World Bank estimate that 95 percent of the populace was in the middle or the upper class. The *Financial Times* said the achievements of Peña Nieto's neoliberal administration would outshine the appeal of the "Latin Left." And businessmen added their two cents: Larry Fink, who heads BlackRock, Inc., the world's largest asset-management company ($4.5 trillion), called Mexico an "incredible growth story."

The U.S. government endorsed the happy talk. In May 2013 President Obama made a high-profile visit to Mexico City. In a speech at the National Anthropology Museum he acknowledged that "there are Mexicans all across this country who are making courageous sacrifices for the security of your country." But he stressed that the world was also seeing "a Mexico that's creating new prosperity: Trading with the world. Becoming a manufacturing powerhouse—from Tijuana to Monterrey to Guadalajara and across the central highlands—a global leader in automobiles and appliances and electronics."

"I see a Mexico," Obama rolled on, "that's lifted millions of people from poverty. Because of the sacrifices of generations, a majority of Mexicans now call themselves middle class, with a quality of life that your parents and grandparents could only dream of." And he insisted that "the relationship between our nations must be defined not by the threats that we face but by the prosperity and the opportunity that we can create together."

Time magazine's veteran correspondent Tim Padgett was one of the few not swept away by irrational exuberance. In a March 2013 piece entitled "Mexico's New Boom: Why the World Should Tone Down the Hype," he expressed reservations about the "overweening boosterism" and the "blood-soaked headlines yielding all of a sudden to rose-colored banners," reminding readers of Mexico's ongoing "mafia bloodletting," vast "social inequality," "corrupt and incompetent judicial system," "shameless business monopolies," and enormous levels of poverty.

Padgett proved prescient. Mexico's economy sagged badly over the rest of Peña Nieto's first year, growing at a rate of only 1.1 percent, well below the regional average, dragged down by the continuing U.S. recession and investor worries about crime. What cream there was floated to the top: the number of Mexican billionaires rose 23 percent between 2013 and 2014, and the top 10 percent harvested 42 percent of all income. Many middle-class families saw their incomes stagnate or even decline. And a report released by CONEVAL (the National Council for the Evaluation of Social Development Policy) splashed cold water on the "middle class nation" notion by showing that approximately fifty-three million Mexicans were living in poverty—around 45 percent of the populace—and that the number had remained fairly constant over two decades, making a hash of the argument that NAFTA had lifted all boats.

Some of the huge discrepancy in observed poverty rates was a function of different measurement systems. CONEVAL employed a multidimensional approach that considered not just income but also access to education, health services, social security, basic services, and food. The income-based piece, taken separately, defined the poverty line (in 2012) as 2,329 pesos ($177) per month in cities and 1,490 pesos ($113) in rural areas, and "extreme poverty" as roughly half those amounts.

Wilson and Silva's analysis of the 2013 CONEVAL report notes that while the middle class had indeed been growing, so too had the numbers of poor Mexicans. They found it "quite troubling" that "poverty as measured by income increased in recent years despite the relative strength of the Mexican economy," and advanced a variety of specific explanations, such as the fact that 71.8 million Mexicans do not get social security, in large part because they work in the "informal sector" (which includes workers in the drug industry). That in turn was because there weren't enough jobs in the "formal sector," which in turn was due to insufficient economic growth.

But Mexico was the only major Latin American country where poverty had grown in recent years. Bolivia, Brazil, Chile, and Colombia had used their economic growth to reduce poverty levels by more than 30 percent in recent years; why had Mexico not?

Perhaps the simultaneous growth of *Progress and Poverty*—as Henry George entitled his 1879 *Inquiry into the Cause of Industrial Depressions and of Increase of Want with Increase of Wealth*—could be traced in part to specific neoliberal policy choices Mexico made. Thomas Friedman noted that Mexican manufacturing growth—a.k.a. the revival of maquiladora sweatshops—was largely due to rising wages in China. But he did not ask why Mexican wages had not gone up too. The stagnation, Paul Imison suggests, was in part related to "labor reform" legislation passed in 2012, at the tail end of the Calderón sexenio, by PAN and PRI Congress members. It effectively tore up Mexico's 1970 labor law, and gave employers greater leverage against workers, notably enhancing their freedom to fire. Corrupt unions, long-time supporters of the PRI, did not help either. Nor did NAFTA provisions. Nor did a minimum wage of sixty-seven pesos a day (less than $5). Nor did the absence of unemployment insurance or having only 30 percent of the workforce covered by social security. As a result, average manufacturing wages were, in 2012, only 18 percent of those in the U.S. And auto jobs were notoriously low-paying. Which is why almost 60 percent of the workforce has opted for the informal economy. So perhaps, pace Friedman, undercutting Chinese wage levels was not something to boast about.

◆ ◆ ◆

On the crime front, Peña Nieto's first two years proved to be an extremely mixed bag.

Ironically, his administration performed best at doing the one thing—catching kingpins—on which he had pledged not to focus. In July 2013, Mexican marines arrested Miguel "Z-40" Treviño Morales— the number one Zeta—without a bullet being fired. U.S. authorities had passed along information that Treviño Morales, famed for burning his victims alive, had been making frequent visits to the Nuevo Laredo border area to see his newborn baby. Duly alerted, marines searched for him from a Black Hawk helicopter, spotted Z-40 riding in a truck, landed, and apprehended him. In February 2014, Treviño's opposite number, El Chapo Guzmán—the number one Sinaloan—was tracked down using DEA data, and arrested while vacationing with his wife at a beachfront condo in Mazatlán; again, no shots fired. March 2014 brought the violent end of El Más Loco, head of the Knights Templar, in Michoacán. In October 2014, Héctor Beltrán Leyva, top man in the cartel that bore his family's name, was captured (again, with no gunplay) while dining on fish tacos at a seafood restaurant in San Miguel de Allende, near the city of Querétaro, where he had been living in plain sight, passing as a moderately wealthy businessman who dabbled in the real estate and art markets. And a little over a week later, Vicente "El Virrey" Carrillo Fuentes, head of the shrunken Juárez Cartel, was reeled in, again, in a bloodless affair. These top-drawer triumphs were also accompanied by a raft of second-stringer arrests.

The impact of all these roundups is unclear. Fears that the Hydra Principle will come into play have not been borne out, though the country continues to be roiled by combat between fragments of former cartels, notably the battles between the Guerreros Unidos and Los Rojos, which figured in the murder of the Forty-Three. Guzmán's well-built cartel, the most business-like of the bunch, seemed to be managing a smooth transition of power, with El Chapo's long-time associate Ismael "El Mayo" Zambada managing to keep billions' worth of drugs moving, his protection by well-rewarded political officials and corrupt businessmen seemingly undiminished. In particular, his Sinaloa Cartel still controls almost all of the Ciudad Juárez *plaza*, though the remnants of the Carrillo Fuentes drug-trafficking organization, notably its enforcement gangs La Línea and Barrio Azteca, are challenging that dominance, with a little help from their newfound friends, Los Zetas. (Should La Línea and Barrio Azteca have a falling out, of course, Ciudad Juárez could again become a war zone.)

More ominous were reports of a June 2014 drug summit meeting in the border town of Piedras Negras between four of the major cartels—somewhat akin to a Marvel Comics' League of Supervillains sit-down—at which the Jalisco New Generation Cartel, the Carrillo Fuentes (Juárez) Organization, the Beltrán Leyva Organization, and Los Zetas explored the possibility of creating an alliance that would reconfigure the drug-trafficking map of Mexico. A donnybrook between Sinaloans and Supervillains would be cataclysmic indeed.

◆ ◆ ◆

Whatever the long-term outcome of Peña Nieto's successes in decapitating cartels, in the short-term laurels were not forthcoming because other types of crime had exploded all over Mexico, with doubts raised about his ability to deal with them. The president could and did point out that the number of homicides in 2013, his first year in office, had declined modestly from the previous year, Calderón's last. Estimates of those killed on his watch ranged from 18,388 to 22,732 (between 8 and 13 percent fewer than the 2012 body count), though the number did not take into account the thousands who had disappeared.[42] But in the same twelve month period Mexico had become a world kidnapping capital, with more than 1,698 reported abductions in 2013, a 20 percent increase over 2012, and the worst year on record. It was made even more nightmarish by expert estimates that more than 80 to 90 percent of kidnappings went unreported, family members being scared to endanger the victims—or themselves—by going to the police, who might well be in bed with the perpetrators. The victims were not only plutocrats—indeed the rich could afford high-caliber security—but also shopkeepers, physicians, carpenters, and taxi drivers, ordinary working people. The perpetrators, ever younger, were satisfied with the lower per unit ransoms, which they made up for with higher volume. 2013 had also been a particularly bad year for the media, the most violent one since 2007: at least ten journalists had been killed, and according to the organization Article 19, 330 non-lethal attacks had been made on the press, 60 percent of them attributed to authorities.

Fear was up, too. Mexico's National Statistics and Geography Institute (*Instituto Nacional de Estadística y Geografía*) Victimization Survey found that people had felt more unsafe in 2013 than in any previously recorded year. The United States State Department, to Mexican officials' dismay, believed fear was an all-too-rational response to reality. Its August 2014 Travel Warning alerted readers that seventy-one U.S. citizens had been reported to the department as having been murdered in Mexico in 2012, and eighty-one in 2013. Travelers had also fallen victim to carjacking, highway robbery, and kidnapping—nearly seventy of the latter had been reported between January and June 2014. U.S. government employees were prohibited from driving on non-official business from the U.S.-Mexico border to or from the interior of Mexico or Central America, as they had been since July 2010.

---

42 Where 12,930 had disappeared over Calderón's sexenio, a rate of 5.9 every day, Peña Nieto's tally stood at 9,384 as of October 2014, a rate of 13.4 every twenty-four hours.

Mexico's forces of order, meanwhile, had received some black eyes. A coalition of national human rights groups had filed a complaint with the office of the prosecutor of the International Criminal Court, asking it to investigate the "systematic and widespread" abuse of thousands of civilians by the army and the police in their fight against organized crime. The federal police had been deluged with widespread accusations of abuse and corruption—particularly with extorting money from migrants in transit through Mexico.

Then, on June 30, 2014, in Tlatlaya, a town in the Estado de Mexico, a squad of eight soldiers on night patrol happened upon a group of twenty-two gang members in an empty warehouse, together with two tied-up rival gangsters and four women (a fifteen-year-old runaway; her mother, a teacher, come to retrieve her; and two tied-up girls that the gang members had snatched off the streets). The army men called on them to come out; they answered with gunfire, slightly wounding one soldier; the army fired back, killing and wounding a few; and after this brief exchange the gang members surrendered and were disarmed. The soldiers, saying "these dogs don't deserve to live," then executed them, one after another, roaring "where are your balls now, you sons of bitches?" They also finished off the runaway, who had been wounded in the crossfire, though they spared her mother and the two remaining women. Then they moved the bodies around and put guns in their hands, rearranging the crime scene to make it appear as if all had been killed while shooting at the soldiers. The State of Mexico's governor, its attorney general, and the army's high command stoutly accepted their story. Indeed the state attorney general's people tortured the two kidnapped women into backing up the lies. The teacher, though released, was similarly terrorized into supporting the coverup.

The charade unraveled when journalists from the Associated Press and *Esquire Latin America* visited the scene and discovered patently obvious signs that the crime scene had been rearranged. They then tracked down the teacher who bravely agreed to tell what had happened. The two imprisoned girls also recanted. Now international human rights organizations demanded a review, and Washington insisted on a "credible" investigation. Finally Peña Nieto ordered the case transferred to federal authorities, who eventually accused three of the soldiers with extrajudicial murder, but no higher-ups; nor have state officials have been charged with coercing witnesses. Human Rights Watch spoke for many when it said that Peña Nieto's reaction had been so halting that "the image of his government is in tatters."[43]

The much touted National Gendarmerie, which arrived in August 2014, proved but a shadow of its much anticipated self. The hoped-for forty-thousand-man organization, independent from both the army and federal police, had been whittled down (at army insistence) to a five-thousand-man subdivision of the federal police. The rank and file were not military veterans, as originally intended, but rather young, well-educated, and intensely screened recruits who had never served in any armed force. They were, however, trained by the Mexican Army, and their commanding officers had gone to school with police forces from Colombia, Chile, Spain, France, and the United States. Their lack of experience would presumably be offset by their freedom from corruption, and rather than replacing military units as primary forces of order, they would be flown into hot-spots (SWAT-team style) where organized crime had all but strangled local or foreign businesses.

But the most momentous moves against organized criminality came from a completely unexpected source—the citizenry itself—in an uprising that forced the federal administration to put front and center what it had hoped to sideline.

◆ ◆ ◆

Autodefensas: Civil Society in Arms
On February 24, 2013, the drug war began to push its way back onto the front pages, with the eruption on the scene of a totally new set of

---

43   In January 2015 Human Rights Watch went further, and urged President Obama to make clear to Peña Nieto "that if Mexico is unable to show significant results in prosecuting human rights crimes, [the U.S.] administration will no longer be able to certify that the human rights requirements in the Merida Initiative have been met."

players—fed-up and outraged citizens who, rather than marching and protesting and demanding state protection against criminal depredations, picked up guns and launched their own offensive against one of the nastiest cartels of all.

What came to be known as the *autodefensa* (self-defense) movement had actually made its first appearance two years earlier, high in the mountains of Michoacán, in the town of Cherán, where indigenous Purépecha people had been under siege by Los Caballeros Templarios, the Knights Templar Cartel. For centuries they had sustained their economy and culture by logging in the surrounding oak forests, but recently outsider loggers had descended like locusts, protected by machine-gun toting gangsters, and had taken away an estimated 70 percent of the trees. The Templarios also extended to Cherán the reign of terror they imposed elsewhere in the state—raping, kidnapping, and murdering at will. Appeals to municipal and state officials proved useless as they (and the police) were securely in the service of organized crime; indeed the cartel *was* the government in much of the region. Cherán was thus like the mountain village in Kurosawa's *Seven Samurai*—beleaguered by bandits—except that no samurai showed up to rescue them, so they decided to rescue themselves.

On April 15, 2011, armed townspeople, women and men of all ages, rose up and expelled the town's entire police force, along with the representatives of established political parties. Reviving an ancient tradition of community policing, which had been given rough sanction in the 1917 Constitution, they turned an institution once used to maintain internal order into a weapon to wield against an external threat. Using captured AR-15 assault rifles, they took the loggers hostage, barricaded all entrances to the town, closed off roads leading to the timber territory, kept hundreds of bonfires blazing all night while they watched for Templario invaders, and successfully established a bandit-free zone.

Roughly two years later, on February 24, 2013, just at the start of Peña Nieto's sexenio, a few dozen residents from two towns in Michoacán's Apatzingán Valley, in the low lying Terra Caliente region, decided to resist Templario exactions by forming an autodefensa. But not being composed of indigenous peoples, they were without benefit of even a quasi-legal cover. The group of lime pickers, ranchers, and small business owners started small, patrolling the streets, setting up roadblocks, and ambushing Knights who cruised through town in black SUVs, culminating in a vicious and victorious gun battle near the town plaza. Over the next eight months other towns followed suit—mobilizing farm hands and factory workers, doctors and taxi drivers—until there were several thousand *comunitarios*, or militias, or vigilantes in the valley. They were financed by donations from residents and businessmen who preferred to support vigilantes rather than pay protection money to the cartel. Weapons were bought in the United States and smuggled south, others were seized from the Templarios. Many of the farmers had learned to shoot in hunting clubs, others now trained with members who had served in the Mexican Army. The citizen-combatant movement spread across Michoacán and into neighboring Guerrero, the vigilantes shooting it out with the Knights and liberating ranches, villages, and towns (though only where local autodefensas had already been established and asked for their help).

The rapid spread of citizen militias startled many, not least the federal government. The Peña Nieto administration's first response was to dismiss them as criminals. Their ranks, it was asserted, harbored members of the Knights' rival from the state just north of Michoacán—the *Cartel de Jalisco Nueva Generación* (Jalisco New Generation Cartel [CJNG]). Their guns, it was feared, had probably been obtained from criminal suppliers. Officials in the capital recalled that La Familia Michoacana had started out promising to be pro-citizen but quickly evolved into bloodsuckers, and Human Rights Watch activists remembered that Colombian paramilitaries had similarly transmogrified into Frankenstein's monsters. Taking a more abstract perspective, some argued that the vigilante movement was a threat to the government's monopoly over the use of force. As one congressional leader put it, "A state that allows citizens to arm themselves to take justice into their own hands is a failed state."

From the perspective of Michoacán's Templario-ridden country-side, it must have seemed risible that the government thought it had a monopoly of violence. A simpler explanation for the state's anxieties, one militia founder suggested, was that "the government has never wanted to recognize that we could do the job that it never wanted to do." And while the militias admitted there were no doubt some bad apples in their barrel—the movement was expanding with such speed it was hard to ensure quality-control—they denied any serious presence of cartelistas, other than small fry who had jumped ship when they saw which way the wind was blowing. Besides, as another senior leader observed: "The great heroes who gave us this country really weren't the best people."

Nevertheless, in March 2013, federal troops were sent in. They arrested scores of militiamen and seized their weapons, only to quickly discover the depth of their support among the populace. In one instance when arrests were made, hundreds of autodefensas poured in and detained the soldiers until their comrades were released. Peña Nieto stood firm, stating that "The practice of taking justice into your own hands is outside the law and my government will combat it."

In May 2013, setting aside his goal of demilitarizing the conflict, Peña Nieto sent in six thousand more troops and federal police. But once on the scene, the army, realizing that dismantling the comunitarios would be vigorously resisted, opted for a de facto alliance with them, in effect covering their backs while they liberated new towns. By October 2013 the militia had completely broken the cartels' grip in several municipalities. "Many of the criminals have fled town since we came in," explained one leader. "We have achieved in weeks what police and soldiers could not do in years." "We are not scared of the cartels," said another, brandishing his weapon. "They have guns but we have guns too. And we are many."

By January 2014, vigilantes were preparing to advance on Apatzingán itself, the city of 120,000 people being the bastion of the Knights, and they were determined to slay the dragon in its lair. Fearing a major bloodbath, Peña Nieto dispatched thousands more troops and federal police. But

he also opted for a more daring initiative. Deciding to treat Michoacán as a bankrupt state, if not a failed one, the president dispatched a
receiver to take control of it. Alfredo Castillo, his former State of Mexico attorney general, was appointed "Commissioner of Security and
Integral Development." A position of doubtful legality, it existed in
no other Mexican state and was reminiscent of the old imperial status
of viceroy. The thirty-eight-year-old Castillo briskly shouldered aside
Michoacán Governor Fausto Vallejo, who seemed powerless to stop
the rising violence, and brought in several dozen other federal officials
to take control of the state police, the prosecutor's office, and other
strategic agencies, confecting an ad-hoc legal framework to legitimize
the process.[44]

Castillo also cut a deal with militia leaders. He offered them
de facto recognition, with the choice of joining one of the revamped
municipal police forces—donning uniforms and receiving salaries—
or doing temporary service in a "rural defense corps" under control
of the army.[45] Hence the new Peña Nieto line: "Those that have the
vocation to participate in security matters, which is the principle that
the self-defense squads have claimed," he told reporters, "should do it
within institutions that are established by law."

---

44   A forerunner of this takeover strategy had been deployed two months earlier when
on November 4, 2013, the government announced that the navy, army, and federal police
would take over security in Lázaro Cárdenas, replacing the local police force (which was
disarmed and taken out of action) and customs officials. The port city had expanded enormously since being opened up to container ships a decade earlier, and its harbor was deep
enough to enable the port to compete with Los Angeles in handling Asian goods bound
for the U.S. market. But that would require breaking the Knights, who were at that point
skimming off an estimated $2 billion per year from its operations. Months later, in May
2014, the city's mayor was arrested over suspected links to traffickers, kidnappers, and
extortionists. The following day, Mexican authorities seized a ship carrying sixty-eight
metric tons of illegal iron ore, totaling since the beginning of 2014 over two hundred
metric tons seized, most on the way to China.

45   Rural defense corps were originally militias formed to control banditry in the nineteenth century, and they played a role in defending cooperative farm communities following the Revolution, but had long since disappeared. Castillo's resurrected structure
would require vigilante leaders to submit a list of members to the army, and register their
weapons. One reason enlistment lagged was that donning uniforms was a surefire way to
attract Templario attention.

The government also announced a $3.4 billion spending plan for Michoacán aimed at building public works and public housing, improving education, and financing social development (though most of these programs, it turned out, were already in the pipeline).

With this detente in place, a new level of collaboration flowered between the militias and federal forces. In January 2014, they began jointly occupying new towns, and in February, they marched into Apatzingán itself. Hundreds of soldiers and cops patrolled the city's streets, while militia gunmen manned checkpoints on the outskirts. A flood of intelligence coming from the liberated locals led to the arrest of several important Templario associates. One of them was the city's mayor—in reality boss of the local *plaza*—who also just happened to be a nephew of the departed Nazario Moreno, "El Más Loco."

Then, on March 9, it turned out that Moreno had not departed after all. Michoacán locals had been saying since his reported death in 2010 that he remained among the living, despite all the shrines Templarios erected to "Saint Nazario," which autodefensas had delighted in smashing to bits as they advanced into each new town. "We always knew his death was a farce because people saw him around," one vigilante leader said, adding that the capo was often sighted at cockfights and parties. But when locals had offered to lead troops to his doorstep, their insistence was treated, condescendingly, as an interesting instance of the power of myth. When the army finally listened to them, Moreno was tracked down and killed—his Second Coming followed swiftly by his Second Going.[46]

By the end of March, marines had also killed Enrique Plancarte, one of Moreno's two top operatives, and had the other, "La Tuta" Gomez Martínez, on the run. Just a few weeks later the federal government took another bold step by arresting Jesús Reyna, Michoacán's interior minister, second only to Governor Fausto Vallejo, accusing him of working with the Knights Templar. Shortly after that the governor

---

46 This time, after having been shot to death by soldiers and marines, Nazario Moreno's autopsy at a hospital in Apatzingán was surrounded by 150 armed guards to ensure that the body would not be snatched by his followers.

resigned, only days after the fugitive "La Tuta" released a photograph of himself having a cozy chat with the governor's son, an image that led to the son's arrest and the father's retirement. "We are very happy that the government is finally doing its job," one vigilante leader said. "We are getting closer and closer, in coordination with the government, to cleaning Michoacán of all the criminals," said another.

The optimism proved premature. Castillo and Peña Nieto, who had never been happy about their Kalashnikov wedding with vigilantes, now desired a divorce. Perhaps because they felt they had the Knights on the run, the government strike force believed it was "reaching a point at which we no longer need them." They worried that the unelected and gun-wielding autodefensas might get out of control (or even break bad); the conversion in Colombia of autodefensas into paramilitary squads was a cautionary tale. They were disturbed that the comunitarios did not share their larger drug war goals, and refused to go after traffickers and producers. "We aren't going to go looking for [meth] laboratories because that's not our responsibility," said one spokesman. Their ambitions were more modest: "We don't want there to be kidnappings, disappearances, extortion." Their reluctance should not have been surprising, given that nearly 35 percent of Michoacán's employed were working in the "informal" economy.

Nevertheless, in early April, Castillo ordered the militias to disarm and demobilize or face arrest, and his forces began targeting militia leadership. Just a few days after El Más Loco was killed, authorities arrested one of the first militia leaders, Hipólito Mora, accusing him of involvement in the murder of a vigilante rival (whatever the real story, longstanding feuds did at times get imported into the leadership). Mora's arrest and others that followed (there were soon over a hundred comunitario prisoners in state and federal prisons) were seen as a betrayal, and deeply embittered many of the autodefensas. Some militias refused to dissolve or turn in their weapons. Yes, they said, thirty or so towns had been liberated, but they wanted to finish the job by cleaning out all 113 of Michoacán's municipalities, capturing or killing La Tuta, and perhaps even marching to the aid of violence-stricken

Acapulco. In June 2014, police and soldiers arrested one of the more obdurate of these vigilante leaders, Dr. Jose Mireles, and locked up more than seventy of his supporters for carrying illegal guns.

The state's abrupt termination of an alliance that had partially dismantled one of the country's most powerful criminal organizations and evicted many of its corrupt protectors from public office, may have been understandable—there was no legal basis for such collaboration—but perhaps tactically premature.[47] With the militia movement in disarray, the crime rate shot up again, according to the government's own figures, with murders and extortion leading the pack. Hundreds, perhaps thousands, of Templar gunmen remained at large elsewhere in Michoacán, among them "La Tuta," despite Castillo's announcement back in March 2014 that he was "cornered and with his hands tied." In September 2014, La Tuta, still at large, offered his own assessment of the situation in an epistle to the citizenry. "Right now," the Teacher admitted, "the Caballeros Templarios cartel is not at its best."

> We've suffered painful casualties, and yet we're still standing, and facing the enemy. They got to us, this we accept. With deceit they were able to enter Michoacán and confuse the people.... Now it's up to us to come back and return order in Michoacán. We know it will be difficult but not impossible. We get pissed off seeing the suffering of our people. We do not forget or forgive treason; the betrayal is punished by death. Many have signed their sentences and will not receive forgiveness.
>
> We have returned to Michoacán with more force than ever, and for example, we're going to really fuck up those fucking

---

47   As well as heavy handed. Mirales was treated worse than some captured drug lords: blindfolded, hooded, cuffed, denied phone calls, denied conferences with his attorney, denied his insulin, his head and face clean shaven, flown blindfolded in a helicopter for five hours, and incarcerated at a Sonora prison one thousand kilometers away from his support and defense team. This triggered extensive human rights protests.

Rurales [the autodefensas]. We're still here in many towns, and we remind you that they haven't gotten rid of us. We're not leaving Michoacán. We keep supporting the Michoacán people and receiving support. We have agreements and support at the highest levels!!!

We understand your confusion. Why you turned your backs to us. We are human and we made mistakes, but [you] are the most important thing for us. We will never let our young people consume the filthy crystal meth. Now…these scourges are poisoning our youth. Gradually, all will return to peace. Little by little, you will see.[48]

But by then the central state's attention had turned to Tamaulipas. In April 2014, faction fights broke out inside the Gulf Cartel, and the Zetas seized the moment to challenge its rival's dominance of particular *plazas*. With the prevailing truce shattered, gun battles left over one hundred dead within weeks. Thousands marched in Ciudad Victoria and Tampico, dressed all in white, demanding government protection.

At the same time, an autodefensa movement grew—hearteningly or alarmingly, depending on one's perspective—putting additional pressure on the federal state to act. Its seedbed was the rural town of Hidalgo, which had been swept, like much of Tamaulipas and indeed

---

48   One wonders if this particular appeal was in part the result of public relations advice he received back in 2013 from two reporters, one of them Televisa's correspondent in Michoacán, whom La Tuta had summoned for a consultation (the ensuing conversation was secretly videotaped and released to the media in September 2014). La Tuta—miffed at all the good press being showered on the autodefensas by the local populace and the national and international press—asked the journalists how to improve his public image. They counseled a better media strategy, making various specific suggestions, including a TV interview they could (and did) arrange with Fox News. The camera also caught him handing them large wads of cash. On release of the tape, the journalists were fired forthwith. Perhaps Tuta's epistle was itself part of his new media strategy, though the real strategy here was his ability to secretly get political and media heavyweights to offer self-incriminatory ruminations, which provided Tuta with leverage—threats to release the tapes—to use against those whose careers he had not yet ruined.

much of the nation, by a wave of extortion and kidnapping in Peña Nieto's first year. A local militia, the Pedro Méndez Column, named after a local general who had fought the French in the 1860s, drew in hundreds of armed men, established a curfew, set up a sandbag perimeter, developed a social media communication network, and executed several Zetas. Criminals submit only to "blood and fire," they declared, and called for "permanent struggle and sustained combat against kidnappers." The Zetas could not penetrate the town, but in May 2014 they shot and burned nine people in an outlying hamlet. They also left a note reading: "People of Hidalgo, don't be involved with the column. The monster has woken up. This is the first test. Attentively: The Zetas."

Aware they were no match for cartel sicarios, the Pedro Méndez Column, like the marchers in white, hoped for outside aid, but of the collaborative variety. "Insecurity, violence, and criminality are only solved," they asserted, "by honest soldiers and an armed people." Others disagreed; one marcher in Victoria said: "I think the self-defense groups are dangerous. A shoemaker makes shoes. A businessman does business. You need trained police officers to fight crime, not just anybody with a gun."

In mid-May 2014, Peña Nieto jumped into Tamaulipas boots first. Secretary of the Interior Miguel Ángel Chong arrived in Reynosa, the state's biggest city, to announce that, as in Michoacán, the federal government was sending in the army, navy, and federal police to restore order. In an effort to differentiate this initiative from Calderón's approach, Chong stressed their intention of making structural transformations. The largely lawless state of over three million residents would be divided into four regions, each with a military man in charge of providing security—24/7 patrols of urban centers and highways (which the cartels had ruled for years), along with the ports and airports. Forty police departments would be dismantled; a training center for new cops would be established; the office of the attorney general would be purged. It would take at least six months for the strategy to produce results, said Chong, and three to four years for Tamaulipas' state and municipal police forces to be reconstituted. There was no sign of any interest in working with autodefensas—indeed this plan might have been promulgated in part to head off another Michoacán scenario.

◆ ◆ ◆

The Forty-Three and the Future

It was at this juncture that Guerrero became the incendiary center of national (indeed global) attention. The forty-three students from Ayotzinapa were taken away in September 2014 and their appalling fate revealed in November. As recounted in our introduction, this triggered a tsunami of protest—the mass murder provoking mass fury—and the emergence of widespread demands for fundamental change. But prior outbursts have come and gone, with the established order weathering each storm, and it is always possible that the newest marches will die down, the media move on to some new horror, the collective energy will dissipate, and prospects for the arrival of an Aztec Spring will wither away. How to channel this energy into long-term structural transformations is the question of the hour, and we will have to see what bubbles up from the ferment now boiling throughout the country. From our perspective, one that flows from the historical analysis we've presented, several broad-brush approaches might deserve popular attention.

It's not enough, we believe, to call for restructuring the country's criminal justice system, or for rooting out corruption from the political system, or for erecting insuperable barriers to money laundering. Worthy and indispensable as these goals are, they've been advocated endlessly and have proved incapable of achievement. Why? Partly of course because the existing arrangements have powerful supporters—politicians and police, gangsters and businessmen—who have profited mightily from the status quo. What's been missing is an efficient mobilizing of the opponents of this narco-order, particularly the millions of members of what goes under the admittedly amorphous term "civil society." It seems to us that a big obstacle to such a rallying—apart from the disparate and divided nature of such a huge aggregate of people—is the disconnect between the state (that portion of it not already gone over to the dark side) and those mass movements that have emerged to challenge existing arrangements (the autodefensas, the Sicilia demonstrators, the student protestors, the human rights activists, the families of the disappeared, the vast numbers propelled into action by the murder of the Forty-Three).

What if the federal state were to help organize these forces, rather than suppress or ignore them? How about trying to find a way to empower grassroot organizations, perhaps along the lines of the short-lived alliance between federal forces and autodefensas in Michoacán that, in an incredibly short space of time, swept an immensely power-ful drug cartel off the board, if admittedly in a delimited area. Perhaps a modus operandi might be found, one that warded off the possible dangers of vigilantism that loomed so large in federal thinking that they aborted the entire enterprise. Perhaps some strategy could be developed that combined federal takeover of corrupt state and local operations (as done in Michoacán, Tamaulipas, and now in Iguala and other municipalities in Guerrero), with a state-assisted mobilization of citizens' action entities? Perhaps ways could be found to involve the public directly in mitigating if not eradicating corruption?

How about revisiting the oft-suggested notion of establishing a Truth Commission. Its multi-faceted project would be to coordinate and amplify the work of existing human rights groups, and other orga-nizations of concerned citizens (notably families of the disappeared), in undertaking a thoroughgoing toting up of the costs of the drug war, and of the Dirty War with which it was intertwined. The goal would be a complete uncovering of the casualties—canvassing the country-side and opening up mass graves, collecting accounts of abductions, refining existing government data, and establishing a national regis-try of the disappeared, with DNA information included, so the dead could be paired with the missing.[49]

---

49   For a demonstration of how such data can be accumulated and presented, see the refinement (done by the DATA4 group) of existing government-provided numbers of the disappeared during the Calderón and Peña Nieto to-date sexenios, in Merino, et.al. And

President Peña Nieto proposed something like this in the reform package he laid out on November 27, 2014, when—feeling the heat of public outrage—he called for creation of a National System for the Search of Lost Persons, and a National System of Genetic Information. The problem is that after so many broken promises of this sort from the state, civil society has no confidence in yet another one. More to the point, a Truth Commission should not be a government operation, run behind closed doors, but an utterly transparent and mass based enterprise, one whose very mode of organization would be a model for a new political order.

The same goes for EPN's support for a National Anti-Corruption System, and the suggestion of naming a special prosecutor as an anti-corruption czar. The problem, again, is that being subject to the attorney general and the president, such a figure would be all too liable to capture by the Executive, hence lack all credibility. An anti-corruption agency should be as autonomous as possible, situated in the space between state and civil society, able to draw on the resources of both.[50] But while the state could provide funding and commence criminal proceedings against accused miscreants, what would the populace at large bring to the table?

◆ ◆ ◆

For one thing, eyes and ears; for another the memories of experienced abuse. Here we think social media could play a larger part in bringing to bear the power inherent in civil society. Consider the phenomenon of witnesses to police or military abuse pulling out their cell phones and posting images and videos to various web sites. Consider

---

on a civil society approach to forensic studies see the work of the Gobernanza Forense Ciudadana (http://gobernanzaforense.org/).

50   A group of eighty intellectuals and representatives of organizations pondering Mexico's corruption problem objected to the special prosecutor proposal on this and other grounds. See, among others, the work of Mauricio Merino and his colleagues at the Network for Accountability: http://rendiciondecuentas.org.mx/somos-2/.

the practice of catching arrogant behavior on camera, and having the posted footage "go viral," something of a spectator sport in Mexico.[51] Consider the impact of the footage filmed by a bystander showing Eric Garner being wrestled to the ground in a chokehold by a New York Police Department officer, after which four other cops pile on, driving his face to the ground as he repeatedly gasps out "I can't breathe"; he died shortly thereafter. That video not only went viral; it also helped galvanize hundreds of physical "I Can't Breathe" die-in demonstrations by tens of thousands in cities across the United States and abroad. It's precisely this ability of the new media to alert vast numbers of citizens that provides new opportunities for citizen intervention, but only if it's organized so as to transcend its scattershot quality.

Perhaps it would be possible to develop a system for receiving eyewitness accounts of abuses in progress. Peña Nieto has proposed establishing a nationwide 911 call-in system but the problem there is who is answering the phone? Citizens are demonstrably and reasonably reluctant to turn to local police for help, and the notion that folding the 1,800 municipal forces into thirty-two state organizations, theoretically making it easier to police the police, overlooks the dangers of centralization, and ignores the truly dismal record of state and federal agencies.[52]

Social media in conjunction with autonomous anti-abuse and anti-corruption bodies might help circumvent these problems. People could anonymously submit accounts of abuse or extortionate demands, not to municipal or state police, but to an autonomous Corruption Complaint Center, or a Police Abuse Center, or perhaps an overarching Citizen's Action Center (its motto: *Quis custodiet ipsos custodes?* [Who will watch the watchmen?]). This institution would be

---

51   See the tweets assembled in this *Gatopardo* article, some outrageous, some hilarious: http://www.gatopardo.com/detalleBlog.php?id=359.

52   The members of the shiny new national gendarmerie, and the graduates of the Merida-funded police training schools, may perhaps turn a new page in police-civilian relations, but Mexico has seen too many such fresh starts turn swiftly sour to warrant getting hopes up.

an autonomous body—headed by elected civic worthies of unimpeachable character, staffed by pro bono lawyers, accountants, and other
professionals, supplemented by an army of student volunteers (perhaps
mobilized through a Peace Corps equivalent: an Anti-Corruption
Corps).

The organization might have three divisions. The first would enter
arriving accusations and any supporting evidence in a database. When
a predetermined number of similar accusations were filed against a
particular individual or organization, thus providing a check against
merely malicious gossip, an investigation would be initiated into the
truth or falsity of the accumulated charges. That would be the province
of the second division, trained investigators given the right to subpoena,
acting somewhat like a grand jury. If there were deemed to be sufficient
grounds for prosecution, a citizen indictment—in effect a pre-prepared
case, complete with evidence and lists of willing witnesses—would be
handed over to the criminal justice system. Now the third division
would take charge of follow-up, tracking the progress (or lack thereof)
in the courts of the case against an accused perpetrator, and if needs
be mobilizing popular response via social media. If done with flair,
such coverage could outdraw "true crime" or "reality TV." This body
would be financed ideally by civic-minded citizens, again using social
media (crowdfunding) to gather the resources. These are just gestures
toward a solution. The mechanics and practicality of such an approach
would have to be worked out by professionals in the field.[53] A similar
procedure could be fashioned for dealing with corruption by high state

53 Professionals like the Red por la Rendición de Cuentas (Network for Accountability); the Laboratory for the Documentation and Analysis of Corruption and Transparency, part of the Institute for Social Research at the National Autonomous University
of Mexico; the Alianza Para El Gobierno Abierto En México (Open Government Partnership); and Transparencia Mexicana, a branch of Transparency International, which
documents corruption levels in countries around the world; Mexico, it calculates, registers
200 million acts of corruption annually.

    Amateurs haven't done too badly, either. Citizen journalists have been organizing
twitter feeds that track corruption—@anticorrupción—and one Monterrey group, the
Via Ciudadana, has begun running a "Corruptour" bus ride, which spotlights eleven "corruption landmarks" in the city. The young activists hope to "place the issue of corruption
at the center of political debate." See: http://nyti.ms/1wW7zof.

officials, though to be effective, the legal immunities they now enjoy would have to be withdrawn. Mayors, governors, and presidents could then become liable to recall referendums at any time in their tenure, not only in the first two years of a term, as is currently the case in Mexico. In the U.S., roughly half the states have recall provisions in their constitutions, and in 2011, of the 150 recall elections in the United States, 75 ended in a removal from office.

More broadly still, picking up on Peña Nieto's proposal for federal seizure of cities where infiltration by organized crime has been demonstrated, why not make this a systematic periodic practice? Franklin Roosevelt, when the public had lost confidence in the banking system, ordered a Bank Holiday, shutting down all banks and reopening only those proven sound. Why not establish a program of regular corruption check-ups with, again, autonomous regulatory bodies sending swarms of lawyers and accountants and students to scrutinize the books? Yes, there's always the danger of regulators being captured by the entities they are regulating, but, again, all these investigations would be done transparently, their data and findings posted online for all to see.

A similar device was used in New York City in the 1990s, during a crackdown on mob infiltration of legitimate industries. Gangsters had established strangleholds over, among others, fish and food markets, garment manufacture, baking, trucking, garbage collection, and construction—some of which had been in place for over half a century. The city established new regulatory procedures requiring that licensees pass background checks, then denied or withdrew licenses to mob related actors. In one instance, to get rid of corrupt employees at the Javits Convention Center, every employee was fired, and had to pass a background check to get rehired. These measures have not worked miracles, but as James Jacobs argues in *Gotham Unbound* they've had a considerable and salutory impact.

On an even grander scale, the call by Cuauhtémoc Cárdenas for Mexicans to write a new Constitution sounds like another empowering project, one in which the population could and should be deeply involved. The old Constitution, with its mandating of social justice provisions, has been end-runned or overturned on a piecemeal basis and by undemocratic methods. This would be the place to reckon up the costs and casualties of the neoliberal regime, and to consider which aspects of the Old Mexico and the New Mexico the populace wish to retain. Constitution-making would be a contentious process, given the existing deep divisions of opinion, but it seems better to put everything on the table and to have a vigorous conversation about the collective future, than to continue along the path the country's been following.

If the notion of engineering a new nexus of state and civil society that would initiate a series of projects which involved and empowered the citizenry is to be more than the latest utopian fantasy to come down the pike, it will have to reckon with the already existing power of the narcos. As long as the drug lords are possessed of virtually unlimited funds with which to bribe governments and buy weapons, the likelihood of successfully eradicating or even moderating them seems unpromising. So our last suggestion, one that follows from our analysis of the U.S.-backed approach to drug use by its citizens—a prohibition/interdiction/incarceration regime—proposes an effort to diminish the resources available to the narco/state complex, one that provides an opportunity for Americans as well as Mexicans to take a hand in altering the unsatisfactory status quo.

CHAPTER TWELVE

New Directions

We have sought to demonstrate that the term "Mexican Drug War" is a misnomer, as the phenomenon to which it refers was a joint construction by Mexico and the United States, erected over the last hundred years. If that's true, then it suggests that ending the "war" would likely require a joint effort from both sides of the border. Are there any signs of this happening?

Actually, there are. Over the past twenty years a conviction has been growing that the prohibitionist policy officially enforced by both nations is deeply flawed and should be modified or repealed. At first, this dissent was voiced by a very few. It was difficult, even dangerous, to challenge the widely held (and strongly policed) consensus. Interdiction of supply and incarceration of users were deemed the best ways, the only acceptable ways, to deal with the growing use of narcotics in the United States. But slowly, step by modest step, then with accelerating speed and growing support as the costly and often horrible consequences of reigning policy became ever more apparent in both countries, a campaign got underway to breach the ramparts of the War on Drugs regime.

Some key moments in this campaign:
1996: Californians adopted Proposition 215, the Compassionate Use Act, which legalized the use of marijuana for medicinal purposes. The local activists who promoted this initiative attacked the prohibitionist

forces at their least defensible position—the Anslinger characterization of cannabis as a deadly menace—and they promoted pot's decriminalization, not for recreational use, but for the relatively unimpeachable purpose of treating cancer and AIDS patients. The new state law could not, however, supersede federal law, and federal authorities under Clinton, Bush, and (despite campaign promises to the contrary) Obama did their best to thwart the spread of state-legalized suppliers through lawsuits, civil injunctions, DEA and SWAT team raids, and enormous numbers of arrests. Despite this, the California victory triggered a chain reaction across the country; thus far, twenty-three states, plus the District of Columbia, have legalized cannabis for therapeutic purposes.

2006: With the clock counting down on his sexenio, President Vicente Fox, theretofore a stalwart promoter of the state's war on drug traffickers, signaled a change of heart and mind by signing legislation that legalized possession of small quantities of narcotics or psychoactives. The new law barred police from penalizing people for carrying up to five grams of marijuana, five grams of opium, twenty-five milligrams of heroin, or five hundred milligrams of cocaine—enough for a few lines—or limited quantities of LSD, hallucinogenic mushrooms, amphetamines, Ecstasy, or peyote. Given that local consumption of any of these was still quite small in Mexico—alcohol remained the overwhelming drug of choice—this measure would not have had much impact beyond the symbolic. It was, after all, gringos who were the big buyers, and the U.S. seemed hardly likely to follow Fox's lead. Quite the reverse: Washington came down on Fox heavily, in a campaign reminiscent of Anslinger's back in the 1930s. The DEA got on the horn to its Mexican counterparts—pointing out, among other things, that its major effect would likely be to send hordes of collegiate spring-breakers pouring across the border to toke up, thus making a hash of efforts to suppress drug use stateside. Within a week, Fox was forced to back down.

2009: In February, Fox's predecessor Ernesto Zedillo, together with former presidents of Colombia and Brazil, convened and co-chaired a commission of Latin American intellectuals and political leaders, which produced a position paper—*Drugs and Democracy: Toward a Paradigm Shift*—that cautiously dissented from the status quo. "Prohibitionist policies based on the eradication of production and on the disruption of drug flows as well as on the criminalization of consumption have not yielded the expected results," they said. Instead, "the 'war on drugs' strategy pursued in the region over the past thirty years" had led to the "corruption of public servants, the judicial system, governments, the political system, and especially the police forces." It was imperative to break the "taboo" on criticism, because acknowledging the failure of "U.S. prohibitionist policies" was the prerequisite for adopting "a new paradigm leading to safer, more efficient and humane drug policies," like those adopted by some European countries, which had changed the status of addicts "from drug buyers in the illegal market to that of patients cared for in the public health system."

One of Europe's poster countries for this approach was Portugal. Hearkening back to Salazar Viniegra's program in 1930s Mexico, the nation by 2001 had "decriminalized" all illicit drugs. Their possession and use remained illegal, but violations were treated as administrative infractions, and users were channeled not to jail but into "dissuasion" sessions, or if struggling with drug dependency were offered therapeutic services. Opponents forecast nightmarish consequences, like a dramatic surge in drug use, which failed to appear. Instead, drug-related pathologies (for example, HIV infection from needles) declined, partly through education campaigns and partly because fear of arrest in the era before decriminalization had hindered addicts from seeking help. Analysts called it a "resounding success," not least for having dramatically reduced the burdens on the criminal justice system.

Also in 2009, President Calderón himself advanced and won passage of a similar decriminalization bill. It allowed the personal use of small drug amounts, though it still banned cultivation and sale. It also unleashed local police to pursue neighborhood dealers (targets previously reserved for federal authorities), providing a rich new field for corrupt cops to exploit. Calderón justified it as a wartime measure that would allow federal forces to redirect resources from small-time consumers to big-time dealers and their drug lord bosses. Here, too, there was no immediate effect on drug use, belying the scare stories that youths would rush for the nearest syringe.

2010: Californians again debated a drug-related ballot initiative, Proposition 19, also known as the Regulate, Control & Tax Cannabis Act. It would have legalized possession and use of small amounts of marijuana, the home-growing of a modest private stash, and the licensing of commercial cultivators and retail distributors. Supporters of Proposition 19 argued that taxes would allow California to harvest $1.4 billion annually in badly needed revenue (the Great Recession being in full swing), save tens of millions wasted on incarcerating nonviolent users, and free police to catch serious criminals.

It would also, some argued, cut off a significant flow of funds to Mexico's violent drug cartels and allow California's southern neighbor to redirect law-enforcement resources to more dangerous crimes like kidnapping and extortion. There were wildly varying estimates of how much marijuana prices might fall upon legalization and regulation. If the White House Office of National Drug Control Policy estimate (as of 2009) was correct, and over half of cartel revenues came from the sale of marijuana to U.S. consumers, a significant chunk of their business would evaporate, and with it the tremendous profits with which they funded recruitment, arms purchases, and bribes.

Calderón nevertheless vigorously opposed Proposition 19, and suggested any softening of the U.S. stance toward drug consumption would undercut his efforts to control organized crime groups in Mexico. Vicente Fox disagreed (there was no love lost between these two PANistas) and said passage of Proposition 19 would be a "great step forward" and could "open the door to these ideas for us." Mexico should legalize the entire production chain, Fox argued, allowing farmers to produce marijuana, manufacturers to process it, distributors to distribute it, and shops to sell it. Throwing off the prohibitionist shackles should be seen as "a strategy to strike at and break the economic structure that allows gangs to generate huge profits in their trade, which feeds corruption and increases their areas of power."

Jorge Castañeda, a former Mexican foreign minister and a proponent of legalization, coauthored a *Washington Post* op-ed piece saying that passage of Proposition 19 would make war-as-usual untenable: "If California legalizes marijuana, will it be viable for our country to continue hunting down drug lords in Tijuana? Will Wild West–style shootouts to stop Mexican cannabis from crossing the border make any sense when, just over that border, the local 7-Eleven sells pot?" The point was mooted, momentarily, when the proposition was defeated with 53.5 percent of California voters voting "No"—but 46.5 percent had voted "Yes."

2011: In June the Global Commission on Drug Policy, an expanded version of the 2009 Latin American–only operation, appeared on the scene. It, too, featured a bevy of former Latin American presidents, including Ernesto Zedillo, and distinguished Latin American cultural figures such as Carlos Fuentes. But it also included "formers" from the United States—including former Secretary of State George Shultz, former Federal Reserve Bank chair Paul Volcker—as well as former United Nations Secretary General Kofi Annan. The report they issued was considerably more forthright than its predecessor's, its palpable sense of urgency in large part a reflection of Mexico's soaring death rate.

"The global war on drugs has failed," the commissioners declared flatly, "with devastating consequences for individuals and societies around the world." It had exacerbated "violence, crime and corruption in Latin America." Its "vast expenditures on criminalization and repressive measures directed at producers, traffickers and consumers" had "clearly failed to effectively curtail supply or consumption." Repression of consumers had impeded public health measures to reduce HIV/AIDS and overdose fatalities. Budgets of the state and local governments had been busted to pay for prison systems and tens of thousands of law enforcement agents.

Recommending a sharp U-turn, they proposed: ending the "criminalization, marginalization and stigmatization of people who use drugs but who do no harm to others"; modifying mandatory sentencing laws and removing penalties for the possession of small amounts of drugs;

and experimenting with regulated commodity markets to undermine the power of organized crime—starting with, but not limited to, cannabis. Harm reduction campaigns should be expanded, but should eschew simplistic "just say no" messages and "zero tolerance" policies in favor of educational efforts grounded in credible information. The flawed scheduling of cannabis, coca leaf, and Ecstasy as dangerous drugs should be revised. The commissioners also urged ending the incarceration of millions—not just end-users, but farmers, couriers, and petty sellers, many themselves victims of violence and intimidation, or drug dependent, or seeking to escape poverty. Prohibition was a policy that "has filled prisons and destroyed lives and families without reducing the availability of illicit drugs or the power of criminal organizations."

Both Washington and Mexico City promptly rejected the report. Both opposed "legal regulation," and declared they would not back away from the war on drugs, which by that time had racked up roughly forty thousand dead. "The Obama administration's efforts to reduce drug use," said the White House, "are not born out of a culture war or drug-war mentality, but out of the recognition that drug use strains our economy, health, and public safety." Calderón said his government "categorically rejects" the notion that "a stronger application of the law" had led to an increase in narco-violence.

2012: More dissent emerged from Latin American elites. In March, when Guatemala's president proposed legalizing drugs, the U.S. embassy there swiftly responded with a stern warning about the "major public health and safety threat" such a policy represented. In April, at the Sixth Summit of the Americas, almost every president in the region was reported to be saying (albeit behind closed doors) that the "U.S.-sponsored-and-dictated" war on drugs was not working, and they needed to try something else. In June, at the gathering of the Organization of American States, Secretary of State John Kerry was on hand to defend existing policy, and the delegates—mindful that they risked U.S. trade sanctions and the loss of military and economic aid—prudently refrained from going public with their discontent.

But then, in November 2012, came the game changer. Residents of Colorado and Washington voted to legalize marijuana for recreational use. Adults would now be allowed to grow and consume their own supply, possess up to one ounce while traveling, and give the same amount as a gift to other adult citizens. Consumption in public remained illegal, and driving under the influence of marijuana would be treated like driving while drunk. More remarkably, the two states legalized cultivation, manufacturing, and selling of cannabis, subject to government licensing, regulation, and taxation. Much of the likely resulting revenue—estimated to be in the tens of millions of dollars—would be earmarked for substance-abuse prevention, research, education, and healthcare.

Colorado and Washington did not have the size or political clout of California, but the reverberations from their decisions would be startling, immediate, and widespread. As Fox and Castañeda had predicted, legalization in the States—any states—prompted a change in official Mexico's rhetoric.

In July, shortly after his election victory but before the U.S. referenda, Peña Nieto announced that while he was not in favor of legalizing drugs himself, "I'm in favor of opening a new debate in the strategy in the way we fight drug trafficking. It is quite clear that after several years of this fight against drug trafficking, we have more drug consumption, drug use, and drug trafficking. That means we are not moving in the right direction. Things are not working." We "should debate in Congress, in the hemisphere and especially [he added pointedly] the U.S. should participate in this broad debate."

Then in November came Washington and Colorado. Peña Nieto, while sticking to his opposition to legalization, said that in view of the two states' decision, an international review of drug policy was more urgent than ever. Aides and allies were more vociferous. The powerful leader of the PRI delegation in Mexico's Congress said: "The legalization of marijuana forces us to think very hard about our strategy to combat criminal organizations, mainly because the largest consumer in the world has liberalized its laws." Peña Nieto's top adviser, Luis

Videgaray, said: "Obviously, we can't handle a product that is illegal in Mexico, trying to stop its transfer to the United States, when in the United States, at least in part of the United States, it now has a different status." More proactive still was Cesar Duarte, governor of Chihuahua and an ally of the new president: "It seems to me that we should move to authorize exports," as then "we would have control over a business which today is run by criminals." Despite these reactions, no actual steps were taken in this direction.

2013: During his south of the border visit in May, Obama gave a speech in which he declared: "We understand that much of the root cause of violence that's been happening here in Mexico, for which so many Mexicans have suffered, is the demand for illegal drugs in the United States. And so we've got to continue to make progress on that front." This was greeted with enthusiastic applause. Then he added: "I honestly do not believe that legalizing drugs is the answer. But I do believe that a comprehensive approach—not just law enforcement, but education and prevention and treatment—that's what we have to do. And we're going to stay at it because the lives of our children and the future of our nations depend on it." No applause.

In August, Obama blinked. The Department of Justice elected not to sue Washington and Colorado over their legalization of marijuana, and not to prosecute its sale and consumption in those states, if cannabis commerce was tightly regulated, did not cross state lines, and was forbidden to minors. Federal law remained unchanged; and cannabis continued to be classified as a dangerous Schedule I substance.

In December, he blinked again. Uruguay—determined to forestall the arrival of Mexican-style violence—legalized and regulated the production, distribution, and sale of marijuana, allowing home cultivation, registration of growers' clubs, licensed sales to adults in pharmacies, and provision of medical marijuana through the Ministry of Public Health. In sharp contrast to the previous year's dressing down of Guatemala, there was nary a peep from the U.S. embassy about the new law.

2014: Obama promulgated a National Drug Control Strategy that left the prohibitionist structure in place, but rejected traditional drug-war rhetoric. The White House was adopting "a twenty-first century approach to drug policy." It would be "science-based," unlike the twentieth century approach, which had been the prisoner of "powerful myths and misconceptions." Back in the day it was believed that addicts were "morally flawed and lacking in willpower," and that their transgressions required a punitive response. (Take *that*, Harry Anslinger!). But modern neuroscience had discovered that addiction is really a disease of the brain, one that like diabetes, asthma, or hypertension could and should be treated (this point was underscored with colorful images of brain scans). That was why his administration would treat addiction as a public health issue. "An enforcement-centric 'war on drugs' approach to drug policy is counterproductive, inefficient, and costly," the White House said, insisting that "we simply cannot incarcerate our way out of the drug problem." On the other hand—"at the other extreme"—the drug legalization approach was equally flawed, as it would lead to more drug use, hence higher health and criminality costs (assertions that, besides being demonstrably false, completely ignored the harm reduction and public health focus of the new state laws). Critiquing the drug war while continuing to wage it had become something of a tradition for the Obama administration; the White House Office of National Drug Control Policy had called for a shift to a public health policy as early as 2009. But the president had nevertheless made a genuine contribution to a non-punitive approach by expanding access to treatment programs for addicts. Twenty-two million Americans, the White House estimated, were in need of such attention, which only two million were receiving. The Affordable Care Act (Obamacare) required insurance companies to cover such services.

On the international front, 2014 brought an escalation of assaults on another stronghold of war on drugs warriors—the United Nations. In 1961, pressed by the United States (with Federal Bureau of Narcotics chief Anslinger leading the charge[54]), the UN had adopted

---

54 After Anslinger retired in 1962, aged seventy, he served as the United States Representative to the United Nations Narcotics Commission for two years, where he exported American prohibitionism to the global level.

a Single Convention on Narcotic Drugs (supplemented by 1971 and 1988 treaties). The long-term announced goal was that "all non-medical use of narcotics" be eventually "outlawed everywhere," leading to a "drug-free world." All signatories agreed to tailor their domestic drug legislation to UN specifications, which dictated criminalization policies. An International Narcotics Control Board was established to ensure compliance. Over the subsequent fifty-odd years, whenever a state considered experimenting with a more tolerant approach to drug use, international diplomatic pressure was applied to "protect the integrity of the Conventions."

In September 2014, a new report from the Global Commission on Drug Policy (*Taking Control: Pathways to Drug Policies that Work*) challenged this status quo, calling for more flexible interpretations or outright revision of the international conventions "to accommodate experimentation with harm reduction, decriminalization and legal regulatory policies." They set their sights on the upcoming (2016) United Nations General Assembly Special Session on Drugs, seeing it as "an historic opportunity to discuss the shortcomings of the drug control regime, identify workable alternatives."

In another important shift of U.S. policy, a high-ranking official responded to this in October by agreeing that the treaty's tight corset needed to be loosened. Assistant Secretary of State for Drugs and Law Enforcement William Brownfield, in addressing a UN committee, said: "How could I, a representative of the government of the United States of America, be intolerant of a government that permits any experimentation with legalization of marijuana if two of the fifty states of the United States of America have chosen to walk down that road?"[55]

---

55   On the other hand, Brownfield wanted the corset itself to remain in place. The international community, he said, should "respect the integrity of the existing UN Drug Control Conventions," even as they allowed for some greater degree of flexibility. Which is why the human rights agency WOLA (Washington Office on Latin America) cautioned that Brownfield's statement was likely mainly aimed at damage control: if the UN conventions could be interpreted to allow for marijuana legalization, now that the U.S. wanted it, perhaps calls for more thoroughgoing revision could be headed off.

In November 2014 two more states (Oregon and Alaska) and Washington, DC chose to walk down the same road—their electorates voting to legalize cannabis for recreational use.

♦ ♦ ♦

So what's next for the United States?
There has clearly been a major change in popular thinking about pot, and it seems to be accelerating. In a 1969 Gallup poll only 12 percent had supported legalization. Then the numbers rose slowly, to 25 percent in 1995 and 36 percent in 2005, then jumped to 48 percent in 2012 and vaulted to 58 percent only a year later, breaking through to majority status. This gives credibility to the widely held belief that upcoming ballot initiatives or legislative proposals proposing legalization—scheduled for 2016 in Massachusetts, Maine, Nevada, Arizona, and, once again, pivotal California—are likely to succeed.

Will marijuana reform then sweep the nation, becoming national policy? That will depend on the outcome of an upcoming political struggle.

There are significant forces lined up to perpetuate the status quo. These include institutions that are themselves products of the war on drugs approach and would not long survive its passing. The Drug Enforcement Administration would be hard-pressed to justify its annual budget of roughly $2.5 billion if the legal ground shifted beneath it. Many police departments and public prosecutors have been in the forefront of lobbying campaigns against marijuana ballot initiatives and legislative drug-law reforms, although others have embraced decriminalization as they consider hunting down tokers a diversion from pursuing serious criminals. The mammoth incarceration complex that has grown up to house a wildly expanded prison population will likely resist any diminution in the production of felons, its lifeblood, as would the many communities that have been forced by deindustrialization to accept the running of jailhouses as their bread-and-butter industry. The gun lobby might not be frontally challenged by drug legalization, but arms manufacturers have made big money from legal and illegal sales to Mexico, and the NRA is hyper-alert to anything that might imperil Smith & Wesson's profits.[56] There are many in faith-based institutions who would decry granting legal absolution to those who indulge in immoral (some would say wicked) behavior. And many in public health institutions would oppose the further diffusion of toxic substances.

Ranged against this formidable congeries of prohibitionists are the increasingly organized forces promoting repeal. These groups include the Drug Policy Association, NORML (National Organization for the Reform of Marijuana Laws), the Marijuana Policy Project, the Marijuana Majority, LEAP (Law Enforcement Against Prohibition), and innumerable local groups like Arkansas CALM (Citizen's Alliance for the Legalization of Marijuana), whose vice president, pastor at the Sabbath Day Church of God in Hot Springs, is promoting an Arkansas Hemp & Marijuana Amendment to the state constitution. Their members contest these arguments and interests, and advance other concerns.

There are proponents of public health who suggest that prohibition has diverted resources from health care to punishment; libertarians who object to governmental intrusion in the private lives of citizens; strapped states seeking to tap potential tax revenues and reduce the costs (in the billions) of enforcing laws on possession; to say nothing of the thirty million Americans who annually smoke weed because they enjoy it.

Spurred by mass protests against militarized policing, led by African Americans, there has also been an increase in public repudiation of the immense expansion of the prison population, and the use of marijuana possession as justification for the mass incarceration that has overwhelmingly (and not coincidentally) ensnared people of color. Nationwide from 2001 to 2010, police made more than 8.2

---

56 Theoretically, a wedge might be driven between gun makers and gun users—the hunters and home-defenders who don't always agree with positions the NRA advances in their name. It might be possible to rally support for limitations strictly aimed at curtailing exports, and thus win ratification of CIFTA. But it's not likely.

million marijuana arrests; almost nine in ten were for possession, not sale. Between 1997 and 2012, New York City alone arrested and jailed more than six hundred thousand for simple possession; 87 percent of those arrested were blacks and Latinos. African Americans, who make up 14 percent of regular drug users, are 56 percent of those in state prison for drug offenses.

Even when their sentences are short ones, those who pass through this gulag are marked for life. As convicted felons they cannot vote, serve on juries, or receive public benefits like food stamps, housing, or education; they are often fired, and their future job prospects crippled. Ironically, the unemployable victims become prime candidates for recruitment by the very drug industry that prohibitionists want to dismantle. "Broken Windows" policing proponents argue that coming down hard on minor crimes prevents future major ones—a theory that bears some resemblance to the argument that marijuana should be proscribed lest users move on to harder stuff—but they take no cognizance of the devastating long-term impact on those arrested, those for whom broken windows mean broken lives.

Legalizers note, too, that moralizers who defend prohibition seldom extend their ethical concerns below the Rio Grande, hence fail to include the mass slaughter of Mexicans in their moral calculus. They also critique those who justify criminalizing drugs on public health grounds by noting that countries adopting harm-reduction strategies have done far better at diminishing drug-related medical damage than punitive-minded states. They also cite the U.S. success with nicotine reduction programs aimed at a lethal but legal drug, which have dramatically reduced smoking to its lowest level since the 1930s. In the case of the alarums raised over marijuana's purported dangers, anti-prohibitionists point to the mortality statistics; as one runs an eye down the Center for Disease Control's annual list of fatalities from drug consumption, the numbers (in 2012) tumble down from the 480,000 deaths chalked up to cigarette smoking, to the 88,000 alcohol-related deaths, through the 3,635 heroin overdoses, to the grand total of marijuana mortalities: zero.

◆ ◆ ◆

Weighing up the pro- and anti-legalization contenders, and factoring in inertia—as the Founding Fathers knew, "experience hath shewn, that mankind are more disposed to suffer, while evils are sufferable, than to right themselves by abolishing the forms to which they are accustomed"—it is hard not to be pessimistic about the possibilities of a wholesale turnabout. On the other hand, there is a strong pragmatic streak running through the American past, alongside an at-times zealous utopianism.

On January 15, 1920, the Anti-Saloon League issued a press statement hailing the imminent demise of legal liquor. Tomorrow at midnight, the victorious prohibitionists rejoiced, a new nation would be born: "Now for an era of clean thinking and clean living!"

Twelve years later, in 1932, John D. Rockefeller, Jr. who with his father had been the biggest single financial backer of Prohibition, now ruefully wrote: "When Prohibition was introduced, I hoped that it would be widely supported by public opinion and the day would soon come when the evil effects of alcohol would be recognized. I have slowly and reluctantly come to believe that this has not been the result. Instead, drinking has generally increased; the speakeasy has replaced the saloon; a vast army of lawbreakers has appeared; many of our best citizens have openly ignored Prohibition; respect for the law has been greatly lessened; and crime has increased to a level never seen before."

Rockefeller was a Johnny-come-lately to the drive for Repeal, as by then a formidable coalition had gathered that was appalled at the amount of vice spawned by the effort to impose virtue, at the level of violence generated by inter-gang warfare, and at the amount of corruption spawned by the state's war against the gangs. New York City Mayor Fiorello La Guardia, who had fought vigorously but unsuccessfully against the dry crusaders, had remarked dryly that "it would take seventy-five thousand coast guardsmen to protect the Florida coastline alone—and then we'd need seventy-five thousand more to watch *them*."

Yet the corruption never came close to the degree of rot that has corroded Mexican institutions. The level of violence attained in the U.S. in the 1920s—all those St. Valentine's Day Massacres—was piddling compared to the mountainous death toll in Ciudad Juárez alone. Nevertheless, despite the Prohibitionists having (so they thought) ensured their proscription's permanence by carving it into the Constitution itself, the United States managed to reverse itself. Despite the embarrassment of having to go through the enormously complex process of inserting an amendment into the Constitution, and one dedicated solely to repealing another amendment, Americans re-legalized a substance that was (and remains) far more dangerous than heroin, or cocaine, or crystal meth, to say nothing of marijuana.

Yes, it's a different time, different circumstances, different players. Yes, the odds are against a twenty-first-century replay of the twentieth century's Repeal; but the fact remains that the U.S. has done it before, and could do it again. Legalization of marijuana (and perhaps other drugs) would not be a magic bullet. Believing it would end the drug wars overnight would be as delusional as was the fantasy of prohibitionists that banning alcohol would usher in "an era of clean thinking and clean living." There are far too many variables involved to say with any surety how it would work out. The possibility of negative as well as positive unanticipated consequences would have to be kept in mind. But given that the damage already wrought by drug prohibitionsts far outweighs the damage done by their anti-alcohol forebears, it's time to consider a change.

◆ ◆ ◆

And what's next for Mexico?
Here the odds against a Uruguayan or Colorado-style reconsideration are considerably higher, given that Mexico remains constrained by American policy, and by the presence of vicious cartels on its soil. But it's possible to hypothesize a route toward revision.

Peña Nieto's administration has been reluctant to do more than speculate about changing the rules. The PRI strategy, after all, had been to avoid dealing with drug war issues as much as possible, and to focus instead on neoliberal economic initiatives. Legalization would require a drastic shift of priorities (though not of ideology, as decriminalization could be packaged as a blow for free trade). But the autodefensa movement, and now the nationwide outrage over the mass murder of the Forty-Three, coupled with the concern of international investors about ongoing rampant criminality, has forced EPN to confront the crime issue. But how? Given that a replay of Calderón's all-out military assault is almost certainly off the table—been there, done that, didn't work—one of the likeliest ways of tackling crime would be to go the decriminalization route, drying up the sea in which the cartel fish swim. But here he would run up against the United States, whose ability to retaliate through decertification and other measures remains unimpaired, as it has for the last century. How to break out of this trap?

One possibility: PRD politicians in Mexico City have said they will submit a legalization package to the city's legislature, where passage would be quite likely. The capital is more liberal than the country on cultural matters, having already accepted legalized abortion and gay marriage.[57] If the city did, the federal government would be confronted with the same quandary the Obama administration faced after Colorado and Washington's breakaway move; they could sue or order arrests, or they could acquiesce. Assume, moreover, that in 2016 California legalizes marijuana production and distribution (current polls show 65 percent in favor). It's just possible that a Mexican legalization of exports might *not* bring down the wrath of the still-in-power Obama administration; indeed the whole war on drugs regime might become destabilized, perhaps unsustainable.[58]

---

57 A Mexican analog of U.S. groups like the Drug Policy Association is CUPIHD (*Colectivo por una Política Integral hacia las Drogas*). The organization includes psychologists, journalists, lawyers, academics, artists, doctors, and civil society activists, including the distinguished historian and sociologist of the drug industry Luis Astorga.

58 Of course it's possible that California might *resist* Mexican imports, preferring to shelter its infant industry from international competition. Or that a movement modeled on those calling for energy independence might emerge, dedicated to freeing the U.S.

There are plenty of U.S. businessmen who are plumping for such an eventuality; one former Microsoft executive is soliciting investors for $10 million in start-up money to create the first U.S. national marijuana brand, which would supply cannabis imported legally from Mexico to recreational and medical outlets. (He has begun buying up dispensaries and touring with Vicente Fox touting his vision.) After New York passed its medical marijuana law in July 2014, and gave the Health Department eighteen months to choose five companies to produce the herb from "seed to sale," it triggered a grass rush of would-be growers, investors, lobbyists, consultants, and branding firms. In October, nine hundred people flocked to a three-day East Coast Cannabis Business Expo, Educational Conference and Regulatory Summit, chockablock with vendors and venture capitalists prepared to shell out $20 million in start-up costs. The venerable counterculture magazine *High Times* announced it planned to create a private equity High Times Growth Fund to invest in cannabis businesses.[59]

But what of the cartels? How are they likely to respond to all this flux? How are they dealing with declining marijuana profits? Some are bailing out. An April 2014 report from the Golden Triangle region of Sinaloa found that farmers were no longer planting marijuana, its wholesale price having collapsed from $100 per kilogram to less than $25. "It's not worth it anymore," said Rodrigo Scilla, fifty, a lifelong cannabis farmer, adding: "I wish the Americans would stop with this legalization."

Are the cartels really ready to abandon marijuana production? Perhaps they could go straight, becoming corporations—Sinaloa Cartel, Inc.? The rate of return on legal weed would be less, but so would overhead—fewer bribes, lower arms-budgets and transport costs. But

---

from dependence on foreign marijuana producers. Or that Republicans would jump on the issue, crying "soft on crime!" and Hillary Clinton or whomever the Democrats nominate would likely cave immediately.

59   This whole scene bears some resemblance to the forces of capital circling Cuba, waiting and hoping for the collapse of existing Cuban and U.S. constraints on their ability to invest—now that a fledgling detente has been achieved.

what about competition? Would the Zetas, turned purveyors of Zeta brand joints, be prepared to join with the makers of "El Chapo brand" reefers in peaceable trade associations? Attend conventions? Would American tobacco corporations flock south and go toe-to-toe with the formerly fearsome killer-businessmen? It doesn't seem likely. But for the moment the issue is not pressing, as the cartels can simply shift to an as yet un-decriminalized product. Indeed, they already have.

Drug farmers in Sinaloa are filling their fields with opium poppies, partly in response to heightened demand in the United States. American authorities, trying to contain an epidemic of prescription painkiller abuse, have tightened controls on semi-synthetic opiates such as hydrocodone and oxycodone. As the pills have become more costly and difficult to obtain, the cartels have adjusted their product line, sending heroin flooding north. Similarly, cartels are experimenting with cultivating coca leaves; in September 2014, 639,000 plants were discovered in Chiapas.

In the long run, however, a half-criminal and half-legal situation probably could not stand, and would likely require a complete dismantling of the anti-drug regime, including the whole spectrum of presently criminalized drugs (as did Mexico's 2009 law, though only for possession of tiny amounts, and as does the full-rigged approach adopted by Portugal). The peaceable production of drug crops would become just another industry—like growing avocados or making tequila—and by providing decently paying agricultural jobs for campesinos, might go partway to reversing some of the damage wrought by NAFTA. In the end, a real recovery would require tackling Mexico's pervasive poverty, unemployment, and economic inequality by providing the citizenry with decent jobs, good educations, and affordable healthcare. This, however, is a social project incompatible with an ongoing commitment to neoliberal demands and continuing fantasies of salvation through oil investment, especially now that the price of oil has collapsed.

Would ending the "Mexican Drug War" by decriminalizing it out of existence be politically conceivable? Perhaps, given the blood-soaked alternative. The hope would be, given the tremendous hit the cartels would take thanks to diminished profitability, that they and their ganglet offspring (like the Guerreros Unidos, who committed the savagery against the Forty-Three in Iguala) might become vulnerable to a focused assault by restructured and less bribable forces of order. If some of civil society's current furious insistence that justice, law, and order prevail were to be channeled into pressing for a structural solution, rather than another short-term fix, there's a chance that Mexico might be able to dig itself out of the mess it has gotten into, courtesy in large part of the U.S.A. Perhaps it's time to say:

¡Ya Basta! One hundred years is enough.

ACKNOWLEDGMENTS

Thanks to John Oakes for persisting in his conviction that a book with this perspective would be a useful contribution to a now global conversation about "warring" on drugs. Thanks also to Samantha Schnee for translating Carmen's initial approach to the topic. Joel Feingold offered trenchant readings of each successive draft, significantly aiding its evolution, while also whipping into shape our bilingual bibliography. Elisa Ríos Simbeck handled complex last-minute editing tasks. And thanks for their help along the way to our friends Alberto Barranco, Ana Luisa Liguori, Lucía Melgar, and Naief Yehya.

This book relies heavily on brave journalists (like Ioan Grillo) who have spent years on the appalling front lines of the "Mexican drug war," and have literally risked (or lost) their lives to bring back their stories. We have also profited from the work of the many scholars (like Luis Astorga) who have examined the phenomenon from innumerable angles.

Neither of us is an expert on the issue, as will no doubt be apparent to the real professionals. We're a bi-national couple—Carmen is a Mexican novelist and poet, Mike is an historian of New York City—who agreed that a book on the interlocking trajectories of the U.S. and Mexico, which led to the current dreadful state of affairs, might be of interest to non-Mexican readers. Hence we have assumed no familiarity with Mexican history, politics, or geography. The titles listed in the bibliography following are works we found particularly useful in constructing our analysis and narrative; we salute the authors and absolve them of all responsibility for our errors.

BIBLIOGRAPHY
English

"Ambassador's Private Dinner with President-Elect Calderon," *Wikileaks.org*, September 29, 2013.

"Mexico Murders at over 101,000 in Past 6 Years, Report Says," *Latino.foxnews.com*, November 27, 2012.

"Mexico's Presidential Election: Back to the Future," *The Economist*, June 23, 2012.

Ahrens, J. M. "The Couple That Danced among the Dead," *El País in English*, October 13, 2014.

——. "Mexicans Say 'Enough Is Enough' at Massive Protest Rally: Tens of Thousands from All Walks of Life Call for Changes to Prevent Another Iguala Case," *El País in English*, November 21, 2014.

Ahrens, J. M. and L. P. Beauregard. "Peña Nieto Sends Troops to Tamaulipas," *El País in English*, May 14, 2014.

Alexander, Michelle. (2010) *The New Jim Crow: Mass Incarceration in the Age of Colorblindness*. New York.

Althaus, Dudley. "How Colorado and Washington Could End Mexico's Drug War," *Globalpost.com*, November 10, 2012.

——. "Even the 99 Percent Get Kidnapped in Mexico," *Globalpost.com*, April 14, 2014.

——. "How Mexico's West Was Won: It Took a Village, and Plenty of Ak-47s," *Globalpost.com*, February 20, 2014.

Althaus, Dudley and Steven Dudley. "Mexico's Security Dilemma: Michoacán's Militias—the Rise of Vigilantism in Mexico and Its Implications Going Forward," *Insightcrime.org & Wilson Center: Mexico Institute*, July 2014.

Alvarez, Lizette. "In Puerto Rico, Cocaine Gains Access to U.S.," *New York Times*, May 29, 2014.

Andreas, Peter. (2013) *Smuggler Nation: How Illicit Trade Made America*. New York.

Archibold, Randal C. "Elite Mexican Police Corps Targets Persistent Violence, but Many Are Skeptical," *New York Times*, August 22, 2014.

———. "Killings Jolt a Family in Mexico," *New York Times*, February 25, 2011.

———. "Drug Gang Killed Students, Mexican Law Official Says," *New York Times*, November 7, 2014.

———. "Mexican Leader, Facing Protests, Promises to Overhaul Policing," *New York Times*, November 27, 2014.

———. "Mexican Soldiers Wage Bloody Battle with Gang," *New York Times*, June 30, 2014.

Arias De Leon, Delia M. "Ayotzinapa: For Better or Worse, Mexico's Turning Point," *Huffingtonpost.com*, November 19, 2014.

Ashby, Paul. (2013) *NAFTA-Land Security: The Mérida Initiative and U.S. Security Projection in Mexico*. Kent, UK.

Associated Press. "Mexican President Backs Off Drug Decriminalization Bill," *Foxnews.com*, May 4, 2006.

———. "Obama, Calderon Pledge Cooperation on Drug Wars: Amid Heightened Tensions, U.S. And Mexico Look to Repair Relations," *Nbcnews.com*, March 4, 2011.

———. "Lazcano's Autopsy: 2 Shots in Head the Killed Mexican Drug Lord," *Voxxi.com*, October 12, 2012.

———. "New Mexican President Could Target Small Gangs," *Foxnews.com*, July 5, 2012.

———. "Drug Empire Will Survive without 'El Chapo,'" *Usatoday.com*, February 25, 2014.

———. "'I've Had Enough,' Says Mexican Attorney General in Missing Students Gaffe," *Theguardian.com*, November 8, 2014.

———. "Mexico Creates Special Federal Force of 5,000 Gendarmes to Combat Widespread Economic Crime," *Foxnews.com*, August 22, 2014.

Astorga, Luís. "Drug Trafficking in Mexico: A First General Assessment: Discussion Paper No. 36," *UNESCO Management of Social Transformations*, 1999.

——. (2001) "Organized Crime and the Organization of Crime." In *Organized Crime and Democratic Governability: Mexico and the U.S.-Mexican Borderlands*, edited by Bailey, John and Roy Goodson. Pittsburgh, PA.

——. (2004) "Mexico: Drugs and Politics." In *The Political Economy of the Drug Industry: Latin America and the International System*, edited by Vellinga, Menno. Gainesville, FL.

AutoObserver Staff. "Navistar Says Mexico Violence Could Cause Pullout," *Edmunds.com*, September 9, 2011.

Avalos, Stephanie. "Final Presentation, Group 7: Cell Phone Use in Mexico," *Prezi.com*, May 6, 2013.

Bagley, Bruce and Woodrow Wilson International Center for Scholars: Latin American Program. (2012) *Drug Trafficking and Organized Crime in the Americas: Major Trends in the Twenty-First Century*. San Diego, CA.

Bailey, John J. and Roy Goodson. (2000) *Organized Crime & Democratic Governability: Mexico and the U.S.-Mexican Borderlands*. Pittsburgh, PA.

Balderrama, Francisco E. and Raymond Rodriguez. (2006) *Decade of Betrayal: Mexican Repatriation in the 1930s*. Albuquerque, NM.

BBC News. "Mayor of Mexico Port City Arrested over 'Cartel Links,'" *Bbc.com*, April 29, 2014.

Beittel, June S. "Mexico's Drug Trafficking Organizations: Source and Scope of the Violence," *Congressional Research Service*, April 15, 2013.

Bender, Steven. (2012) *Run for the Border: Vice and Virtue in U.S.-Mexico Border Crossings*. New York.

Bertram, Eva. (1996) *Drug War Politics: The Price of Denial*. Berkeley, CA.

Bewley-Taylor, David R. (2002) *United States and International Drug Control, 1909-1997*. New York.

Booth, William. "Mexico's Crime Wave Has Left About 25,000 Missing, Government Documents Show," *Washington Post*, November 29, 2012.

——. "Senate Report Says Mexico Must Focus on Cops and Courts, Not Army," *Washington Post*, July 11, 2012.

Booth, William and Nick Miroff. "Mexico's President-Elect Wants Close Security Ties with U.S., with Limits," *Washington Post*, July 5, 2012.

Borderland Beat Reporter "Buggs." "Knights Templar—Caballeros Templarios," *Borderlandbeat.com*, June 13, 2009.

———. "La Familia Michoacana," *Borderlandbeat.com*, May 11, 2009.

Borderland Beat Reporter "Chivis." "Mexico's Presidential Election: Drugwar Security Plan of Each Candidate," *Borderlandbeat.com*, February 8, 2012.

———. "Narco Homicides: 'The Real' Number 100-200+ Thousand," *Borderlandbeat .com*, August 19, 2012.

———. "The Juarez Cartel Sinks into Oblivion since the Death of Rodolfo Carrillo Fuentes," *Borderlandbeat.com*, September 18, 2013.

———. "Analysis: Sinaloa Cartel Losing Power in Juárez," *Borderlandbeat.com*, April 18, 2014.

———. "Coahuila: A Drug Summit of Z's, BLO, CJNG Juarez Cartels Seeking an Alliance," *Borderlandbeat.com*, August 29, 2014.

———. "Dr. Mireles May Be Released on September 17th," *Borderlandbeat.com*, September 12, 2014.

———. "Michoacán Hit with Record Breaking Crime, Circuit Court Allows Appeal, Mireles Sends Second Message," *Borderlandbeat.com*, August 9, 2014.

———. "Tuta Message to Michoacán: 'We Have Suffered Painful Casualties, but We Are Still Standing,'" *Borderlandbeat.com*, September 10, 2014.

———. "Video: Televisa and Esquema Journalists Give La Tuta 'PR Advice' against AD, Tuta Gives Them Money," *Borderlandbeat.com*, September 22, 2014.

Borderland Beat Reporter "Itzli." "The Pineda Villa Clan," *Borderlandbeat.com*, October 24, 2014.

Borderland Beat Reporter "Tijuano." "The War for Tijuana, a 20+ Year Conflict, Part 3," *Borderlandbeat.com*, August 15, 2013.

Borderland Beat Reporter "Un Vato." "Pena Nieto Has Been Unable to Decrease Homicides," *Borderlandbeat.com*, August 25, 2014.

Borderland Beat Reporter "Un Vato" and El Diario/Proceso. "Their Dreams Ended in the San Fernando Massacre," *Borderlandbeat.com*, August 24, 2012.

Borderland Beat Reporter "Un Vato" and Jose Gil Olmos. "Fausto Vallejo: A Governor of the Narco and for the Narco," *Borderlandbeat.com*, June 24, 2014.

Borderland Beat Reporter "ValorxTruth." "The Autodefensas of Tierra Caliente and the Example of Cherán," *Borderlandbeat.com*, January 30, 2014.

Bowden, Charles and Julián Cardona. (2010) *Murder City: Ciudad Juárez and the Global Economy's New Killing Fields*. New York.

Bright, Kimberly J. "Narcocorridos: The Outlawed Commercial Jingles of Violent Mexican Drug Lords," *Dangerousminds.net*, August 27, 2013.

Brooks, Emily. (2013) Marijuana in La Guardia's New York City: The Mayor's Committee on Marijuana and Federal Policy, 1938–1945. New York.

Brownfield, William R. "Trends in Global Drug Policy," *Fpc.state.gov*, October 9, 2014.

Calderón, Felipe. "Todos Somos Juarez: An Innovative Strategy to Tackle Violence and Crime," *Harvard Kennedy School: Latin America Policy Journal*, 2013.

Campbell, Howard. (2011) "No End in Sight: Violence in Ciudad Juarez." *NACLA Report on the Americas* 44: 19–38.

——. (2012) "Narco-Propaganda in the Mexican 'Drug War': An Anthropological Perspective." *Latin American Perspectives* 41: 60–77.

Campo-Flores, Arian and Zusha Elinson. "Heroin Use, and Deaths, Rise: The Death of Philip Seymour Hoffman from an Apparent Heroin Overdose Underscores the Drug's Resurgence," *Wall Street Journal*, February 3, 2014.

Campos, Isaac. (2012*) Home Grown: Marijuana and the Origins of Mexico's War on Drugs*. Chapel Hill, NC.

Carless, Will. "5 Key Takeaways from Uruguay's Push to Legalize Marijuana," *Globalpost.com*, August 1, 2013.

Carlsen, Laura. "Congress Sends Drug War South, Taxpayer Money to Defense Firms," *Huffingtonpost.com*, June 20, 2009.

——. "Mexico's Oil Privatization: Risky Business," *Fpif.org*, May 27, 2014.

Carroll, Rebecca. (2004) "Under the Influence: Harry Anslinger's Role in Shaping America's Drug Policy." In *Federal Drug Control: The Evolution of Policy and Practice*, edited by Erlen, Jonathon and Joseph F. Spillane. New York.

Carruth, Bruce, and Nicholas Rowe. (2011) Mexico's Oportunidades: Conditional Cash Transfers as the Solution to Global Poverty? Claremont, CA.

Cave, Damien. "How a Kingpin above the Law Fell, Incredibly, without a Shot," *New York Times*, February 23, 2014.

Cawley, Marguerite. "Groups Ask International Criminal Court to Investigate Mexico Military Atrocities," *Insightcrime.org*, September 15, 2014.

Centers for Disease Control and Prevention. "Adult Cigarette Smoking in the United States: Current Estimates," *Cdc.gov*, February 14, 2014.

——. "Fact Sheets: Alcohol Use and Your Health," *Cdc.gov*, August 19, 2014.

——. (2014) "Increases in Heroin Overdose Deaths—28 States, 2010 to 2012." *Morbidity and Mortality Weekly Report* 63: 849–54.

——. "Smoking & Tobacco Use: Fast Facts," *Cdc.gov*, April 24, 2014.

Chapa, Sergio. "Border Battleground Series—Day Two: Living on the Edge: Deaths Mounting on Mexico's Border Security Watch," *The Brownsville Herald*, August 14, 2005.

——. "San Fernando Body Count Climbs to 193," *Valleycentral.com*, June 7, 2011.

Chesnut, R. Andrew. (2012) *Devoted to Death: Santa Muerte, the Skeleton Saint.* New York.

Chicago Alliance Against Racist and Political Repression. "Summary of the Draft Legislation for an Elected Civilian Police Accountability Council Enabling Prosecution of Criminal Police Abuse of Human Rights," *Naarpr.org*, October 2, 2013.

Collins, Michael. "U.S. State Dept. Calls for Reforming International Treaties That Support the Global Drug War," *Drugpolicy.org*, October 16, 2014.

Committee to Protect Journalists. "Valentín Valdés Espinosa: Zócalo De Saltillo, January 8, 2010, in Saltillo, Mexico," *Cpj.org*, January 2010.

Corcoran, Katherine. "How a Ruthless Cartel Was Beaten," *Associated Press*, November 9, 2013.

——. "Top Mexico Cartel to Keep on Despite Capo Capture," *Bigstory.ap.org*, February 25, 2014.

Corcoran, Patrick. "What Mexico's Elections Mean for Crime Policy: Part I," *Insightcrime.org*, July 19, 2012.

——. "What Mexico's Elections Mean for Crime Policy: Part II," *Insightcrime.org*, July 19, 2012.

Corkery, Michael and Elisabeth Malkin. "Citigroup Says Mexican Subsidiary Was Defrauded of as Much as $400 Million," *Dealbook.nytimes.com*, February 28, 2014.

Council on Hemispheric Affairs. "A Perspective on President Calderón's Militarized 'Drug Conflict,'" *Truth-out.org*, February 22, 2011.

Courtwright, David T. (2001) *Dark Paradise: A History of Opiate Addiction in America.* Cambridge, MA.

Craig, Richard B. (1978) "La Campana Permanente: Mexico's Antidrug Campaign." *Journal of Interamerican Studies and World Affairs* 20: 107–31.

——. (1980) "Operation Condor: Mexico's Antidrug Campaign Enters a New Era." *Journal of Interamerican Studies and World Affairs* 22: 345–63.

Daly, Michael. "Mexico's First Lady of Murder Is on the Lam," *Thedailybeast.com*, October 29, 2014.

Davidson, Thomas S. II. "Operation Secure Mexico," *Foreign Military Studies Office*, June 2005.

Deibert, Michael. (2014) *In the Shadow of Saint Death: The Gulf Cartel and the Price of America's Drug War in Mexico*. Guilford, CT.

Dellios, Hugh. "Draft Faults Presidents in 'Dirty War': Conclusions of Mexico's Probe into 1960s and '70s Atrocities Are Leaked before Being Sent to President Fox Because of Concerns the Final Report Might Be Toned Down," *Chicago Tribune*, February 28, 2006.

Dorocki, Sławomir and Paweł Brzegowy. (2014) "The Maquiladora Industry Impact on the Social and Economic Situation in Mexico in the Era of Globalization." In *Environmental and Socio-Economic Transformations in Developing Areas as the Effect of Globalization*, edited by Wójtowicz, Mirosław and Anna Winiarczyk-Raźniak. Kraków, Poland.

Doyle, Kate. (2006) Impunity's Triumph: The Failure of Mexico's Special Prosecutor. Washington, DC.

——. "Draft Report Documents 18 Years of 'Dirty War' in Mexico: Special Prosecutor: State Responsible for Hundreds of Killings, Disappearances," *National Security Archive Electronic Briefing Book*, February 26, 2006.

Drukier, Wendy. (1996) "Understanding Mobilization: Urban Popular Movements and Mexico's Lost Decade." Thesis, Carleton University.

Dudley, Steven. "Zeta Testimony Solves Mystery of Mexico Bus Massacres," *Insightcrime.org*, June 27, 2011.

——. "Why Mexico Police Reform Could Defeat Even Colombia's Ex–Top Cop," *Insightcrime.org*, July 19, 2012.

——. "'Chapo' Guzman Capture Provides Glimpse of Mexico's Past, Future," *Insightcrime.org*, February 22, 2014.

Dudley, Steven and Sandra Rodriguez. "Civil Society, the Government and the Development of Citizen Security," *Wilson Center: Mexico Institute*, August 2013.

Edmonds-Poli, Emily. "The Effects of Drug-War Related Violence on Mexico's Press and Democracy," *Wilson Center: Mexico Institute*, April 2013.

Eisenstadt, Todd A. and Alejandro Poiré. (2006) Explaining the Credibility Gap in Mexico's 2006 Presidential Election, Despite Strong (Albeit Perfectable) Electoral Institutions. Washington, DC.

Ellingwood, Ken. "Mexico's President Calderon Has Few Choices in Drug War," *Los Angeles Times*, October 1, 2008.

Epatko, Larisa. "Legalizing Drugs: Why Some Latin American Leaders Are Ok with It," *Pbs.org*, April 16, 2012.

Epstein, Edward Jay. (1990) *Agency of Fear: Opiates and Political Power in America*. London.

Erlen, Jonathon and Joseph F. Spillane. (2004) *Federal Drug Control: The Evolution of Policy and Practice*. New York.

Estévez, Ariadna. (2008) *Human Rights and Free Trade in Mexico: A Discursive and Sociopolitical Perspective*. New York.

Estévez, Dolia. (2010) "Protecting Press Freedom in an Environment of Violence and Impunity." In *Shared Responsibility: U.S.-Mexico Policy Options for Confronting Organized Crime*, edited by Olson, Eric L., David A. Shirk, and Andrew Selee. San Diego, CA.

Estrella, Alfredo. "Mexico Dissolves Equivalent of FBI," *Za.news.yahoo.com*, July 27, 2012.

Farooq, Umar and Connor Guy. "The Movement for Peace and Justice in Mexico," *The Nation*, June 5, 2012.

Ferragut, Sergio. (2007) *A Silent Nightmare: The Bottom Line and the Challenge of Illicit Drugs*. Reston, VA.

Finnegan, William. "Silver or Lead: The Drug Cartel La Familia," *The New Yorker*, May 31, 2010.

———. "The Drug War and Mexico's Election," *The New Yorker*, July 2, 2012.

Flannery, Nathaniel Parish. "Mexico: Is the Aztec Tiger Starting to Whimper?," *Forbes.com*, August 27, 2013.

Fox, Edward. "Mexico Military Sees over 56,000 Desertions under Calderon," *Insightcrime.org*, April 19, 2012.

Friedman, Thomas L. "How Mexico Got Back in the Game," *New York Times*, February 23, 2013.

Frontera NorteSur News. "Rage and Fury Sweep Mexico, the World: Justice for Ayotzinapa," *Fnsnews.nmsu.edu*, October 10, 2014.

Frontline. "Interview: Guillermo González Calderoni," *Pbs.org*, January 2001.

Gagne, David. "Amnesty Tracks Rise of Torture in Mexico," *Insightcrime.org*, September 5, 2014.

Gardner, David. "Captured with $2million in Cash, the Drugs Baron Who Stewed Enemies in Boiling Oil and Beheaded Hundreds," *Daily Mail UK*, July 16, 2013.

Gaspar de Alba, Alicia and Georgina Guzmán. (2010) *Making a Killing: Femicide, Free Trade, and La Frontera*. Austin, TX.

Gibler, John. (2011) *To Die in Mexico: Dispatches from inside the Drug War*. San Francisco, CA.

——. "The Disappeared: The Story of September 26, 2014, the Day 43 Mexican Students Went Missing—and How It Might Be a Turning Point for the Country," *The California Sunday Magazine*, January 4, 2015.

Global Commission on Drug Policy. (2011) *Report of the Global Commission on Drug Policy*. Rio de Janeiro, Brazil.

——. (2014) Taking Control: Pathways to Drug Policies That Work. Rio de Janeiro, Brazil.

Global Direct Investment Solutions. "Ciudad Juarez, Chihuahua, Mexico: fDi City of the Future 2007 / 2008," *Gdi-solutions.com*, April 23, 2007.

Gobernanza Forense Ciudadana. "Gobernanza Forense Ciudadana: Video," *Gobernanzaforense.org*, June 5, 2014.

Gomez, Robert. (2012) A New Visual Regime: Narco Warfare through Social Media. San Francisco, CA.

González de Bustamante, Celeste. (2012) *"Muy Buenas Noches": Mexico, Television, and the Cold War*. Lincoln, NE.

Goodman, Adam. "Mexico Economic Reality Doesn't Fit 'Aztec Tiger' Narrative," *America.aljazeera.com*, November 14, 2013.

——. "A Long Series of Uncertainties," *The Nation*, September 22, 2014.

Goodman, J. David. "In Mexico, Social Media Become a Battleground in the Drug War," *Thelede.blogs.nytimes.com*, September 15, 2011.

Gould, Jens Erik. "Mexico Oil: Awakening the 'Aztec Tiger,'" *Thefinancialist.com*, June 23, 2014.

Graham, David. "Chinese Iron Trade Fuels Port Clash with Mexican Drug Cartel," *Reuters.com*, January 1, 2014.

Grant, Will. "Heriberto Lazcano: The Fall of a Mexican Drug Lord," *Bbc.com*, October 13, 2012.

Grayson, George W. "Los Zetas: The Ruthless Army Spawned by a Mexican Drug Cartel," *Foreign Policy Research Institute*, May 2008.

———. (2010) *La Familia Drug Cartel: Implications for U.S.-Mexican Security*. Carlisle, PA.

———. (2011) *Threat Posed by Mounting Vigilantism in Mexico*. Carlisle, PA.

———. (2013) *The Impact of President Felipe Calderón's War on Drugs on the Armed Forces: The Prospects for Mexico's "Militarization" and Bilateral Relations*. Carlisle, PA.

———. (2014) *The Cartels: The Story of Mexico's Most Dangerous Criminal Organizations and Their Impact on U.S. Security*. Santa Barbara, CA.

Grayson, George W. and Samuel Logan. (2012) *The Executioner's Men: Los Zetas, Rogue Soldiers, Criminal Entrepreneurs, and the Shadow State They Created*. New Brunswick, NJ.

Greenwald, Glenn. (2009) Drug Decriminalization in Portugal: Lessons for Creating Fair and Successful Drug Policies. Washington, DC.

Grillo, Ioan. "Drug Cartels to Mexican Businesses: Pay Up," *Globalpost.com*, December 14, 2009.

———. (2011) *El Narco: Inside Mexico's Criminal Insurgency*. New York.

———. "Mexico's Ex-President Vicente Fox: Legalize Drugs," *TIME*, January 19, 2011.

———. "Calderon's Legacy of Blood and Busts," *Globalpost.com*, November 30, 2012.

———. "Mexico's Zetas Rewrite Drug War in Blood," *Reuters.com*, May 23, 2012.

———. "Mexican Vigilantes Beat Back Ruthless Knights Templar Cartel," *TIME*, January 29, 2014.

———. "Mexico's Cartel-Fighting Vigilantes Get Closer to Texas Border," *Nbcnews.com*, July 9, 2014.

———. "Mexico's Craziest Drug Lord 'Died' Twice and Used to Dress as God," *TIME*, March 11, 2014.

———. "Mexico's Deadly Narco-Politics," *New York Times*, October 9, 2014.

——. "Mexico's Drug War Leads to Kidnappings, Vigilante Violence," *TIME*, January 17, 2014.

——. "Tourists Are Pouring Back to Mexican Beaches after a Security Image Facelift," *Globalpost.com*, August 31, 2014.

Grillo, Ioan and Dolly Mascareñas. "Mexico Goes after the Narcos—before They Join the Gangs: The Country's Latest Addition to Its Anticrime Strategy Is Stopping Kids from Joining Cartels," *TIME*, February 25, 2013.

Guillermoprieto, Alma. "A Hundred Women," *The New Yorker*, September 29, 2003.

——. "Mexico: 'We Are Not Sheep to Be Killed,'" *New York Review of Books*, November 5, 2014.

Gutierrez, Raul. "Leaking Secrets, Leaking Blood: Blog Del Narco, the Anonymous Tracker of Mexico's Ultraviolent Drug War," *Boingboing.net*, September 14, 2010.

Heinle, Kimberly, Octavio Rodríguez Ferreira, and David A. Shirk. (2014) *Drug Violence in Mexico: Data and Analysis through 2013*. San Diego, CA.

Hennessey, Kathleen and Tracy Wilkinson. "Obama, Visiting Mexico, Shifts Focus from Drug War," *Los Angeles Times*, May 2, 2013.

Henry, James S. "The Theft of Mexico: How the 1988 Mexican Presidential Election Was Rigged," *Bloodbankers.typepad.com*, March 10, 2004.

Hernández, Anabel. (2013) *Narcoland: The Mexican Drug Lords and Their Godfathers*. London.

Hickey, Walter. "How the Gun Industry Funnels Tens of Million of Dollars to the NRA," *Business Insider*, January 16, 2013.

Hodges, Donald Clark and Ross Gandy. (2002) *Mexico under Siege: Popular Resistance to Presidential Despotism*. New York.

Holden, Stephen. "Singing of the Cartels, and Investigating Them: 'Narco Cultura,' a Documentary About Music and Drug Cartels," *New York Times*, November 21, 2013.

Hollersen, Wiebke. "'This Is Working': Portugal, 12 Years after Decriminalizing Drugs," *Der Spiegel Online International*, March 27, 2013.

Hootsen, Jan-Albert. "'Blood Avocados': The Dark Side of Your Guacamole," *Vocativ.com*, November 18, 2013.

Horwitz, Sari and Joshua Partlow. "U.S. And Mexican Authorities Detail Coordinated Effort to Capture Drug Lord," *Washington Post*, February 23, 2014.

Imison, Paul. "The Ultimate Mexican Hype Machine: The Myth of the Aztec Tiger," *Counterpunch.org*, March 29–31, 2013.

Inside Story Americas. "Is Mexico's War on Drugs Close to a Real End?," *Aljazeera.com*, February 15, 2013.

International Center for Analysis of Transnational Criminal Networks. "Conferenza Roma: Video," *Scivortex.org*, March 26, 2013.

Jacobs, James, Coleen Friel, and Robert Radick. (2001) *Gotham Unbound: How New York City Was Liberated from the Grip of Organized Crime*. New York.

Jacobs, Ron. "A War on People: Drug Wars and Neoliberalism," *Counterpunch.org*, December 19–21, 2014.

Jacobson, Roberta S. "Merida Initiative: Remarks," *State.gov*, April 22, 2010.

Jamasmie, Cecilia. "Mexican Police Seized 68,000 Tonnes of Iron Ore Mined by Drug Lords," *Mining.com*, May 5, 2014.

Jimenez, Guillermo. "Mass Graves, Murderous State-Cartel Alliance Revealed in Guerrero: Hundreds of Bodies Found near Iguala, Mexico, but Not the 43 Students," *Panampost.com*, October 30, 2014.

Kane, Michael. "Peña Nieto Discusses Proposed Security Force," *Insightcrime.org*, July 19, 2012.

Karlin, Mark. "Fueled by War on Drugs, Mexican Death Toll Could Exceed 120,000 as Calderon Ends Six-Year Reign," *Truth-out.org*, November 28, 2012.

Keefe, Patrick Radden. "Cocaine Incorporated," *New York Times Magazine*, June 15, 2012.

Kenny, Paul, Mónica Serrano, and Arturo Sotomayor. (2012) *Mexico's Security Failure: Collapse into Criminal Violence*. New York.

King, Nicole B. (2007) "An Economic History of Modern Ciudad Juarez, 1960–2006." Thesis, University of Texas at El Paso.

Knowlton, Brian. "At White House, Fox Urges Accord on Workers," *New York Times*, September 6, 2001.

Krauze, Enrique. (1997) *Mexico: Biography of Power: A History of Modern Mexico, 1810–1996*. New York.

——. "Mexico's Barbarous Tragedy," *New York Times*, November 10, 2014.

Krauze, Enrique and Hank Heifetz. "Mexico at War," *New York Review of Books*, September 27, 2012.

Kuzmarov, Jeremy. (2009) *The Myth of the Addicted Army: Vietnam and the Modern War on Drugs*. Amherst, MA.

Kyvig, David E. (2000) *Repealing National Prohibition*. Kent, OH.

La Botz, Dan. "Financial Crisis Hits Mexico: Social Crisis on the Horizon?," *Monthly Review*, October 8, 2008.

Latin American Commission on Drugs and Democracy. (2009) *Drugs and Democracy: Toward a Paradigm Shift*. Rio de Janeiro, Brazil.

Lee, Martin A. "Let a Thousand Flowers Bloom: The Populist Politics of Cannabis Reform," *The Nation*, November 18, 2013.

Leland, John and Mosi Secret. "For Pot Inc., the Rush to Cash in Is Underway: A Competition to Get a Medical Marijuana License in New York," *New York Times*, October 31, 2014.

Lerner, Michael A. (2007) *Dry Manhattan: Prohibition in New York City*. Cambridge, MA.

Levine, Harry. "The Scandal of Racist Marijuana Arrests," *The Nation*, November 18, 2013.

Livingston, Jessica. (2004) "Murder in Juarez: Gender, Sexual Violence, and the Global Assembly Line." *Frontiers: A Journal of Women Studies* 25: 59–76.

Logan, Samuel. (2012) "The Future of Los Zetas after the Death of Heriberto Lazcano." *CTC Sentinel* 5: 6–9.

Lohmuller, Michael. "Is Tamaulipas Becoming Peña Nieto's Ciudad Juárez?," *Coha. org*, May 27, 2014.

Longmire, Sylvia. "Mexico's Drug War—TCO 101: The Juarez Cartel," *Borderviolenceanalysis.typepad.com*, June 2009.

——. (2013) *Cartel: The Coming Invasion of Mexico's Drug Wars*. New York.

——. (2014) *Border Insecurity: Why Big Money, Fences, and Drones Aren't Making Us Safer*. New York.

López, Enrique. "The Pineda Clan: A Criminal Dynasty in Mexico," *Dw.de*, October 24, 2014.

López, Oscar. "Mexican Drug War News: DEA Reveals Cartels Use Drones to Transport Drugs from Mexico into US," *Latintimes.com*, July 10, 2014.

Lupsha, Peter A. and Kip Schlegel. (1980) The Political Economy of Drug Trafficking: The Herrera Organization (Mexico & the United States). Albuquerque, NM.

Mabry, Donald J. "Father of a Mexican President: Luis Calderón Vega," *Historicaltextarchive.com*, July 18, 2006.

Marentes, Luis A. "Returning Migrants and the Michoacán Autodefensas: An Entangled Past, Present, and Future," *Huffingtonpost.com*, February 3, 2014.

Marks, Josh. "NRA's Top 5 Gun Industry Donors," *Nationalmemo.com*, January 11, 2013.

Martínez, Chivis. "You F***** with me, so I will have the pleasure of killing you"…said mayor of Iguala before shooting activist," *Borderlandbeat.com*, October 5, 2014.

Marquis, Christopher. "A Spicy Welcome to the White House," *New York Times*, September 6, 2001.

Martínez, Oscar. (2011) "The Border: Funneling Migrants to Their Doom." *NACLA Report on the Americas* 44: 5–8.

———. (2013) *The Beast: Riding the Rails and Dodging Narcos on the Migrant Trail*. London.

Mazzetti, Mark and Ginger Thompson. "U.S. Widens Role in Mexican Fight," *New York Times*, August 25, 2011.

McCleskey, Claire O'Neill. (2012) "Fighting for the *Plaza* and the Pueblo: Assessing the Role of 'Hearts and Minds' in the Mexican Drug Conflict." Thesis, Georgetown University.

McCoy, Alfred W. (2003) *The Politics of Heroin: CIA Complicity in the Global Drug Trade: Afghanistan, Southeast Asia, Central America, Colombia*. Chicago, IL.

McDougal, Topher, David A. Shirk, Robert Muggah, et al. (2013) *The Way of the Gun: Estimating Firearms Traffic Across the U.S.-Mexico Border*. San Diego, CA.

McKinley, James C. Jr. "With Beheadings and Attacks, Drug Gangs Terrorize Mexico," *New York Times*, October 26, 2006.

McWilliams, John C. (1990) *The Protectors: Harry J. Anslinger and the Federal Bureau of Narcotics, 1930–1962*. Newark, DE.

Meyer, Maureen, Coletta Youngers, and Dave Bewley-Taylor. "At a Crossroads: Drug Trafficking, Violence and the Mexican State," *Beckley Foundation & Washington Office on Latin America*, November 2007.

Miroff, Nick. "Tracing the U.S. Heroin Surge Back South of the Border as Mexican Cannabis Output Falls," *Washington Post*, April 6, 2014.

Miroff, Nick and William Booth. "Mexico's Drug War Is at a Stalemate as Calderon's Presidency Ends," *Washington Post*, November 27, 2012.

Miron, Jeffrey A. "The Budgetary Implications of Marijuana Prohibition," *Prohibitioncosts.org*, June 2005.

Molzahn, Cory, Octavio Rodriguez Ferreira, and David A. Shirk. (2013) *Drug Violence in Mexico: Data and Analysis through 2012*. San Diego, CA.

Moore, Gary. "Ending the Zetas Killing Spree: An Invisible Success Story," *Insightcrime.org*, September 22, 2011.

——. "Unravelling Mysteries of Mexico's San Fernando Massacre," *Borderlandbeat .com*, September 19, 2011.

——. "Gaze Not on the Face of Evil: Massacre by Assembly Line," *Garymoore22 .wordpress.com*, May 26, 2012.

Moreno, Alejandro. (2007) "The 2006 Mexican Presidential Election: The Economy, Oil Revenues, and Ideology." *PS: Political Science and Politics* 40: 15–19.

MSNBC News Services. "Fox Balks at Signing Drug Decriminalization Law: Mexican President Wants Changes in Measure He Previously Said He'd Sign," *Nbcnews.com*, May 3, 2006.

MSNBC Staff. "Blogger on Mexico Cartel Beheading: 'Cannot Kill Us All,'" *Nbcnews.com*, November 10, 2011.

Musto, David F. and Pamela Korsmeyer. (2002) *The Quest for Drug Control: Politics and Federal Policy in a Period of Increasing Substance Abuse, 1963–1981*. New Haven, CT.

National Institute on Alcohol Abuse and Alcoholism. "Alcohol Facts and Statistics," *Niaaa.nih.gov*, July 2014.

Nazario, Sonia. "The Children of the Drug Wars: A Refugee Crisis, Not an Immigration Crisis," *New York Times*, July 11, 2014.

Niblo, Stephen R. (1999) *Mexico in the 1940s: Modernity, Politics, and Corruption*. Wilmington, DE.

Noriega, Roger F. and Felipe Trigos. "Why Isn't Mexico's Security Strategy Working?," *Aei.org*, June 12, 2014.

North American Congress on Latin America. (2011) "Introduction Mexico's Drug Crisis: Alternative Perspectives." *NACLA Report on the Americas* 44: 12–13.

O'Neil, Shannon K. (2013) "Mexico Makes It: A Transformed Society, Economy, and Government." *Foreign Affairs* 92: 52–63.

O'Reilly, Andrew. "Mexico's Drug Death Toll Double What Reported, Expert Argues," *Latino.foxnews.com*, August 10, 2012.

Obama, Barack. "Remarks by the President to the People of Mexico: Anthropology Museum, Mexico City, Mexico," *Whitehouse.gov*, May 3, 2013.

Ochoa, Enrique C. and Gilda L. Ochoa. "The Ties That Bind: Ferguson and Ayotzinapa," *Counterpunch.org*, December 12–14, 2014.

Olson, Eric L., David A. Shirk, and Andrew Selee. (2010) Shared Responsibility: U.S.-Mexico Policy Options for Confronting Organized Crime. San Diego, CA.

OpenNet Initiative. "Mexico (2013): Opennet Initiative Country Profile," *Opennet .net*, July 15, 2013.

Osorno, Diego Enrique. "How a Mexican Cartel Demolished a Town, Incinerated Hundreds of Victims, and Got Away with It," *News.vice.com*, December 31, 2014.

Pachico, Elyssa. "How the Beltran Leyva, Sinaloa Cartel Feud Bloodied Mexico," *Insightcrime.org*, February 1, 2011.

Padgett, Tim. "Mexico's New Boom: Why the World Should Tone Down the Hype," *TIME*, March 8, 2013.

Padgett, Tim and Ioan Grillo. "Mexico's Meth Warriors," *TIME*, June 28, 2010.

Paley, Dawn. (2014) *Drug War Capitalism*. Oakland, CA.

Pansters, W.G. (2012) *Violence, Coercion, and State-Making in Twentieth-Century Mexico: The Other Half of the Centaur*. Stanford, CA.

Pantaleo, Katherine. (2010) "Gendered Violence: An Analysis of the Maquiladora Murders." *International Criminal Justice Review* 20: 349–65.

Payan, Tony, Kathleen A. Staudt, and Z. Anthony Kruszewski. (2013) *A War That Can't Be Won: Binational Perspectives on the War on Drugs*. Tucson, AZ.

Philip, George and Susana Berruecos. (2012) *Mexico's Struggle for Public Security: Organized Crime and State Responses*. New York.

Pineda, Leticia. "Mexico Arrests Beltran Leyva Cartel Chief," *News.yahoo.com*, October 2, 2014.

Planning Division of the Development Services Department of the City of El Paso. "El Paso–Juarez Regional Historic Population Summary," *Elpasotexas.gov*, August 2007.

Poppa, Terrence E. (1990) *Drug Lord: The Life and Death of a Mexican Kingpin: A True Story*. New York.

Preston, Julia and Randal C. Archibold. "U.S. Moves to Stop Surge in Illegal Immigration," *New York Times*, June 20, 2014.

Preston, Julia and Sam Dillon. (2004) *Opening Mexico: The Making of a Democracy.* New York.

Priest, Dana. "U.S. Role at a Crossroads in Mexico's Intelligence War on the Cartels," *Washington Post*, April 27, 2013.

Pueblita, Jose Carlos R. (2013) Screening Seguro Popular: The Political Economy of Universal Health Coverage in Mexico. Cambridge, MA.

Ramsey, Geoffrey. "U.S. Legalization Takes a Toll on Mexico Drug Profits," *Thepanamericanpost.com*, December 3, 2014.

Recio, Gabriela. (2002) "Drugs and Alcohol: US Prohibition and the Origins of the Drug Trade in Mexico, 1910–1930." *Journal of Latin American Studies* 34: 21–42.

Reding, Andrew. "Favorite Son," *Mother Jones*, November 1988.

——. "How to Steal an Election: Mexico, 1988," *Mother Jones*, November 1988.

Redmond, Helen. "The Political Economy of Mexico's Drug War," *International Socialist Review*, July 2013.

Reporters Without Borders. (2013) 2013 World Press Freedom Index: Dashed Hopes after Spring. Paris.

Reuters. "2 Mexican Policemen Beheaded in Acapulco: Drug Gangs Eyed as Likely Suspects," *Boston Globe*, April 21, 2006.

——. "Severed Head Found in Acapulco Marks Grisly Trend," *The New Zealand Herald*, June 30, 2006.

——. "Mexico: Emotions Run High as Embattled President Felipe Calderon Meets Crusading Poet and Activist Javier Sicilia to Discuss the Nation's Descent into Violence and an Increasingly Unpopular Drugs War," *Itnsource.com*, October 15, 2011.

Riggs, Mike. "Obama's War on Pot," *The Nation*, October 30, 2013.

Rincón Parra, Juliana. "Mexico: Citizen Video and Drug Trafficking," *Globalvoicesonline.org*, August 10, 2010.

Robles, Frances. "Fleeing Gangs, Children Head to U.S. Border," *New York Times*, July 9, 2014.

Rodriguez, Olga R. "Hugo Hernandez: Mexico Cartel Stitches Rival's Face on Soccer Ball," *Huffingtonpost.com*, March 18, 2010.

Roig-Franzia, Manuel. "U.S. Officials Laud Transfer of Mexican Drug Suspects," *Washington Post*, January 21, 2007.

Rolles, Steve, George Murkin, Martin Powell, et al. (2012) *The Alternative World Drug Report: Counting the Costs of the War on Drugs*. Bristol, UK.

Romero, Simon. "Brazil Releases Report on Past Rights Abuses," *New York Times*, December 10, 2014.

Ross, John. (2009) *El Monstruo: Dread and Redemption in Mexico City*. New York.

Rowe, Thomas C. (2006) *Federal Narcotics Laws and the War on Drugs: Money Down a Rat Hole*. Binghamton, NY.

Sadler, Louis R. (2000) The Historical Dynamics of Smuggling in the U.S.-Mexican Border Region, 1550–1998. Pittsburgh, PA.

Saliba, Frédéric. "Les Troubadours Du Narcotrafic," *Lemonde.fr*, November 30, 2012.

Scenario Team of the Organization of American States. (2013) *Scenarios for the Drug Problem in the Americas, 2013–2025*. Washington, DC.

Schaffer Library of Drug Policy. "How Many People Are Actually Killed by Drugs?," *Druglibrary.org*, September 2006.

Schiller, Dane. "Mexican Crook: Gangsters Arrange Fights to Death for Entertainment," *Houston Chronicle*, June 11, 2011.

Schneider, Eric C. (2008) *Smack: Heroin and the American City*. Philadelphia, PA.

Scott, Peter Dale and Jonathan Marshall. (1998) *Cocaine Politics: Drugs, Armies, and the CIA in Central America*. Berkeley, CA.

Shannon, Elaine. (1989) *Desperados: Latin Drug Lords, U.S. Lawmen, and the War America Can't Win*. New York.

Shipley, Joe C. (2011) "What Have We Learned from the War on Drugs? An Assessment of Mexico's Counternarcotics Strategy." Thesis, Naval Postgraduate School.

Shirk, David A. and Center for Preventive Action. (2011) *The Drug War in Mexico: Confronting a Shared Threat*. New York.

Shirk, David, Duncan Wood, Eric L. Olson, et al., "Building Resilient Communities in Mexico: Civic Responses to Crime and Violence," *Wilson Center: Mexico Institute*, March 2014.

Sicilia, Javier. "Javier Sicilia's Open Letter to Mexico's Politicians and Criminals," *Narconews.com*, April 4, 2011.

Sidaoui, José, Manuel Ramos-Francia, and Gabriel Cuadra. "The Global Financial Crisis and Policy Response in Mexico," *Bank for International Settlements*, December 2010.

Simmons, William Paul. (2006) "Remedies for Women of Ciudad Juárez through the Inter-American Court of Human Rights." *Northwestern Journal of International Human Rights* 4: 492–517.

Simons, Marlise. "Mexican Rights Groups File Suit for 'Systematic and Widespread' Abuse by Army and Police," *New York Times*, September 12, 2014.

Sklair, Leslie. (1989) *Assembling for Development: The Maquila Industry in Mexico and the United States.* Boston, MA.

Smith, Benjamin T. "The End of the Drug War—or a New Cartel of Cartels?," *Dissent*, November 3, 2014.

Southwick, Natalie. "Can Mexico Break Knights Templar's Hold on Michoacan Port?," *Insightcrime.org*, November 5, 2013.

Staudt, Kathleen A., Tony Payan, and Z. Anthony Kruszewski. (2009) *Human Rights Along the U.S.-Mexico Border: Gendered Violence and Insecurity.* Tucson, AZ.

Steinberg, Nik. "Vanished: The Disappeared of Mexico's Drug War," *Human Rights Watch*, January 8, 2014.

Stevenson, Mark. "Mexican Candidates Tough on Drug Issue," *Washington Post*, June 18, 2006.

——. "At 20 Years, NAFTA Didn't Close Mexico Wage Gap," *Bigstory.ap.org*, December 31, 2013.

——. "Mexico Opens Debate over Low Minimum Wage," *Bigstory.ap.org*, August 8, 2014.

——. "Mexico to Draw Line on Vigilantes," *Bigstory.ap.org*, March 14, 2014.

Storrs, K. Larry. "Mexican Drug Certification Issues: U.S. Congressional Action, 1986–1998," *Congressional Research Service*, April 9, 1998.

Sugarmann, Josh, Ilana Goldman, Violence Policy Center, et al. (2013) *Blood Money II: How Gun Industry Dollars Fund the NRA.* Washington, DC.

Sugarmann, Josh, Marty Langley, and Violence Policy Center. (2011) *Blood Money: How the Gun Industry Bankrolls the NRA.* Washington, DC.

Sweig, Julia E. (2013) A Strategy to Reduce Gun Trafficking and Violence in the Americas: Council on Foreign Relations Policy Innovation Memorandum No. 36. New York.

Syal, Rajeev. "Drug Money Saved Banks in Global Crisis, Claims UN Advisor: Drugs and Crime Chief Says $352bn in Criminal Proceeds Was Effectively Laundered by Financial Institutions," *The Observer/The Guardian*, December 12, 2009.

Székely, Miguel. (1995) "Poverty in Mexico During Adjustment." *Review of Income and Wealth* 41: 331–48.

T. W. "Crime in Mexico: The Governor's Miraculous Achievement," *Economist.com*, September 22, 2011.

Tate, Katherine, James Lance Taylor, and Mark Q. Sawyer. (2013) *Something's in the Air: Race, Crime, and the Legalization of Marijuana*. New York.

Tegel, Simeon. "Can Bolivia Teach the US How to Fight Drugs?," *Globalpost.com*, March 24, 2013.

Thomasson, James, William Foster, and Laurence Press. (2002) *The Diffusion of the Internet in Mexico*. Austin, TX.

Thompson, Ginger. "Mexico President Urges U.S. To Act Soon on Migrants," *New York Times*, September 6, 2001.

———. "Rival Drug Gangs Turn the Streets of Nuevo Laredo into a War Zone," *New York Times*, December 4, 2005.

———. "Mexican Vote Hinges on Conflicted Middle Class," *New York Times*, July 2, 2006.

Thompson, Ginger, Randal C. Archibold, and Eric Schmitt. "Hand of U.S. Is Seen in Halting General's Rise in Mexico," *New York Times*, February 4, 2013.

Thomson, Adam. "Mexico: Aztec Tiger," *Ft.com*, January 30, 2013.

Timoshenkov, Miguel. "Criminals Winning, Guv Says 'México Seguro Is Ineffective,'" *Laredo Morning Times*, February 12, 2006.

Toro, María Celia. (1995) *Mexico's 'War' on Drugs: Causes and Consequences*. Boulder, CO.

Travis, Jeremy, Bruce Western, and Steve Redburn, eds. (2014) The Growth of Incarceration in the United States: Exploring Causes and Consequences. Washington, DC.

Tuckman, Jo. "Mexico Changes Stance in Drug War—but Little Difference Seen from Calderón: Mexico's President Enrique Peña Nieto Talks of End to Military Crackdown against Drug Cartels That Has Left up to 100,000 Dead," *Theguardian .com*, December 18, 2012.

——. "Mexican Drug Lord Nazario Moreno's Killing May End Knights Templar Cartel: It Seems 'the Craziest One,' Whose Death Had Been Announced before in 2010, Really Is Dead—Pleasing Anti-Cartel Vigilantes," *Theguardian.com*, March 10, 2014.

——. "Mexican Gang Suspected of Killing 43 Students Admits to Mass Murder," *Theguardian.com*, November 7, 2014.

——. "Mexican Police Injured in Acapulco During Protests over Student Massacre," *Theguardian.com*, November 10, 2014.

——. "Mexico: Protests at Admission That 43 Missing Students Were Massacred," *Theguardian.com*, November 9, 2014.

Turati, Marcela. "Death Threats, Then Red Tape: Exiled Mexican Journalists Face Red Tape and Doubt in U.S.," *New York Times*, June 21, 2014.

U.S. Department of State. "Mexico Travel Warning," *Travel.state.gov*, August 15, 2014.

U.S. Department of State and Bureau for International Narcotics and Law Enforcement Affairs. "2014 International Narcotics Control Strategy Report, Volume I: Country Report: Mexico," *State.gov*, March 2014.

Ulrichs, Martina and Keetie Roelen. (2012) Equal Opportunities for All?—a Critical Analysis of Mexico's Oportunidades. London.

UN News Centre. "UN Human Rights Office Concerned About Killing of Journalists in Mexico," *Un.org*, September 30, 2011.

Valentine, Douglas. (2006) *The Strength of the Wolf: The Secret History of America's War on Drugs*. London.

Veeravagu, Anand and Robert M. Lober. "Heroin: America's Silent Assassin," *Thedailybeast.com*, February 3, 2014.

Villarreal, M. Angeles. "The Mexican Economy after the Global Financial Crisis," *Congressional Research Service*, September 16, 2010.

——. "NAFTA and the Mexican Economy," *Congressional Research Service*, June 3, 2010.

Villegas, Paulina. "Mexican Drug Lord Taunts the Authorities with Videos," *New York Times*, July 31, 2014.

Villegas, Paulina and Randal C. Archibold. "Keeping Mexico's Revolutionary Fires Alive," *New York Times*, November 2, 2014.

Violence Policy Center. "National Rifle Association Receives Millions of Dollars from Gun Industry 'Corporate Partners' New VPC Report Reveals," *Vpc.org*, April 13, 2011.

Wald, Elijah. (2001) *Narcocorrido: A Journey into the Music of Drugs, Guns, and Guerrillas.* New York.

Walker, William O. (1989) *Drug Control in the Americas.* Albuquerque, NM.

——. (1996) *Drugs in the Western Hemisphere: An Odyssey of Cultures in Conflict.* Wilmington, DE.

——. "Narcotics Policy," *Encyclopedia of American Foreign Policy,* 2002.

Warner, Margaret. "Mexico's President-Elect: Legalization Should Be Part of Drug Strategy Debate," *Pbs.org,* July 3, 2012.

Watt, Peter and Roberto Zepeda Martínez. (2012) *Drug War Mexico: Politics, Neoliberalism and Violence in the New Narcoeconomy.* London.

Wedge, Captain Gary R. "Drug Decriminalization in Mexico," *California Commission on Peace Officer Standards and Training,* August 2007.

Wegman, Jesse. "The Injustice of Marijuana Arrests," *New York Times,* July 28, 2014.

Weinberg, Bill. (2008) "Guns: The U.S. Threat to Mexican National Security." *NACLA Report on the Americas* 41: 21–26, 38–39.

Weiner, Tim. "Mexico's Image Is Buffed and Tarnished with Military Drug Arrests," *New York Times,* April 7, 2001.

——. "Slump in U.S. Drags Mexico, and Fox's Agenda, Down," *New York Times,* August 21, 2001.

Weissenstein, Michael. "Mexico Pres Front-Runner Promises to Cut Violence," *Bigstory.ap.org,* May 25, 2012.

Weissmann, Jordan. "Whom Does the NRA Really Speak For?," *The Atlantic,* December 18, 2012.

White House Office of the Press Secretary. "Fact Sheet: U.S.-Mexico Partnership," *Whitehouse.gov,* May 2, 2013.

Whitehouse.gov. "President Obama's Trip to Mexico & Costa Rica: May 2–4, 2013," *Whitehouse.gov,* May 2013.

——. "A Drug Policy for the 21st Century," *Whitehouse.gov,* July 9, 2014.

Wilkinson, Tracy. "Governor in Mexico's Troubled Michoacan State Steps Down," *Los Angeles Times,* June 18, 2014.

Wilkinson, Tracy and Ken Ellingwood. "Mexico President-Elect Peña Nieto's Win Is Weaker Than Expected," *Los Angeles Times,* July 2, 2012.

Williams, Dennis A. and Sylvester Monroe. "Busting the Heroin Pipeline," *Newsweek*, May 22, 1978.

Wilson, Christopher and Gerardo Silva. "Mexico's Latest Poverty Stats," *Wilson Center: Mexico Institute*, August 12, 2013.

Worthman, Shaye. "The Rise of the La Familia Michoacana," *E-ir.info*, December 16, 2011.

Zabludovsky, Karla. "Reclaiming the Forests and the Right to Feel Safe," *New York Times*, August 2, 2012.

◆ ◆ ◆

Spanish

"Bases de datos sobre personas desaparecidas en México 2006–2012," *Desaparecidosenmexico.wordpress.com*, December 20, 2012.

"Tú y yo coincidimos en la noche terrible," *Nuestraaparenterendicion.com*, 2013.

"Tamaulipas, propiedad criminal," *El Diario de Coahuila*, January 26, 2014.

Adnpolitico.com. "5 Claves de cooperación Federal por violencia en Michoacán," *Adnpolitico.com*, January 13, 2014.

Aguilar Camín, Héctor. "La captura criminal del Estado," *Nexos.com.mx*, January 1, 2015.

Aguilar Camín, Héctor, Eduardo Guerrero, Alejandro Madrazo, et al. (2012) *El informe Jalisco: Más allá de la Guerra de las Drogas*. México DF.

Aguilar, Rubén and Jorge G. Castañeda. (2009) *El Narco: La guerra fallida*. México DF.

Aguirre Botello, Manuel. "Evaluacion de la pobreza de acuerdo a los ingresos, México, 1992 a 2012," *Mexicomaxico.org*, June 2014.

Astorga Almanza, Luis Alejandro. (2005) *El siglo de las drogas: El narcotráfico, del porfiriato al nuevo milenio*. México DF.

Baltazar, Elia, Lydiette Carrión, Thelma Gómez Durán, et al. (2012) *Entre las cenizas: Historias de vida en tiempos de muerte*. Oaxaca de Juárez, México.

Beith, Malcolm. (2011) *El último narco*. México DF.

Blancornelas, Jesús. (2010) *El Cártel: Los Arellano Felix, la mafia más poderosa en la historia de América Latina*. México DF.

Bosch, Lolita and Alejandro Vélez. (2012) *Tú y yo coincidimos en esta noche terrible*. México DF.

Buscaglia, Eduardo. (2010) "México pierde la guerra." *Esquire Latinoamérica*. March 2010: 95–101.

Caballero, José Luis. "Deterioro social: la herencia que recibe Peña Nieto," *El Economista*. November 30, 2012.

Calderón Hinojosa, Felipe. (2014) *Los retos que enfrentamos: Los problemas de México y las políticas públicas para resolverlos*. México.

Comisión Mexicana de Defensa y Promoción de los Derechos Humanos. "147° Período de sesiones de la Comisión Interamericana de Derechos Humanos (CIDH): Situación general de Derechos Humanos en México," *Comisión Mexicana de Defensa y Promoción de los Derechos Humanos*, March 2013.

Comisión Nacional Contra las Adicciones and Secretaría de Salud. (2002) *Encuesta Nacional De Adicciones, 2002*. México DF.

———. (2008) *Encuesta Nacional De Adicciones, 2008*. México DF.

———. (2011) *Encuesta Nacional De Adicciones, 2011: Drogas ilícitas*. México DF.

Comisión Nacional de los Derechos Humanos. (2011) *Informe especial sobre secuestro de migrantes en México*. México DF.

Contreras, Sergio Octavio. "La semántica del Blog del Narco," *Etcetera.com.mx*, November 11, 2010.

Corchado, Alfedo and Juan Elías Tovar Cross. (2013) *Medianoche en México: El descenso de un periodista a las tinieblas de un país*. México DF.

Cordero, Laura. "El regreso de Calderón para dar recetas es 'cinismo,' dicen líderes sociales y víctimas de la violencia en su sexenio," *Sinembargo.mx*, August 13, 2014.

Dávila, Darío. "Las vacantes del 'Señorío,'" *Periodismoindeleble.com*, November 16, 2012.

Díaz, Gloria Leticia. "Primer año de Peña, el más violento para la prensa desde 2007: Artículo 19," Proceso.*com.mx*, March 18, 2014.

Enciso, Froylán. (2010) "Los fracasos del chantaje: Régimen de prohibición de drogas y narcotráfico." In *Seguridad Nacional y seguridad interior: Los grandes problemas de México, V. 15*, edited by Arturo Alvarado and Mónica Serra. México DF.

Escalante Gonzalbo, Fernando. "Homicidios 2008–2009: La Muerte tiene permiso," *Nexos.com.mx*, January 1, 2011.

———. "Crimen Organizado: La dimensión imaginaria," *Nexos.com.mx*, October 1, 2012.

Esmas. "'México Seguro' para Michoacán," *Esmas.com*, September 18, 2005.

Fernández, Leticia. "ONC: En enero, un secuestro cada seis horas," *Milenio.com*, March 19, 2014.

Fernández Menéndez, Jorge. (2001) *El otro poder: Las redes del narcotráfico, la política y la violencia en México*. México DF.

———. (2012) *La batalla por México: de Enrique Camarena al Chapo Guzmán*. México DF.

Ferri Tórtola, Pablo. "Testigo revela ejecuciones en el estado de México," *Esquirelat.com*, September 19, 2014.

Flores Pérez, Carlos Antonio. "El tráfico de drogas en México: Condiciones generales de evolución y estrategias de respuesta del Estado," *Norlarnet.uio.no*, May 6, 2009.

Garay, Luis Jorge, Eduardo Salcedo-Albarrán, Luis Astorga, et al. (2012) *Narcotráfico, corrupción y estados: Cómo las redes ilícitas han reconfigurado las instituciones en Colombia, Guatemala y México*. México DF.

García Cruz, Fernanda. "Los multimillonarios en México crecen, dice estudio; y también los pobres: Coneval," *Sinembargo.mx*, October 2, 2014.

Gobierno del Estado de Coahuila de Zaragoza. (2012) *Programa especial de prevención social de la violencia y la delincuencia 2011–2017*. Saltillo, México.

Gómez, María Idalia and Dario Fritz. (2006) *Con la muerte en el bolsillo: seis desaforadas historias del narcotrafico en Mexico*. México DF.

González Rodríguez, Sergio. (2014) *Campo de guerra*. Madrid.

———. (2009) *El hombre sin cabeza*. Madrid.

Grillo, Ioan. "Michoacán: Deportados en las filas de las autodefensas," *Letraslibres.com*, January 28, 2014.

Guerrero, Héctor and Rolando Herrera. "Matan a 21 cada día," *Reforma*, November 30, 2012.

Hernández, Anabel. (2010) *Los señores del Narco*. México DF.

Hernández, Anabel and Steve Fisher. (2014) "Iguala: La historia no oficial." *Proceso* 1989: 6–11.

Hope, Alejandro. "Iguala o la impunidad," *Eluniversalmas.com.mx*, October 9, 2014.

Illades, Esteban. "Iguala: El polvorín que nadie olió," *Nexos.com.mx*, October 20, 2014.

———. "La noche más triste," *Nexos.com.mx*, January 1, 2015.

Indigo Staff. "Hallan cultivo de coca en Chiapas," *Reporteindigo.com*, September 11, 2014.

Instituto Nacional de Estadística y Geografía. "Encuesta nacional de victimización y percepción sobre seguridad pública 2013 (ENVIPE)," *Inegi.org.mx*, September 30, 2013.

Instituto Nacional de Salud Pública, Carlos Oropeza Abúndez, Gabriel Nagore Cázares, et al. (2008) *Encuesta nacional de adicciones 2008*. Cuernavaca, México.

InsurgentePress. "Rompen códigos cárteles en Michoacán," *Insurgentepress.com.mx*, November 20, 2013.

Jiménez, Carlos. "Osiel supo de la extradición desde noviembre; reacomodó su cártel en el norte del país," *Cronica.com.mx*, January 23, 2007.

Luna, Camila. "Alfredo Castillo condiciona justicia a Cherán a cambio del mando unificado," *Michoacantrespuntocero.com*, June 3, 2014.

Martínez, Paris. "4 Presidenciables y sus números contra la delincuencia," *Animalpolitico.com*, August 25, 2011.

———. "Esclavos Del Narco: Profesionistas forzados," *Animalpolitico.com*, October 30, 2012.

Mauleón, Héctor de. (2010) *Marca de sangre: Los años de la delincuencia organizada*. México DF.

Merino, José, Jessica Zarkin, and Eduardo Fierro. "Desaparecidos," *Nexos.com.mx*, January 1, 2015.

Murillo Karam, Jesús. "Conferencia de prensa del Procurador General de la República, Jesús Murillo Karam," *Pgr.gob.mx*, November 7, 2014.

Ortiz León, Ramón Eduardo. "Muerte de un activista," *Noticias de Caborca*, September 2, 2013.

Ortiz Pinchetti, Francisco. "Sinaloa: un trasplante de Sudamérica: La Operación Cóndor, letanía de horrores," *Proceso*, October 7, 1978.

Osorno, Diego Enrique. (2010) *El Cartel de Sinaloa*. México DF.

Periódico ABC de Sevilla. "Eisenhower recibió a Johnson y a López Mateos," *Hemeroteca Periódico ABC de Sevilla*, February 23, 1964.

Periódico La Jornada. "A la luz, video de La Tuta con dos periodistas michoacanos," *La Jornada*, September 23, 2014.

Proal, Juan Pablo. "Los jóvenes mexicanos abrazan el suicidio," *Proceso.com.mx*, January 11, 2013.

Proceso. "Medio país bajo el poder Narco," *Proceso, Edición especial*, October 24, 2010.

———. "Herencia ineludible de Peña Nieto: Los desaparecidos, los muertos," *Proceso (Edición especial)*, December 30, 2012.

———. "Los amos de Michoacán," *Proceso (Edición especial)*, November 3, 2013.

Proceso.com.mx. "Historia: se acercaba el final de sexenio," *Proceso.com.mx*, September 27, 2014.

Quintana S., Víctor M. "Juárez: Lo que Calderón no enseña en Harvard," *La Jornada*, March 1, 2013.

Ravelo, Ricardo. (2012) *Narcomex: Historia e historias de una guerra*. Madrid.

Rea Gómez, Daniela, Marcela Turati, Elia Baltazar, et al. (2012) *Entre las cenizas: Historias de vida en tiempos de muerte*. Oaxaca de Juárez, México.

Red Nacional de Organismos Civiles de Derechos Humanos. "El derecho a defender los Derechos Humanos en México: Informe sobre la situación de las Personas Defensoras 2011–2013," *Red Nacional de Organismos Civiles de Derechos Humanos*, January 9, 2014.

Resa Nestares, Carlos. (1999) *Sistema político y delincuencia organizada en México: Caso de los traficantes de drogas*. Madrid.

Reveles, José. (2010) *El Cártel Incómodo: El fin de los Beltrán Leyva y la hegemonía del Chapo Guzmán*. México DF.

———. (2011) *Narcoméxico*. Madrid.

———. (2014) *El Chapo: Entrega y traición*. México DF.

Rincón Gallardo, Gilberto, Adolfo Aguilar Zinser, et al. (2014) ¡*Ya Basta! El despertar de un país: a diez anos de la marcha contra la inseguridad*. México DF.

Sánchez Treviño, Martín. "Confirma Egidio Torre Cantú que ya opera otro cuartel militar en el Estado," *La Jornada*, February 28, 2012.

Sarmiento, Sergio. "El Tata y las drogas," *El Reforma*, February 19, 2014.

Sinembargo.mx. "Lo que empezó como hechos aislados, se extiende como epidemia por el país: Los grupos de autodefensa se disparan," *Sinembargo.mx*, February 2, 2013.

———. "La cifra de homicidios rebasa los 30 mil en el sexenio, con Edomex como el más violento," *Sinembargo.mx*, September 24, 2014.

———. "La Violencia hace de México el país más peligroso para los Clérigos: Estudio Del Vaticano," *Sinembargo.mx*, January 2, 2015.

Soto Espinosa, Angélica Jocelyn. "Anuncian madres de Ayotzinapa despliegue de movilizaciones," *Cimacnoticias.com.mx*, January 2, 2015.

Székely, Miguel. "20 años de pobreza," *Mexicosocial.org*, October 1, 2013.

Turati, Marcela. (2011) *Fuego cruzado: Las víctimas atrapadas en la Guerra del Narco*. México DF.

———. "…Y todos somos Juárez, gran negocio," *Proceso.com.mx*, November 8, 2012.

———. "San Fernando-Ayotzinapa: Las similitudes," *Proceso.com.mx*, December 22, 2014.

Valdés Castellanos, Guillermo. (2013) *Historia del narcotráfico en México*. México.

Velázquez, Carlos. "Todo Narco, todo Narco," *Gatopardo.com*, March 2, 2012.

Villalobos, Joaquín. "El infierno al sur de México," *Nexos.com.mx*, September 1, 2014.

Zepeda Patterson, Jorge. "Narcovideos y el peligro de informar," *Jorgezepeda.net*, April 22, 2007.

———. "Dos toneladas sin respuesta," *El País*, January 7, 2015.

GANGSTERISMO
The United States, Cuba and the Mafia, 1933 to 1966
♦ Jack Colhoun
ISBN 978-1-935928-89-8 (paperback)
ISBN 978-1-935928-90-4 (e-book)

"Gangsterismo brilliantly unravels the bizarre tale of the Mafia army the Kennedy brothers recruited in their manic determination to rid Cuba of Castro."
—Martin J. Sherwin, co-winner of the Pulitzer Prize (together with Kai Bird) for *American Prometheus: The Triumph and Tragedy of J. Robert Oppenheimer*

"Colhoun damningly documents the pathetic, incompetent and sometimes comic, but always inappropriate and anti-democratic, attempts by the CIA and/or its confederates, working in tandem with members of the mob, to assassinate Castro and overthrow the Cuban revolution." —Victor S. Navasky, publisher emeritus, *The Nation*; professor, Columbia University Graduate School of Journalism

♦ ♦ ♦

METHOD AND MADNESS
The hidden story of Israel's assaults on Gaza
♦ Norman G. Finkelstein
ISBN 978-1-939293-71-8 (paperback)
ISBN 978-1-939293-72-5 (e-book)

"Mr. Finkelstein['s] ... research is certainly thorough. His characterizations, too, can be brilliant, and he spares nobody ..." —*The Economist*

"As a work of scholarship and commentary, *Method and Madness* is simply outstanding." —Mouin Rabbani, Senior Fellow, Institute for Palestine Studies

CARMEN BOULLOSA is an award-winning Mexican novelist, poet, newspaper columnist, and Emmy-winning TV show host. She's been a Guggenheim and Cullman Center Fellow. Of her seventeen novels, four are available in English: *Texas: The Great Theft*; *They're Cows, We're Pigs*; *Leaving Tabasco*; and *Cleopatra Dismounts*.

www.carmenboullosa.net | @carmenboullosa

MIKE WALLACE, Distinguished Professor of History at John Jay College of Criminal Justice of the City University of New York and the CUNY Graduate Center, and founder of the Gotham Center for New York City History, won the Pulitzer Prize for History for his book *Gotham: A History of New York City to 1898*, co-authored with Edwin Burrows.

Printed in the USA
CPSIA information can be obtained
at www.ICGtesting.com
JSHW081030140724
66374JS00001B/1